HANNAH ARENDT AND THE
POLITICS OF TRAGEDY

Hannah Arendt
and the
Politics of Tragedy

ROBERT C. PIRRO

Northern Illinois University Press

DeKalb

Library of Congress Cataloging-in-Publication Data

Pirro, Robert.

Hannah Arendt and the politics of tragedy / Robert Pirro.

p.   cm.

Includes bibliographical references and index.

ISBN 0-87580-268-0 (alk. paper)

1. Arendt, Hannah—Contributions in political science.

2. Legitimacy of governments. 3. Tragic, The—Political aspects.

JC251.A74P56 2000

320.5'092—dc21   00-036149

Contents

Acknowledgments

An early version of this work benefited from the comments of Hanna Pitkin and Michael Rogin, who served on my dissertation committee in the Department of Political Science at the University of California, Berkeley. I am thankful for their help. I want also to express my appreciation to the anonymous readers who reviewed my manuscript on behalf of Northern Illinois University Press for their many helpful suggestions.

The task of finding a publisher was greatly facilitated by Neil Jumonville, a longtime friend, who gave me the benefit of his experience. The historian George Rawlyk was a mentor and friend whose reassuring presence has been sorely missed since his sudden, unexpected death in November 1995. For their generous and timely support in lean times, I am very grateful to my in-laws, Dieter and Helena Schmidt. Julia Schmidt-Pirro has been a partner in this project from its beginnings. Without her, it and I would both have turned out differently. The largest portion of thanks are due my parents, Costantino Pirro and Filomena Silvestri, for their many sacrifices and their unfailing encouragement. This book is dedicated to them.

HANNAH ARENDT AND THE
POLITICS OF TRAGEDY

Introduction

In May 1941 Hannah Arendt, German Jewish refugee, together with her husband, Heinrich Blücher, arrived by passenger ship to safe haven in New York City. Less than two years before, when hostilities were officially declared between Germany and France in September 1939, the life they had previously made together in Paris as longtime exiles from Nazi Germany lost whatever stability it had once possessed. From that time until they managed to obtain rare U.S. visas and cross the French border en route to the port city of Lisbon in January 1941, they separately endured periods of internment by French authorities and, after a chance reunion in the main square of a town in southern France, months of anxious waiting and uncertainty.[1]

Uprooted as she was, it was not long before Arendt tried to make sense of recent events. Among the earliest of Arendt's writings published in English in the United States, "We Refugees" (*Menorah Journal*, January 1943) stands as a powerful, concentrated expression of the concerns and themes that would occupy her centrally over the course of a productive career as American scholar and teacher of political theory. The essay derives much of its dramatic power from its hybrid status as both personal testimony and theoretical prolegomenon. A German Jewish refugee recently arrived in the United States, she testifies to terrible experiences of loss and deprivation, and her matter-of-fact, staccato-like recounting of the various dimensions of these experiences is suggestive of a fierce effort to keep the anguish of loss under tight control.

> We lost our home, which means the familiarity of daily life. We lost our occupations, which means the confidence that we are of some use in this world. We lost our language, which means the naturalness of reactions, the simplicity of gestures, the unaffected expression of feelings.

We left our relatives in the Polish ghettos and our best friends have
been killed in concentration camps.[2]

In other parts of her testimony as a Jewish refugee, marked by irony
and sarcastic phrasing, Arendt appears to give freer rein to another
emotion—anger. The subject of this anger, curiously enough, is not
the Nazi regime or its agents of Jewish mass expulsion and murder
but, rather, what she holds to be the inappropriate spirit in which
her fellow German Jewish refugees had responded to the catastrophic upheaval of their lives. This spirit finds expression in what
she considers her fellow refugees' false optimism that eliminating
the burdens imposed by the condition of statelessness is mainly a
matter of making personal adjustments to the requirements of polite
society. Thus, the purveyors of "optimism" act as though they can
shed any personal attributes that might recall or draw attention to
their condition as refugees—their native language, their memories of
home, even their identities as Jews.

Arendt wants nothing to do with this kind of optimism, which
lends itself to a worldview that dangerously underestimates the anti-
Semitism of the powers that be and which dangerously overesti-
mates Jews' capacity to renounce their identity in a way that would
be acceptable to those powers that be. The project of changing one's
identity as a Jew strikes her, in the first place, as difficult and fraught
with risks to one's inner balance and sense of personal integrity: "the
recovering of a new personality is as difficult—and as hopeless—as a
new creation of the world" ("We Refugees," 63).

She finds Jewish refugees' attempt to discard their Jewish identity
objectionable for a further reason: that it has the perverse effect of
eroding the power of Jews collectively to resist the forces that have
made them international outlaws. "We fight like madmen for private
existences with individual destinies. . . . we don't feel entitled to
Jewish solidarity; we cannot realize that we by ourselves are not so
much concerned as the whole Jewish people" ("We Refugees," 60).
In the willingness of German Jews to discard their Jewish identity,
Arendt additionally sees an instance of the oppressed accepting the
standards of the oppressors. The debilitating effects imposed by this
acceptance on Jews' self-worth, solidarity, and fighting spirit are, for
her, not new. They have long been present, in less exaggerated form,
as by-products of the assimilationist strategy Jews were employing in

Germany for generations before the National Socialists' rise to power. "Whatever we do, whatever we pretend to be, we reveal nothing but our insane desire to be changed, not to be Jews. . . . We don't succeed and we can't succeed; under the cover of our 'optimism' you can easily detect the hopeless sadness of assimilationists" (63). For Arendt, the central problem with the strategy of assimilation, which the harsh experiences of German Jewish refugee life had so painfully pointed up, is its having accustomed Jews to set few—if any—limits to the extent of personal adjustment they were willing to make to be counted as Germans. "With us from Germany the word *assimilation* received a 'deep' philosophical meaning. . . . We adjust in principle to everything and everybody" (63).

In situating her attack on the ineffective and unworthy "tricks" of adjustment resorted to by German Jewish refugees within the context of a critique of assimilation in pre-Nazi Germany, Arendt testifies to the influence of Kurt Blumenfeld, a leading Zionist activist and thinker, who became her political mentor after they met in 1929. According to the Zionist critique promoted by Blumenfeld and others, the problem with assimilation was that it wrongly encouraged German Jews to comport themselves according to the social mores and standards of bourgeois Gentiles, who if not anti-Semitic themselves were susceptible to anti-Semitic appeals. Under such conditions, entry into bourgeois Gentile social circles could normally be gained only by "exception" Jews or by Jews who could pass as Gentiles. In either case, the price of entry was a psychologically distortive repression of personality and a politically isolating disassociation from other members of the Jewish community.

Blumenfeld's critique of assimilation not only provided a conceptual framework through which Arendt could make sense of the demoralizing contradictions and maddening ironies that afflicted her life and the lives of her fellow German Jewish refugees; it also set the basic terms she would use to theorize for the next thirty years about the nature and meaning of politics in the modern world. In particular, this critique anticipated her later conceptualization of the "political" (a citizen realm of individuation and collective self-determination) in opposition to the "social" (a clientilistic realm of conformity and collective drift). Arendt's concern about the encroachment of society's mores and imperatives into areas where political relationships ought to hold would find its most conceptually weighted expression in such works as *The Human Condition* and *On Revolution* (first published in 1958 and 1963, respectively). At the time of writing "We Refugees," Arendt's firsthand experiences of utter dependence and extreme vulnerability as a stateless person are still painfully fresh. The result is a narrative that both conveys the shocking novelty of the experiences it recounts and asserts a claim for their exemplary significance.

> If we should start telling the truth that we are nothing but Jews, it would mean that we expose ourselves to the fate of human beings who, unprotected by any specific law or political convention, are nothing but human beings. I can hardly imagine an attitude more dangerous, since we actually live in a world in which human beings as such have ceased to exist for quite a while; since society has discovered discrimination as the great social weapon by which one may kill men without bloodshed; since passports or birth certificates, and sometimes even income tax receipts, are no longer formal papers but matters of social distinction. (65)

If "We Refugees" can be said to have the character simultaneously of a personal testimony *to* events and a theoretical ordering *of* events, it is due in important part to aspects of the essay's narrative construction, especially the switching back and forth between the "we" of experience and the "I" of theoretical assessment. The "we" of experience consists of German Jewish refugees. Arendt's pointed deployment of the pronoun signals her choice to acknowledge the identity she shares with them, to recognize in her predicament the predicament of an entire people, and to accept her share of the collective responsibility for her and their inadequacies in responding to that predicament. In using "we" to insist on her Jewish identity and the collective dimensions of the stateless condition imposed on bearers of that identity, Arendt seems intent on demonstrating a more politically aware and group-conscious response than she thought possible if one started from assimilationist premises.

Appearances of the "I" who "speak[s] of unpopular facts" ("We Refugees," 58) and who disposes of the telling anecdote about personal experiences in an internment camp—"At the camp of Gurs, for instance, where I had the opportunity of spending some time, I heard only once of suicide" (59)—mark those instances of theoretical distancing and reflection that afford Arendt the opportunity to assess critically the spirit in which German Jewish refugees have responded to their predicament. So, for example, Arendt implicitly criticizes those refugees who out of fear of social stigmatization choose to remain silent about their past experiences. She does so by expressing a consolatory wish in the first-person singular: "But sometimes I imagine that at least nightly we think of our dead or we remember the poems we once loved" (57).

Such obvious—and, at times, jarring—shifts of narrative voice attest to the difficult task Arendt has apparently set herself in this essay: to maintain solidarity with her fellow German Jewish refugees while critically reflecting on their beliefs and actions. In both its thematic concern and its narrative technique, "We Refugees" stands as an important signpost indicating the future direction and mode of Arendt's thought about the nature and meaning of public life. The struggle both to be part of and to stand apart from a group of people with whom one identifies would remain a central thematic preoccupation, animating her later efforts to envision and promote a republican form of public- and critical-minded democratic citizenship. Those efforts would find stylistic expression in a mode of theorizing that increasing numbers of democratic theorists and sympathetic readers of Arendt have come to characterize under the rubric of storytelling.

Many prominent American political and moral theorists writing in the last quarter of the twentieth century—including Alasdair MacIntyre, Judith Shklar, Michael Walzer, and Martha Nussbaum—have drawn inspiration, if not direction, from forms of storytelling such as Greek tragedy and the novel in considering how best to reconcile the critical demands of theory and the solidary requirements of political commitment. Take Michael Walzer for a representative example. He rejects "the claim that moral principles [are] necessarily external to the world of everyday experience, waiting *out there* to be discovered by detached and dispassionate philosophers." Drawing on the life and career of Ignazio Silone, a twentieth-century Italian political activist and novelist, Walzer argues that storytelling is the better way to convey the "infinite entanglement and subtle constraint" so characteristic of that world.[3]

Although the endorsements of storytelling modes of moral and political theory to be found in books such as Alasdair MacIntyre's *After Virtue* (1981), Judith Shklar's *Ordinary Vices* (1984), and Martha

Nussbaum's *Poetic Justice* (1995) have found and duly impressed many readers, it seems increasingly clear that within the burgeoning field of studies focused on the narrative or literary dimensions of politics and political theory Arendt's legacy looms the largest.[4] To contemporary proponents of storytelling modes of theory, Arendt stands as a trailblazing political theorist of the twentieth century, in significant part because she recognized, in forms of imaginative literature such as the novel, short story, poetry, and drama, resources for critically engaging traditional metaphysical approaches to politics and their monologically premised, deductively generated accounts of the nature of political life. Arendt drew examples, lessons, and techniques from storytelling forms in her search for a theoretical practice that was able to generate insights sufficiently attentive to the particularities, varieties, and novelties of human action and yet that was also solicitous of general assent.

Storytelling elements of the sort identified in Arendt's later works are not hard to find in "We Refugees." They include narrative shifts of voice, a device associated more with works of literature than with works of social science, and her giving heavy weight to personal anecdote. In addition, there is a passage in which Arendt refers to a character from Greek epic (by his Latin moniker) in order to evoke both the plight of German Jewish refugees and the inadequacies of their response to this plight. "The desperate confusion of these Ulysses-wanderers who, unlike their great prototype, don't know who they are is easily explained by their perfect mania for refusing to keep their identity" ("We Refugees," 64). References to characters and story lines from works of imaginative literature would constitute perhaps the most noticeable storytelling aspect of Arendt's later theoretical practice.

Theorists who read Arendt for insights into the uses of storytelling have carefully delineated the literary aspects of Arendt's thought, revealing how the impact of the traumatic political events and momentous social developments of the first half of the twentieth century impelled her consideration of the storytelling possibilities of theory. They have also begun to assess the implications of Arendtian storytelling for analyzing and implementing public policy.[5] Accepting the Arendtian idea of the political efficacy and desirability of storytelling modes of theory, Arendt scholars have, however, neglected to make a systematic inquiry into the basic human impulses that storytelling is supposed to activate and channel so satisfyingly. In the present work I attempt to compensate for this neglect by indicating how an unacknowledged theory of Greek tragedy—inherited by Arendt from her philhellenic predecessors in the German tradition of philosophy and letters—shaped her understanding of storytelling and its relevance to democratic citizenship in a disenchanted world. In pursuing a line of inquiry focused on the Greek dimensions of Arendt's political thought, this book moves against the dominant current of contemporary Arendt criticism. Many readers of Arendt (especially those who consider her thought systematically flawed and wholly compromised by its entanglement in a suspect tradition of German philosophy and letters) have dismissed Arendt's affirmative assessments of polis life in classical Athens as anachronistic, if not politically pernicious.[6]

Although much insightful work has been done by readers who have chosen to focus solely on the non-Hellenic aspects of Arendt's thought[7] and by those who have made her sometimes inconsistent use of Hellenic categories the starting point for investigating alternative sources of her thinking,[8] there remain important elements of her work that are best accessed through direct and systematic consideration of her mostly admiring vision of classical Athens. In the analysis of this vision to be undertaken in the following pages, my focus will be on her sense of classical Athens as exemplary site for the exercise of practices both political and cultural. For, given the central role played by the literary relics of such Athenian practices as epic recital and tragic drama in the evolution of Western understanding of what it means to tell a meaningful story or to form a narrative capable of moving an audience, it seems incumbent on those who would more fully grasp the bases of storytelling's promise as understood by Arendt to consider closely and systematically her numerous references to characters and scenes from, and conventions and theories of, Greek tragedy.

Taking as its starting point the inspiration drawn by contemporary theorists from Greek tragedy and other storytelling forms in their attempts to situate the critical function of theory in a democratic setting of plurality, Chapter 1 considers the role of Arendt's work as a touchstone in this literature. Chapter 2 situates Arendt in a German philosophical tradition of tragic engagement whose bearers have concerned themselves with Greek tragedy and theories of tragedy in response to what they have considered disabling tensions or divisions or deficits in German (or European) politics or culture. Chapters 3 and 4 take up authority and judgment, two central concepts of Arendt's political thought. The chapters identify certain puzzles raised by her treatment of these concepts and consider how attention to and reformulation of the tragic elements of her thought provide compelling ways both to resolve those puzzles and to reveal the theory of sublimation that underlies her storytelling practice. Reconsidering Arendt's tragedy-inflected thought in the context of wider debates about the nature and meaning of democratic citizenship, Chapter 5 holds out the possibility of a form of political heroism that is compatible with a notion of democratic citizenship requiring significant levels of both critical reflectiveness and solidary feelings.

In formulating an Arendtian theory of tragedy from materials scattered throughout her writings and in reconsidering some central dilemmas she raised about the nature and meaning of authority and judgment, I will in this book place special significance on the concluding passage of *On Revolution*, an instance in Arendt's writings when her claims about the life-affirming promise of political freedom achieve an unusual dramatic intensity:

> Sophocles in *Oedipus at Colonus*, the play of his old age, wrote the famous and frightening lines:
>
> *Mē phūnai ton hapanta nikā logon. to d'epei phanē, bēnai keis' hopothen per hēkei polu deuteron hōs tachista.*
>
> "Not to be born prevails over all meaning uttered in words; by far the second-best for life, once it has appeared, is to go as swiftly as possible whence it came." There he also let us know, through the mouth of Theseus, the legendary founder of Athens and hence her spokesman, what it was that enabled ordinary men, young and old, to bear life's burden: it was the *polis*, the space of men's free deeds and living words, which could endow life with splendour—*ton Bion Lampron poieisthai*.[9]

On first consideration (and keeping in mind the prevailing view of Arendt as somewhat compromised by a romantic attachment to mythic polis heroes), so conspicuous an invocation of the legendary founder of Athens in the coda of a book about the lost promise of revolutions in the modern age could well seem irrelevant to the contemporary project of understanding the nature and meaning of democratic citizenship. After all, what lessons (other than negative ones) are to be learned by theorists of democracy from Theseus, a mythic Athenian king?

It will be one of my tasks in this book to show that there are positive lessons to be learned from Theseus. These lessons will remain one-sided and incomplete, however, as long as the lessons of another mythic king, whose fate finds its final enactment in Sophocles' last drama, go unrecognized. The absence of old, blind Oedipus, Theban outcast-turned-suppliant at Colonus, from the Sophoclean scenes evoked by Arendt first in her 1963 book on revolution is telling. Twenty years earlier, at a time when she herself had only recently ended a period in her life of forced emigration and statelessness, it apparently also did not occur to her to connect her condition with Oedipus's. Instead, the figure from Greek myth to whom she has occasion to refer is Ulysses, the famous wanderer who after ten years' dangers and distractions finally returns home to Ithaca.

Plainly intended as a reproach to those of her fellow German Jewish refugees who had responded to their stateless condition in what Arendt considered to be an assimilationist spirit (trying to pass oneself off as a person one is not, such as a Gentile, a Frenchman), the reference to Ulysses could be taken to stand as an unintended mark of continuity in a life that had undergone significant disruption. A love of the classics and a readiness with references to ancient Greek and Roman characters and verse were, after all, characteristic of the Germans (both Jew and Gentile) who had been educated according to the humanistic ideals of the *Bildung* tradition. It may also have been that the reference to a character whose story had been told and retold for almost three thousand years provided Arendt with a consoling intimation of survival and the power of remembrance. That such an intimation might serve political needs, in addition to personal ones, is a possibility best appreciated upon a more systematic and comprehensive consideration of Arendt's work.

CHAPTER ONE

Greek Tragedy, Storytelling, and Political Theory

In Search of an Intuitive Basis for Democratic Citizenship

> Political philosophy is tragic thought. Without a dramatic sense of fate and mutability no rational intelligence would turn to this hideous subject.
>
> —Judith Shklar, "Hannah Arendt's Triumph"

Many contemporary theorists profess to be deeply suspicious of the theoretical impulse. Apparently taking to heart the lessons of Nietzschean skepticism (or the skepticism of any number of his postmodern heirs), they steel themselves against theory's temptation not merely to rationalize the world but to rationalize the world *away* by not taking due account of its variety and difference, its particularities and contingencies. Coeval with theorists' self-professed aversion to the totalizing, universalizing, rationalizing excesses to which they are by vocation inclined is their sense that theory can and should make a difference in how people act. Accepting plurality as a basic condition of human affairs cannot mean accepting all particular manifestations of human plurality as equally deserving of preservation. Respecting basic differences in perspective, position, desire, and need cannot mean abdicating the responsibility to discriminate between the better and the worse as a prelude to taking action. To the extent that human existence entails membership in community, the range of permitted expressions of human plurality will always be narrower than the range of potential expressions.

The challenge of respecting human plurality without wholly giving way to it, of remaining open to multiple perspectives without losing the capacity to discriminate between them, has been framed, in recent years, as one of reconciling postmodern insights into the conventionality of human experience—"the constructed character of 'man,' 'humanity,' 'human nature,' 'self'"—with neohumanist concerns to preserve, renew, or construct convention.[1] For postmodern theorists, human liberation fundamentally consists of freeing oneself from the authority of convention. For neohumanists, the promise of human liberation lies more in the establishment of conventions that are capable and worthy of appealing for and eliciting general and sustained support.

Greek tragedy has provided an important touchstone for some contemporary theorists to think through the challenge of fostering an adequately critical theoretical spirit compatible with a viable democratic community. For example, J. Peter Euben (1990) argues that Greek tragedy can provide inspiration and instruction to contemporary theorists because of its distinctive role in the classical Athenian polis as both challenger to and supporter of some of the basic conceptual and institutional boundaries that structured thought and action.

> From inside the polis tragedy questions the divisions between inside and outside. Part of the city's order, it "problematized" the idea of order, contesting as it constructed, challenging what it helped to sustain, presenting transgression, paradoxes, and archaisms to disrupt civic teleologies which it eventually reaffirmed.[2]

Tracy Strong (1990), in his ongoing attempts to show how "political theorists [might] enlist the service of dramatists to further them in their aim [of] defin[ing] and formulat[ing] what it means to be a human being with other human beings" (40), repeatedly invokes, by way of Nietzsche's *Birth of Tragedy*, the example of Greek tragedy. Strong finds particularly significant Greek tragedy's role as promoter of individuals who were capable both singly and collectively of interrogating the nature and meaning of the conventions that governed their common affairs without being immobilized by their "profound insight . . . into the basic unjustifiability of any given configuration of events."[3]

In the above readings, it is tragedy's capacity both to confound settled beliefs and assumptions and to put audience members in a kind of intuitive contact with the limits of human knowledge and powers that centrally determined its role as instrument of education and empowerment in the polis. Why should the intuition of human frailty achieved through the witness of representations of intense human suffering lend itself to empowerment rather than resignation? The answer, Strong implies, has something to do with tragedy's capacity to put the imagination in play.

It is through the working of the imagination or intuition that aspects of the world are made present to the audience in a way that enables the world seemingly to sponsor itself. Drawing on Ralph Waldo Emerson's "Divinity School Address," Strong refers to this self-sponsoring experience as an "instance of transparency" and describes its effect as one in which spectators of a tragedy are put in touch with something inside themselves that corresponds to something outside.[4] "Tragedy *establishes* the authority of a human sense before the audience in a manner that this sense can be experienced both as something external and found in oneself." To the extent that achievement of this intuition of correspondence is shared with fellow spectators, "one [can] . . . recognize one's experience with others as authoritative." The role of the tragic theater as occasion for noncoercively provoking intuitions capable of renewing an audience's sense of community is the lesson Strong draws from Nietzsche's *Birth of Tragedy*.[5] If one were to pursue the implications of Strong's reading, the great advantage of founding or renewing a sense of community through the aesthetic activation of intuition would appear to be that membership is experienced as resulting from something more than physical threat, the compulsion of a moral or religious truth, material profit, or routine. To the extent that intuition is felt to originate from within rather than from without, aesthetically activated or supported membership would be founded on voluntary commitment, rather than (or, in addition to) being founded on submission, utilitarian calculus, or habit.

A similar understanding of the power of representations of human suffering to evoke noncoercively an intuitive response that is capable of changing the way people think or act is discernible in the work of Judith Shklar, although she articulates this promise under the rubric of storytelling, not Greek tragedy per se. Shklar was an early and notable proponent and practitioner of storytelling among American political theorists. In her book *Ordinary Vices* (1984) Shklar holds that telling stories provides the political theorist with a means for better thinking about and discussing the irrational, conflictual aspects of human conduct, which are typically missed or ignored or misrepresented by more abstract, generalizing modes of theory. "The great intellectual advantage of telling stories is that it does not rationalize the irrationality of actual experience and of history. Indecision, incoherence, and inconsistency are not ironed out or put between brackets. All our conflicts are preserved in all their inconclusiveness."[6]

Taking a more direct and unmediated account of the irrationalities of human conduct and their unfortunate consequences for people requires the skills of a "novelist" more than of a "theologian" and results, Shklar suggests, in a kind of theory that makes its points less by "fixing exactly the grounds of praise and blame in politics" (*Ordinary Vices*, 231) than by illustrating and illuminating. By *illustration,* Shklar means the presentation of story incidents that serve to exemplify "some general moral and political proposition" (229). In describing the nature and significance of the illuminating function of storytelling, Shklar evokes an effect similar to what Strong claims follows from Emerson's instance of transparency:

> Among the stories, there are some that do not serve to illustrate anything. They are told in order to reveal something directly. These illuminations are not meant to prove anything or to make it easier to grasp some general idea. They are there for their own sake, for their ability *to force us to acknowledge what we already know imperfectly.* (229, emphasis added)

As in Strong's reading (via Nietzsche) of the political relevance of Greek tragedy, Shklar's account of the illuminating role of storytelling rests on a notion of the latent correspondence between what people (on some perhaps nonrational level) understand or sense about the world and what the world is. Here, again, storytelling is seen as promoting increased understanding in a facilitative rather than a transmissive manner. Stories "impose understandings on us, sooner or later, by removing the covers *we may have put* on the mind's eye" (229, emphasis added).

If Shklar clearly appreciates the advantages of telling stories as a means of theorizing more concretely about politics, she does not consider it the only appropriate way of theorizing. Storytelling is, for her, "an addition not a substitute for more abstract modes of analysis. To establish general laws or models, to explain and judge political conduct is particularly necessary for assessing the rational consistency of specific decisions or policy choices" (231).[7] Nor does Shklar apparently harbor robust hopes for effecting democratic political change through storytelling; she has told stories, she says, "in the hope that they could carry messages to the reader and then suggest some more" (228).

Fellow proponents of storytelling among Shklar's political theory colleagues have shown themselves, by and large, to be less sanguine about the utility and desirability of more abstract modes of theory and more hopeful about the promise of storytelling to promote political changes in the direction of more extensive and direct democratic participation. For Ronald Beiner (1995), for example, nothing less than political theory's ability to "engage the grand questions of human nature and human destiny" (14) in ways that foster a kind of thoughtfulness conducive to participatory citizenship is at stake in the theorist's choice to tell stories. For Beiner, no less than for Shklar and Strong, the significance of storytelling as a means of promoting understanding is its capacity to activate intuition. Stories do not so much impart knowledge to audience members as recover it from within their consciousness. "Political philosophy, at its best, can be like a story that *reminds* us of forgotten needs and longings. . . . [It] *restores* to collective consciousness our rational needs and desires."[8]

Beiner reveals a second characteristic he has in common with both fellow proponents of storytelling and theorists of Greek tragedy in his wish to foster more direct participation in politics. For example, MacIntyre—along with Shklar one of the early proponents of storytelling in American political theory circles—ends his influential book *After Virtue* by calling for the "construction of local forms of community within which civility and the intellectual and moral life can be sustained" as an alternative to the remote, centralizing instrumentalities of modern representative government.[9] And between the philhellenist promoters of tragedy, Euben and Strong, a common sympathy for the flowering of new forms of participation in the 1960s provides evidence of democratic-participatory leanings.[10]

While opening new vistas on the problem of negotiating a way between the extremes of tyrannizing abstractness on the one hand and immobilizing open-endedness on the other, the resort to intuition by contemporary political theorists in pursuit of a kind of theory compatible with, if not promotive of, democratic participatory politics invites its share of questions. For example, Lisa Disch (1994) raises the question of how adoption of storytelling as a mode of theory is compatible with the theorist's role as critic.[11] If the boundary-setting, distinction-making, definition-posing functions of abstract theory threaten inappropriately to insulate the theorist from the particularities, contingencies, and irrationalities of human affairs, the character-drawing, plot-forming functions of storytelling might be seen conversely to bind the theorist too closely to the particularities, contingencies, and irrationalities of the affairs of a given community. The trick, Disch suggests, is to conceive and practice a storytelling mode of theory that "manages to be both engaged and critical."[12]

Answering the question of how storytelling modes of political theory encourage political engagement while promoting critical thinking about both the promise and the limits of that engagement may partly depend on understanding more clearly the role of intuition in theory. The preceding accounts share a notion of the distinctive power of storytelling to illuminate something about the world. This power provokes an intuitive recognition on the part of spectators or readers. A correspondence between inside and outside that was latent becomes actualized in a way that is personally transforming partly because it is shared by others. A sense of the associational effects of intuition is conveyed suggestively by Victor Turner as a "flash of lucid mutual understanding on the existential level" and "an intersubjective illumination," formulations to which he resorts in describing the power of social dramas to create or renew a sense of meaningfulness among members of a community.[13] What is less clear from the preceding accounts is what this "inside" is that storytelling (or Greek tragedy in its time) presumably contacts or activates or actualizes in and between members of an audience.

A fuller and more illuminating perspective on the connection provided by intuition between storytelling and participatory democracy may be had by recourse to the political thought of Hannah Arendt. For if the work of any political theorist in the twentieth century functions as theoretical touchstone—in the contemporary project of fostering an adequately critical spirit compatible with membership in a viable democratic community through the mediation of Greek tragedy or storytelling—it is the work of Arendt. This should come as no surprise given the central place of notions of aesthetic judgment in her attempts to conceptualize new forms of democratic individuality and community for the modern world: "it is as though taste decides not only how the world is to look, but also who belongs together in it."[14] To the extent that contemporary political theorists make Arendt a companion in their search for a mode of theory capable of putting readers' imaginations in play, consideration of her work may shed light on what politically relevant effect theory in a storytelling mode is supposed to have.

Among the political theorists who look to Greek tragedy as an institution of political education in the classical polis with important lessons to teach contemporary democrats, Arendt's influence is pervasive. In Euben's book, for example, no other contemporary political thinker is cited as often as Arendt. In fact, Arendt citations serve in many instances to confirm insights he has drawn from a work of Aeschylean or Sophoclean drama.[15] Arendt's informing influence is less pervasively, but no less strategically, present in Strong's analysis of the political relevance of Greek tragedy and theater generally.[16] It is also worth noting that, in her comparative study of politics and theater, Karen Hermassi (1977) envisions the central political promise of Greek tragedy—responding to "the need for a new birth or new beginning"—in explicitly Arendtian terms.[17]

If Arendt is an informing presence in political theory analyses of Greek tragedy, she stands as nothing less than a life-giving presence in contemporary studies of storytelling modes of political theory. Recent theorists of storytelling, including Beiner (1995) and Frederick Dolan (1994), invoke Arendt and engage her work in depth.[18] For them, Arendt's work serves as a paradigm, illuminating what it means to think and write about politics in a storytelling mode. Theorists who investigate the promise and limits of storytelling through the prism of Arendt's thought have noted three aspects of Arendt's storytelling or narrative mode of theory:[19] her frequent deployment of characters and story lines from works of fiction; her use of narrative conventions and devices associated more with literature than with social science; and her heavy weighting of personal anecdote and quotable utterance in assessing the nature and meaning of historical events and periods.

That Arendt draws upon the fictive worlds of novelists, short-story writers, dramatists, and poets for exemplary characters and scenes is evident from even a cursory survey of her writings. Sympathetic and unsympathetic commentators alike have long noted the unorthodox literary qualities of *The Origins of Totalitarianism* (1973).[20] In this work Arendt recurs to Marcel Proust's *Remembrance of Things Past,* Joseph Conrad's *Heart of Darkness,* and Rudyard Kipling's *Kim* for insights concerning the nature and political significance of (respectively) anti-Semitism in western European bourgeois society (*OT* 80–88), racism among European settlers and adventurers in sub-Saharan Africa (189–91), and the sense of political unaccountability fostered in promoters and agents of British empire in the late nineteenth century (216–18).

A second way she manifests a storytelling dimension in her practice as a political theorist is in her use of narrative devices characteristic more of fictional works than of conventional social science writing. Disch (1994) draws attention to Arendt's striking use of oxymoron (the "incongruous juxtaposition of opposites" contained in the formulation "'extermination factories'") and moral hyperbole ("the Nazis' '*deformed* wickedness'") in her early writings on totalitarianism.[21] Whitfield (1980) notes Arendt's ironic treatment of selected themes in *Eichmann in Jerusalem.*[22]

A third storytelling dimension of Arendt's theoretical practice noted by readers is her heavy weighting of personal anecdote and quotable reference, her "taking particular incidents or statements of historical figures as in some sense paradigmatic of vital stages of the emerging pattern."[23] Arendt's use of anecdote and quotable utterance is memorably evident in the preface to *Between Past and Future* where a citation of verse from French poet and Resistance fighter René Char—*Notre héritage n'est précédé d'aucun testament*—serves to encapsulate for her the nature and meaning of the actions of members of the French Resistance during Nazi occupation. The same citation would later do similar service in the final chapter of *On Revolution.*

Why does Arendt borrow characters and stories from literary sources, adopt devices associated with literature, and rely heavily on anecdote and quotable utterance in order to discuss the nature and meaning of politics in contemporary times? Arendt's frequent resort to stories and storytelling devices is understood in the literature as being significantly conditioned by her sense of the "dark times" afflicting the contemporary Western world. "Dark times" was a term she borrowed from a Bertolt Brecht poem to refer to the absence of political or public freedom, the lack of public spaces of speech and action whereby citizens could reveal their unique individualities and have a say in the conduct of public affairs. The lack of a "public realm [capable of] throw[ing] light on the affairs of men by providing a space of appearances in which they can show in deed and word . . . who they are and what they can do" (viii) meant that direct apprehension of the nature and life-affirming meaning of politics that might be gained through participating in public affairs had become a remote possibility.[24]

The contemporary problem of understanding the nature and promise of politics in the absence of genuine politics was further compounded, in Arendt's view, by the serious inadequacy of prevailing social scientific and ideological modes of political analysis. She held social scientific and ideological approaches to be deficient because they tended to construe the individual primarily as a product of social forces or trends, recognizing his or her actions and sufferings as significant only derivatively. Against the background of her deeply felt awareness of the related crises of politics and political understanding, critics perceive her as adopting a theoretical approach to politics that aims at recalling people to the revelatory potential of particular events. It is by recourse to the revelatory capacity of particulars, the argument goes, that Arendt hopes to reveal and preserve the potentially self-sponsoring significance of the deeds and sufferings of individual human beings.

It is in the context of Arendt's setting of the task of political theory as the mustering of significance from particulars, *as* particulars, that many of her readers have understood her needing to resort frequently to fictional characters and scenes, narrative devices, and personal anecdote and quotable utterance. In the face both of the denaturing collectivism of mass politics and the denaturing abstractness of prevailing scientific and ideological modes of understanding politics, Arendt resorts to literary examples and devices as a means of recapturing the concreteness, particularity, and contingency of human affairs. To take just one of the previous examples, Disch argues that Arendt's use of moral hyperbole in her analysis of the concentration camps ("the Nazis' crime is not just wicked but 'deformed wicked-

ness'") served to call attention to the terrible novelty of a phenomenon whose unprecedented nature was less apprehensible "in terms
of traditional categories such as guilt and innocence."[25]

Critics see in Arendt's recurrence to a storytelling mode of theory
an appropriate and effective means of achieving a "'transparent display of the inner truth of the event'" through the illumination of
the contingency that human plurality endows to human affairs.[26] To
them, Arendt's resort to fictional characters, literary devices, and
anecdote makes sense in a world where politics has largely lost its
revelatory power and where prevailing modes of political analysis
are incapable of witnessing or even remembering that power. The fitness of Arendt's use of storytelling is apparent to Seyla Benhabib,
who suggests that "the method of political theory as storytelling . . .
in Arendt's hands, is transformed into a redemptive narrative, re-
deeming the memory of the dead, the defeated and the vanquished
by making present to us once more their failed hopes, their untrod-
den paths, and unfulfilled dreams."[27]

Many Arendt interpreters (like Benhabib above) locate the redemptive appeal of Arendtian storytelling in its remembrance of the
aspirations and deeds of historical "losers," those individuals and
groups whose efforts to win some degree of justice or a share of
power or, at the barest minimum, recognition of their right to survive come to naught. Arendt's stories are seen as offering the consolation of remembrance as compensation for military or political defeat. In this vein, Beiner (1982) suggests that Arendt's mode of
storytelling theory, by inviting us to "reflect on the miraculousness
of human freedom as instantiated in particular moments of the
past," gives us cause to "hope" rather than to "despair."[28] Beiner offers little in the way of systematic argument about the nature or
sources of the reconciliatory effects of Arendtian storytelling, beyond this ad hoc reference to hope, however. Why should stories of
failed strivings and ruined aspirations foster a sense of hope rather
than despair? After all, remembrance of a lost cause seems a slender
reed on which to rest one's hopes.

With Beiner, consideration of how Arendtian storytelling affects its
audience comes to a premature halt, resting merely on an appeal to
an unexamined power of stories to inspire hope. Other commentators substitute an appeal to ontology in the place of an adequate investigation of the grounds of storytelling effect. This kind of circular

reasoning sneaks its way, for example, into Benhabib's otherwise care-
ful and insightful essay. In one strategic passage, Benhabib suggests
that Arendt's use of narrative rests on the notion that storytelling is
significant to living a human life because the activity is ontologically
grounded in human nature. "The narrative structure of action and of
human identity means that the continuing retelling of the past, its
continued reintegration into the story of the present, its reevaluation,
reassessment, and reconfiguration are ontological conditions of the
kinds of beings we are."[29]

To Benhabib's credit, she does not conclude her argument with
this appeal to ontology but follows up with a set of pointed questions about the criteria by which the Arendtian storyteller shapes
her narrative. "But what guides the activity of the storyteller when
tradition has ceased to orient our sense of the past? What structures
narrative modes when collective forms of memory have broken
down, have been obliterated, or have been manipulated beyond
recognition?" Unfortunately, the answer Benhabib elicits from
Arendt—poetic inspiration—lacks specificity.[30] In the absence of a
more thorough analysis isolating the specific poetic qualities of
Arendt's storytelling method of political theory, the nature of the relationship between narrative composition and audience response remains obscure.

In a way similar to Benhabib, David Luban, an early and insightful commentator on Arendt's storytelling approach to theory, pushes
his analysis only so far. Noting Arendt's claim that it is "'poetry' in
the broadest sense" that gives rise to a "*formed* narrative," Luban
goes on briefly to consider her analysis of the distinctive power of
poetry to convey the "ineffable meaning of events" through
metaphor.[31] However, beyond this appeal to the redemptive power
of poetic metaphor to convey meaning, Luban offers no specifics
other than to suggest that Arendt ambivalently modeled her storytelling mode of theory on Homeric poetry.

However unsatisfactory the analyses of Benhabib and Luban are
in delineating the relationship between Arendt's approach to forming historical or literary material into a narrative and the intended
effect on the narrative audience or readership, they do suggest a
promising line of investigation. With their pointed references to issues of narrative form and structure, they invite us to consider
Arendt's storytelling practices at a different level of analysis. They in-

vite us to consider those practices in terms of the conventions of genre or plot type.

The materials for providing a fuller account of how storytelling works politically relevant effects on an audience are not lacking in Arendt. Those materials have escaped analytical attention partly because a *fourth* storytelling dimension of Arendt's theoretical practice has drawn little sustained attention or systematic study. The other three dimensions are the use of story characters and events, the employment of literary devices, and the heavy reliance on personal anecdote and quotable utterance. The fourth is her sometimes self-conscious shaping of historical material according to the conventions of a particular plot type.

As Hayden White (1978) has reminded us, the historian, in formulating his or her story of the past, has recourse to a fund of inherited conventions about the different ways of organizing past events into a narrative. These *"mythoi"* or *"'pre-generic plot-structures'"* or "modes of emplotment" (as White variously calls them) "indicate, 'formally, the appropriate gravity and respect' to be accorded by the reader to the species of facts reported in the narrative."[32] One could say, with regard to these "modes of emplotment," that they embody various assumptions about what effect on the reader's imagination is to be aimed for and what narrative means are to be employed to achieve it. With White in mind, political theorists interested in exploring the promise of Arendt's storytelling mode of political theory to foster critical and connected political membership might consider her theory in terms of its possible modes of emplotment.

A general survey of the critical literature focused on the storytelling or narrative aspects of Arendt's theory shows that references are not lacking to Arendt's theoretical methods and aims in terms of genre or plot categories. These references, typically made in passing, generally associate her with the tragic composers of ancient Greece, Homer and the fifth-century tragedians. Shklar (1977), for example, after situating Arendt's distinctive methodological practice of "epic history" between the genres of philosophy and poetry, links Arendt's achievement to the specific poetic genre of tragedy: "To write epic history . . . one must make one's peace with the masters of tragedy."[33] In his analysis of Arendt's storytelling approach to

theory, Melvyn Hill (1979) applies standards implicitly derived from
Aristotle's theory of tragedy in order to distinguish Arendtian "stories of men" from ideological "fictions of mankind. . . . How can we
distinguish a story from a fiction? Only by whether we recognize
the experiences and events in its telling rather than a series of unified abstractions. Here the criteria of the possible and probable
come into play, which, according to Aristotle, make up the realm
that poetry illuminates."[34]

In her recent book about Arendt's storytelling practices, Disch
notes some significant parallels between the kind of "spontaneous
critical thinking" taught by Arendt and the inductive, egalitarian
form of paideia that Martha Nussbaum in *The Fragility of Goodness*
claims as the distinctive achievement of Greek tragedy. "The implicit
claim of Arendt's earliest writings and final work on judgment
echoes Nussbaum's argument that storytelling both exhorts and
teaches spontaneous critical thinking."[35] Referring to Arendt as "our
poet of political life," Kimberley Curtis makes Arendt's engagement
with the theater critic and playwright G. E. Lessing and his notion of
"tragic pleasure" the starting point for her consideration of the aesthetic dimensions of Arendt's promise to democratic theory. Curtis is
particularly concerned to understand Arendt's sense of the relationship between citizens' acceptance of difference ("a real gladness in
the recalcitrant and plural quality of the world") and the effect Lessing believed was called forth in spectators to tragedy.[36]

Significantly, in these and other instances in which readers attribute a tragic quality to Arendt's aims, methods, and achievement,
one also finds hopeful readings of the promise of Arendtian theory
to foster political freedom in contemporary times. Thus, Shklar reads
Arendt as a proponent of freedom who, while holding no illusions
about the extent of the obstacles to freedom in the contemporary
world, was nonetheless intent on exploiting what opportunities
there were by retelling history as a chronicle of great deeds and sufferings. "Monumental history salvages whatever can still be praised,
and cultivates whatever can still be found at hand to nourish us in a
very dry season. This is a service to a reality that indulges in no illusions about the distant future, but reconciles us to a living past and
teaches us to concentrate on the best conceivable present."[37]

In a similar spirit, Hill allows a substantial role for Arendt's political thought in "keeping the political imagination alive to the possi-

bility and requirements of freedom." For him, Arendt's narrative re-membrance of past instances of freedom credibly aims at inspiring future instances of freedom through activation of the faculty of political judgment. "In making his selection [of significant stories] . . . the political thinker offers a disclosure of reality on which to base judgment and [thereby] attempts to provide a record of experience that will stir the political imagination of future generations into life."[38]

The contemporary efficacy and relevance of Arendt's theoretical partisanship for freedom is likewise apparent to Disch and Curtis. Convinced of the promise of Arendt's writings to contribute "to contemporary attempts to specify radical democratic practices" (19), Disch formulates a procedural model of political judgment ("situated impartiality" [20]), which she claims is both achievable under present conditions and consistent with the requirements of an activist, pluralist citizenry. For Curtis, proper consideration of Arendt's aestheticism can provide readers with a fuller appreciation of the significance of radical democratic practices, especially their promise to "intensify our awareness of reality."[39]

Although Sheldon Wolin (1977) cannot fully be assimilated to the literature emphasizing the "narrative" or "storytelling" dimensions of Arendt's theoretical practice (he characterizes this practice in terms of "truthtelling"), it is still noteworthy that he—like Shklar, Hill, and Disch—seems also to read Arendt's theory as both politically hopeful and akin to tragedy as well as to epic. "She elevated politics and political action to the level of epic and tragedy, not in order to exonerate actors from their misdeeds or to glorify a particular nation, but to impose a demand upon those who presumed to decide great public matters and upon those who presumed to theorize about political actors and actions." To Wolin's piece, we can also add Alfred Kazin's review of Young-Bruehl's biography, in which Arendt's "Antigone-like" sense of the relationship between freedom and thinking is described as endowing "an unceasing seriousness of tone and inflexibility of judgment fundamental to the tragic vision of our age behind everything she wrote." Kazin concludes the review by implicitly evoking the activist orientation of Arendt's theoretical efforts: "That there has been a 'break,' that we live in truly 'dark times,' no one confronted by her was allowed to doubt. Arendt's greatest value, her distinct example, was that she *could not accept this break*, as most of us do."[40]

Conversely, commentators who read Arendt as being more pessimistic about the prospects for fostering political freedom tend to assimilate her kind of storytelling to genres other than tragedy. Luban, who argues that Arendt's search for reconciliation through poetic storytelling presupposes acceptance of the fact that public spaces of speech and action no longer exist to provide citizens with the promise of a meaningful illusion of immortality, assimilates Arendtian storytelling to Homeric epic in its pre-political, pre-polis manifestation.[41] Luban states, "Arendt has indeed gone into the past for her version of 'explanation': but since *die Vaterstadt* has collapsed she has gone into the Age of Poetry, the Homeric world preceding the polis, and not into the more recent past of historical narratives that depend, albeit indirectly, on the experience of the polis for their validity." Similarly reading Arendt as a pessimist about the prospects for freedom in the modern world, Benhabib also assimilates Arendt's narrative mode of theorizing to a depoliticalized storytelling genre, fragmentary historiography. "Arendt was well aware that by arguing that the activity of storytelling was like that of the pearl diver and of the collector, she was consciously leaving out poetry. . . . [B]etween the poet who sings to eternalize the city and save from oblivion those deeds of human greatness and the modern storyteller who has no identifiable city, there is no more kinship."[42]

These correlations in the literature, between assessments of Arendt's hopes for the possibility of fostering political freedom in contemporary times and assimilations of her storytelling mode of political theory to specific storytelling genres, suggest an approach to Arendt's work that promises not only to illuminate an underexamined aspect of her work (the political role and significance of intuition) but also to supplement contemporary efforts to conceptualize a role for intuition in the promotion of a critical and connected democratic political membership. However offhanded or implicit the various references to Arendt's thought in terms of tragedy (and Greek tragedy in particular), they nonetheless suggest a starting point for investigating the political significance of imagination or intuition in Arendt's thought: the tragic theater in fifth-century Athens. For Greek tragedy has traditionally been seen as existing interdependently with the institutions of polis citizenship in Athens's democratic heyday, promoting that rare combination of critical insight about human convention and voluntary, sustainable commitment to human convention that contemporary theorists such as Nussbaum, Strong, and Euben (in the spirit, if not in the footsteps of Aristotle) have sought to conceptualize. And theories of tragedy have, since Goethe's time, provided German theorists with an important means for thinking about and acting on the promise of fostering meaningful and viable forms of political life.

CHAPTER TWO

Arendt's Resort to Greek Tragedy in the Context of German Philhellenism

What you write about the American Founding Fathers and what you convey about them is completely new to me. You will have made historical discoveries here that will rouse the Americans out of their self-forgetfulness. Your comparison and identification of the meaning of the "workers' and soldiers' councils," the "small republics," the beginnings and truth of all revolutions since the American one, were familiar to me from your Hungary essay. That essay left me hesitant; but now I am convinced of the parallels of meaning and of the opportunity you see in them, though that opportunity has so far always been lost.

In the course of your presentation, the greatness to which you give expression is a source of encouragement. Ultimately, the whole is your vision of a tragedy that does not leave you despairing: an element of the tragedy of mankind.

—Karl Jaspers to Hannah Arendt, May 16, 1963

Karl Jaspers's May 1963 epistolary assessment of Hannah Arendt's book *On Revolution* is notable in several respects. While he read and praised to Arendt all the books she published during his lifetime, Jaspers reserved his highest and most unconditional praise for her revolution book. Typically sober and measured in his judgments of her work, Jaspers apparently felt that Arendt had, in the execution of this book, somehow surpassed her previous efforts.[1]

A second noteworthy feature of Jaspers's report is his categorization of Arendt's achievement in terms of "tragedy." There is good reason to suspect that his use of this term is neither casual nor diffuse. In the first place, he had previously considered, systematically and at length, the nature and significance of tragedy in his book *Von der Wahrheit* (1947). His discussion of "tragic knowledge" eventually appeared as a book in its own right in the United States in 1952 under the title *Tragedy Is Not Enough*. In this book about the nature and meaning of tragedy, whose publication by an American publishing house Jaspers owed in part to Arendt's efforts, he attempted to clarify the basic features of a tragic vision and the promise and dangers of adopting such a vision.[2] Jaspers held that tragedy works when it reveals "some particular truth in every agent and at the same time the limitations of this truth, so [as] to reveal the injustice in everything." According to Jaspers, encounter with tragic stories, in which human hopes come to naught against the limits imposed by the plurality of human agents, could foster those very qualities that might lead to an authentic (philosophical) attachment to existence: "If preserved in purity, the original vision of the tragic already contains the essence of philosophy: movement, question, open-mindedness, emotion, wonder, truthfulness, lack of illusion."[3]

In delineating the nature and promise of tragic knowledge, Jaspers singled out the contributions made by Greek tragedy. In his view, Greek tragedy's privileged status as a paradigmatic tragic genre was manifest in that "all later tragedy [was] either dependent on it . . . or inspired by it." Even compared with preexistent forms of tragic insight such as Homeric epic, Greek tragedy won special mention because its tragic vision fostered qualities that enabled people not only to endure heroically a fundamentally conflicted and contradictory world but also to interrogate ceaselessly the grounds and meaning of that world. "Greek tragedy takes its raw material from this [heroic] world of myth and epic. But there is a difference. Men no longer bear their tragic knowledge calmly, but pursue their questions ceaselessly." Alongside the high promise of Greek tragedy (and of tragedy in general) to promote a questioning of the nature and meaning of human suffering, Jaspers considered in his book the dangers of tragedy. In particular, he warned of the possible misuse of tragedy as a "prop" for either aesthetic renunciation of responsible worldly action or nihilistic "destruction for its own sake."[4]

If Jaspers's own intellectual concerns conditioned him to be especially alert to the tragic aspects of literature, *On Revolution* and the Arendtian text he associates with it (the "Hungary essay") also invited application of a concept of the tragic. For example, in Arendt's "Hungary essay," which introduced the theme of council democracy (whose further development Jaspers so unconditionally praises

in his assessment of *On Revolution*), Arendt explicitly deploys a notion of tragedy in the course of reflecting on the nature, outcome,
and significance of the 1956 Hungarian "revolution." Arendt describes the Hungarian revolutionary outbreak as "a true event
whose stature will not depend upon victory or defeat" because "its
greatness is secure in the tragedy it enacted."[5] Arendt characterizes
the revolution in Hungary as a "stark and sometimes sublime
tragedy" not only for its being a notable example of the defeat of
human aspirations but also because this defeat might still serve to
"illuminate" something Arendt considered worthy of notice and remembrance, a basic human aspiration to exercise freedom of
thought and action.[6]

Jaspers probably also did not fail to notice that references to revolutions as tragedies are not lacking in *On Revolution* either. For instance, Arendt introduces her discussion of the unfulfilled promise of
the French Revolution to institute a lasting realm of public freedom
with the declaration that, "We know what happened in France in the
form of a great tragedy" (*OR* 132). Drawing upon Herman Melville's
story "Billy Budd," she discusses in explicitly tragic terms the incompatibility of absolute goodness with the fundamental relativism of
political affairs: "The tragedy is that the law is made for men, and
neither for angels nor for devils" (*OR* 84). The failure of the U.S. Constitution to recognize and incorporate those spaces of direct political
participation manifested in the New England township form of government is also, for Arendt, a "tragedy," of which, "only Jefferson
among the founders had a clear premonition" (*OR* 235).

If Jaspers missed these examples of Arendt's use of "tragedy" as
metaphor for revolutionary promise and failure, he surely could not
have overlooked the reenactment of Greek tragedy that occurs in the
book's final passage. For there, Arendt chooses to quote, at some
length and in Greek script with accompanying English translations,
a famous section of choral verse and a line of dialogue from Sophocles' last drama, *Oedipus at Colonus,* as a last effort at "approximately
articulating the actual content of the lost treasure" of the "revolutionary tradition" (*OR* 280). As Arendt's Theseus tells us, it is the fulfillment of the aspiration to found and sustain a "space of free men's
deeds and living words that enabled ordinary men, young and old,
to bear life's burden." Political freedom "endow[s] life with splendour—*ton Bion Lampron poieisthai*" (*OR* 281).[7]

In so conspicuously deploying elements of a Sophoclean drama in the coda of *On Revolution*, Arendt grounds her prior invocations of revolution-as-tragedy in what might be considered a highly resonant historical conjunction. As Jaspers had noted in his book on tragedy, Greek or Attic tragedy stands, in an important sense, as the original, paradigmatic tragic genre. Arendt's reference to an example of Greek tragedy as a means of affirming the distinctive revelatory status of the classical polis citizenry's achievement of political freedom may indicate an intention to supplement the appeal of her dramatic quotation by indirect reference to the simultaneous and, perhaps, interdependent presences of tragedy and institutions of political freedom such as the citizen assembly and citizen juries in the fifth-century Athenian polis.

That Jaspers saw Arendt's adoption of a tragic vision in *On Revolution* as dependent on the legacy of Attic tragedy is strongly suggested in the concluding passage of his letter of May 16, 1963: "I sometimes think in reading your book that Greece is there for you: without your homeland among the Greeks you would hardly have been able to find the form, without them you could not have found the perspective that allowed you to perceive the marvelous significance of the American Constitution and its origins." In his May 19 follow-up letter, which arrived together with his May 16 letter, Jaspers also implicitly endorses Arendt's use of a tragic perspective in *On Revolution* as a means of promoting political freedom:

> I continue reading your book with a steady enthusiasm that never flags. I wonder if your dream and mine, different as they may appear to be, don't really belong together after all, and, in any case, have the same base: the dream of political freedom which, as your book so enchantingly shows, has indubitably appeared here and there in this world in thought and reality.

For her part, Arendt, in her May 29, 1963, epistolary reply, enthusiastically endorsed Jaspers's initial impressions of *On Revolution*, particularly his detection of the tragic dimension of her story about revolution and freedom: "every word you wrote strikes to the very heart of what I meant to say. A tragedy that warms and lightens the heart because such great and simple things were at stake. Heinrich's experience, of course, *and* the experience of America."[8]

Arendt's confirming response to Jaspers's initial impressions of the tragic framework of *On Revolution* and her familiarity with Jaspers's book on tragedy might be taken as evidence that they were singing from the same hymnbook when it came to understanding the nature and significance of tragedy in modern times.[9] However, the previously noted indications of mutual recognition of Arendt's tragic perspective on revolution should be balanced against evidence of divergence. In *On Revolution,* the promotion of direct participation in public affairs appears to be the ultimate goal informing Arendt's telling of the "tragedy of Western revolutions in the modern age" ("What Is Authority?" *BPF* 140).[10]

Jaspers held that the experience of genuine tragedy ought to inspire the spectator to become involved: "Tragedy wants more: the catharsis of the soul. . . . It makes him more deeply receptive to reality, not merely as a spectator, but as a man who is personally involved."[11] It is, however, questionable whether the involvement he had mainly in mind at the time of his first composing his thoughts on tragic knowledge was citizen participation in political affairs. Jaspers's concept of the tragic seems to be informed more by a desire to promote the philosophic quest, in dialogue with others, for clarity about the limits of human truth than by a primary commitment to citizen involvement in politics of the kind that presumably existed in the fifth-century Athenian polis.

Such a difference in perspectives on the significance of tragedy is implied, for example, in Jaspers's and Arendt's divergent treatments of Sophocles' drama *Oedipus at Colonus.* Jaspers focuses on the Theban exile Oedipus as an example of tragic hero as truth seeker. Oedipus's "unrelenting thirst for knowledge and [his] unconditional acceptance of its consequences all the way to disaster—these create another truth. A new value is divinely bestowed upon Oedipus, he who had been cursed through knowledge and through fate. His bones confer blessings upon the land where he is laid to rest. Men care for his remains and make his grave a hallowed place. Oedipus himself has achieved an inner reconciliation, and this at last finds outward expression: his tomb becomes a shrine."[12] Arendt puts Theseus, king and founder of Athens, at center stage as heroic witness to the preeminent rewards of political action. The distinctively activist orientation of Arendt's notion of tragedy is further evidenced by her ready resort to characters from Homeric epic such as Ulysses and

Achilles as examples of tragic heroes.[13] Jaspers judged Homeric epic to be deficient as tragedy because it fostered modes of tragic insight— "the sheer joy of seeing, worship of the gods, unquestioned steadfastness and endurance"—of limited relevance to philosophical activity.[14]

What one might conclude from Jaspers's book on tragedy, Arendt's revolution book, and their May 1963 correspondence is that Jaspers was onto something important concerning Arendt's aims and method in *On Revolution* when he referred to the book as a "tragedy." His May 1963 letter exchange with Arendt alerts us to the possibility that she thought about the promise and limits of revolutions through a prism significantly conditioned by an appreciation of Greek tragedy. However, we cannot know from their correspondence the extent and significance of Arendt's reliance on tragedy in her theorizing about politics. And the prospects of easily achieving such knowledge does not seem promising in light of the fact that she does not offer in *On Revolution* or any other of her writings a systematic, extended analysis of the origins, nature, variety, and meaning of tragedy of the kind provided by Jaspers in *Tragedy Is Not Enough*.

If Arendt's presentation of a tragic vision in *On Revolution* lacks the explicit systematization of a Jaspers, it does bear clear resemblances to the use of tragedy made by her other intellectual mentor, Martin Heidegger. In the afterword included in the 1943 edition of *Was ist Metaphysik?* Heidegger closes his reflections on the differences between philosophical and poetic approaches to "being" with a quotation, in Greek script, of the closing choral utterance of *Oedipus at Colonus*. One thing this deployment of Sophoclean verse apparently signals is Heidegger's sense of ancient Greece, particularly ancient Greek theater, as a privileged site of contact with "being."[15]

In his celebrated set of lectures given at the University of Freiburg in 1935—and later published, with Arendt's encouragement and active support, in an American edition, under the title *Introduction to Metaphysics* (1959)—Heidegger refers to several Sophoclean tragedies by way of exemplifying the ancient Greeks' success at achieving appropriately meaningful contact with "being" through a kind of poetic thinking. For Heidegger, fragments of pre-Socratic wisdom such as Parmenides' maxim "There is a reciprocal bond between apprehension and being" and examples of tragic versification such as the famous choral utterance of tragic wisdom "Incomparably best is not to be" of *Oedipus at Colonus* and the second choral ode of the

Antigone, "There is much that is strange, but nothing that surpasses man in strangeness"[16] give telling witness to an original and revelatory insightfulness into man's unique and "uncanny" ability to approach "being" and, yet, also to let this approach lead to a falling away from "being." According to Heidegger, particularly manifest in the meditation of the *Antigone* chorus on man's status as *to deinotaton* (the strangest of the strange) is the insight that genuine contact with "being" or the "essent" lies at the basis of human beings' power to create a meaningful world for themselves—a world of poetry, thought, architecture, and politics, among other things. "The violence of poetic speech, of thinking projection, of building configuration, of the action that creates states is not a function of faculties that man has, but a taming and ordering of powers by virtue of which the essent opens up as such when man moves into it. This disclosure of the essent is the power that man must master in order to become himself amid the essent, i.e. in order to be historical."[17] At the same time, human beings' contact with "being," their "being-there," exposes them to the dangers of a hubristic forgetfulness of the true origin and basis of their powers and a self-destructive employment of them:[18]

> The *violent one,* the creative man, who sets forth into the un-said, who breaks into the un-thought, compels the unhappened to happen and makes the unseen appear—this violent one stands at all times in venture (*tolma,* line 371). In venturing to master being, he must risk the assault of the nonessent, *me kalon,* he must risk dispersion, in-stability, disorder, mischief.[19]

Although it is a text of Greek tragedy that provides the occasion for Heidegger to affirm this fundamental dialectic of man's relation to "being," he does not here formulate this dialectic explicitly in terms of a notion of "the tragic." In other words, he does not draw the conclusion from the Sophoclean chorus's characterization of man as "the strangest of the strange" that man is a fundamentally tragic being.

Heidegger's explicit formulation of the tragic as the one decisive feature of man's relation to "being" does occur in his 1937 lectures on Nietzsche's notion of eternal return. He starts with a Nietzschean aphorism from *Beyond Good and Evil:* "Everything in proximity to the hero becomes tragedy; everything in proximity to the demigod

becomes satyr-play; and everything in proximity to God becomes . . .
what? 'world' perhaps?"[20] Heidegger argues that Nietzsche's Zarathustra fulfills the role of tragic hero. The tragedy of which Zarathustra is
a hero is "the tragedy of beings as such," the tragedy of beings' implication in the eternal coming and passing away of existence.[21] In
other words, as a human being, Zarathustra must confront the inevitable facts of suffering and death. Nietzsche's Zarathustra becomes
a hero, according to Heidegger, when he becomes able to affirm the
eternally recurring cycle of change, thereby to be reconciled to suffering and death.

Can Heidegger's Sophoclean-occasioned 1935 meditation on the
dialectic of being, his 1937 analysis of the tragic aspect of this dialectic, and his 1943 citation of *Oedipus at Colonus* shed any light on
whether a notion of the tragic significantly informs Arendt's study of
revolutions or her political thought in general? The frequency and
context of her references to the "famous chorus of *Antigone*" suggest
that Heidegger's discussion of the ancient Greek insight into the dialectic of "being" did have its impact. For example, in the essays that
compose *Between Past and Future,* invocation of the *Antigone* chorus
becomes a standard way for Arendt to illustrate the ancient Greek
understanding of human beings' power to establish a discernible
and lasting presence against the background of the cyclical processes
of nature:

> When Sophocles (in the famous chorus of *Antigone*) says that there is
> nothing more awe-inspiring than man, he goes on to exemplify this
> by evoking purposeful human activities which do violence to nature
> because they disturb what, in the absence of mortals, would be the
> eternal quiet of being-forever that rests or swings within itself. ("The
> Concept of History," *BPF* 42)[22]

Arendt goes on to argue, in "The Concept of History," that ancient
Greek bards and writers formulated the "task" of poetry- or history-
writing as the assurance of lasting remembrance of men's words and
deeds because they accepted the "tragic" paradox that while "everything was seen and measured against" the eternity that characterized
the processes of nature, human greatness "reside[d] in deeds and
words," which resulted from "the most futile and least lasting activities of men" (*BPF* 45–46).

These passages suggest that Heidegger's interpretation of the second choral ode of *Antigone* as a preeminent expression of man's power to become historical by creating lasting sites of the disclosure of "being" may have shaped Arendt's characterization of ancient Greek poetry as a response to the condition of mortality. Arendt's choice to invoke a Sophoclean tragedy at the conclusion of *On Revolution* suggests, in addition, that Heidegger's 1935 commentary on Sophocles—with its solemn invocations of original Greek terminology and its resonant appropriation of the vocabulary of Hölderlin's famous translation of the Sophoclean text—and his 1943 appropriation of the concluding choral utterance from *Oedipus at Colonus* provided her with models for exploiting some of the expressive power of Greek tragedy. In both Arendt's *On Revolution* and Heidegger's 1935 lecture and 1943 afterword, extended quotations (from ancient Greek language texts or translations) of Sophoclean tragic verse signal efforts at recovering what are considered original and preeminent Greek insights into fundamental modes of affirming life in the face of the burdens of human existence, including mortality. If (as George Steiner has suggested) the second choral ode of *Antigone* can be seen to serve Heidegger as "the inherent talisman, the proof that 'Being', so largely lapsed from western life and thought, was radiantly immanent in certain speech-acts and recapturable," then the choral utterance of tragic wisdom—together with Theseus's affirmation of the revelatory quality of action—can be seen analogously to serve Arendt as a kind of "proof" that the human capacity for political freedom, largely forgotten and unfulfilled since the time of the classical polis, could once again be lastingly remembered and exercised.[23]

Recognition of the parallel uses made of Sophoclean passages by Arendt and Heidegger as means of recovering fundamental human capacities for affirming life should not obscure a significant difference, however. Arendt seemingly places her tragic invocation squarely in the service of promoting political freedom as that life-affirming capacity, whereas Heidegger harnesses his invocation to a different task, the task of fostering an exclusively contemplative, unremittingly solitary relationship to "being."[24] As Dana Villa has recently suggested, Heidegger's affirmation of the disclosive power of Sophoclean tragedy—and Greek poetry generally—rests on his identification of "the illuminative activity of the Greeks not with doxastic political action, but rather with the poetic or creative activity that 'wrests' the truth of being concealed by the 'dimmed down' appearances of the public realm."[25]

It may be that Heidegger's meditation on the meaning of the second choral ode of *Antigone*, his use of the closing verses of *Oedipus at Colonus*, and his analysis of the tragic significance of Nietzsche's Zarathustra significantly contributed to Arendt's sense of the ancient Greek tragic perspective on human greatness and inspired her telescoped reenactment of a Sophoclean tragedy as a means of restoring her readers' memory of, and taste for, political freedom in the final passage of *On Revolution*. It may also be that Jaspers's analysis of the nature and significance of tragic knowledge in *Tragedy Is Not Enough* informed Arendt's conceptualization of revolution as tragedy in *On Revolution*. Even granting these possibilities, the reader might still be left to wonder whether Arendt's application of tragedy as a metaphor for revolution or her resort to a Greek tragedy for politically inspirational verse manifests a significant conceptual framework in her political thought. After all, she could have meant by her characterization of revolution as tragedy nothing more than that revolutions tend to have "sad end[ings]" (*OR* 246, 255). She could have cited passages from *Oedipus at Colonus* in her revolution book solely for their poetic expressiveness rather than for their being, in addition, markers for the distinctive association between Greek tragedy and the democratic polis. Even granting that Arendt's writings contain a fairly substantial, albeit widely dispersed, number of references to Greek tragedies, to tragedy as a literary genre, and to the tragic as a category of historical description, what indications are there that these references manifest the working of a theoretically consequential concept of tragedy?[26]

At least two aspects of Arendt's political thought suggest that her references to tragedy reflect the presence of a tragic framework. In the first place, there is Arendt's tendency to conceptualize the political realm as a kind of theater, a "political theatre" (*OR* 108). To understand the essential nature of the phenomenon of politics is, for Arendt, to understand the kinship of that phenomenon with theatrical drama. In the second place, there is Arendt's tendency, in her references to tragedy, implicitly to evoke the authority of a German tradition of philhellenism characterized by a "tenacious preoccupation with the theory of drama and the idea of the 'tragic.'"[27]

Arendt's emphasis on the dramatic or theatrical aspects of politics is obvious enough and has been amply noted by both sympathetic and unsympathetic readers.[28] The term *public* means for Arendt "that everything that appears in public can be seen and heard by everybody and has the widest possible publicity" (*HC* 50). For her, the "function of the public realm [is] to throw light on the affairs of men by providing a space of appearances in which they can show in deed and word . . . who they are and what they can do" (*MDT* viii). The political actor who inhabits the public realm is a potential "hero," that is, a potential subject of the unique story of his or her own deeds and sufferings ("The Web of Relationships and the Enacted Stories," *HC* ch. 25). And just as "performing artists—dancers, play-actors, musicians, and the like—need an audience to show their virtuousity, [so] acting men need the presence of others before whom they can appear" ("What Is Freedom?" *BPF* 154).

Among the several witnesses Arendt brings forward to attest to the performative nature of political action and the stagelike aspects of the public realm are the eighteenth-century revolutionaries, who "preferred to draw their images from the language of the theatre" (*OR* 106). In addition, Arendt offers etymological evidence of the ancient Roman republican experience of the theaterlike aspects of politics: "The profound meaningfulness inherent in the many political metaphors derived from the theatre is perhaps best illustrated by the history of the Latin word *persona*." Originally, *persona* referred to the theatrical "mask affixed to the actor's face by the exigencies of the play." Later, according to Arendt, it came to mean, legal personality, in reference to the cluster of rights and duties that indicated to the citizen "the part he was expected to play on the public scene" (*OR* 106–7).

In the Greek polis Arendt saw, perhaps, the most compelling historical example of the public realm in its kinship with the theatrical stage. "The Greek polis was precisely that 'form of government' which provided men with a space of appearances where they could act, with a kind of theater where freedom could appear" (*BPF* 154). The reference to theater is doubly evocative, on one level referring to the polis's aspect as political performance space for citizens and on another level evoking the Athenian's polis's sponsorship of dramatic performances in the city theater. Arendt explicitly connects the political freedom of the polis and the polis's sponsorship of dramatic performance when, drawing explicitly on the authority of Aristotle's *Poetics*, she affirms the preeminent capacity of theatrical drama to "represent" the essence of what citizens do in politics:

> The specific revelatory quality of action and speech . . . is so indissolubly tied to the living flux of acting and speaking that it can be represented or "reified" only through a kind of repetition, the imitation or *mimesis*, which according to Aristotle prevails in all arts but is actually appropriate only to the *drama*, whose very name (from the Greek verb *dran*, "to act") indicates that play-acting actually is an imitation of acting. (*HC* 187)

Arendt's explicit reliance on Aristotle's *Poetics* in this instance—mention of the text comes in a series of footnotes (*HC* 187 nn. 11, 12)—constitutes only one of several in which Arendt refers to Aristotle's analysis of Attic or Greek tragedy as poetic genre. In her other references to Aristotle in his role as analyst of tragedy, Arendt reveals in an explicit way what she merely implies in the above reference; that the writing and reception of tragedies, in whatever form, serves important political functions:

> To the extent that the teller of factual truth is also a storyteller, he brings about that "reconciliation with reality" which Hegel, the philosopher of history *par excellence*, understood as the ultimate goal of all philosophical thought. . . . We may see, with Aristotle, in the poet's political function the operation of a catharsis, a cleansing or purging of all emotions that could prevent men from acting. The political function of the storyteller—historian or novelist—is to teach acceptance of things as they are. ("Truth and Politics," *BPF* 262)

Whether implicit or explicit, Arendt's several references to Aristotle in his role as author of the *Poetics* cast a revealing light on her tendency both to cite Sophoclean tragic verse and to characterize political events and developments as tragedies.[29]

These references suggest, in the words of M. S. Silk and J. P. Stern, the working in Arendt's political thought of "a particular tradition within German thought . . . a tradition of theoretical inquiry into the nature of tragedy—Greek tragedy, above all." These authors go on to list some basic features of this tradition:

This tradition goes back at least to Herder and Lessing in the eighteenth century; and it continues beyond Nietzsche to Johannes Volkelt
and Bertolt Brecht in our time. Common to all contributors . . . is their
profound interest in the literature of ancient Greece. They all take issue, in a variety of ways, with the classic theory of tragedy propounded in Aristotle's *Poetics*; they all, in the wake of Herder, make
some attempt to relate the achievements of the Greek tragedies to the
religious or social facts of Greek life; and they all consider the dramas
of Aeschylus, Sophocles, and Euripides to form one of the summits of
world literature.[30]

German men of letters' long-standing affirmation of the preeminent value of Greek tragedy and its lasting relevance for German
and European culture and politics has been analyzed by both the
bearers and the historians of the tradition. Literary critics and historians of ideas have usually identified German political and economic backwardness as a main factor in the emergence within German letters of the idea that the literary survivals of Greek tragedy
could serve as valuable prisms through which to understand—even
act on—contemporary personal and political predicaments. Arguments of this kind suggest that the Thirty Years War, in intensifying
Germany's condition of political fragmentation, hindered the rise
of a middle class with sufficient resources and elan to unify the
country and institutionalize middle-class citizenship.[31] Unable to
exercise a degree of political influence and power comparable to
their counterparts in England and France, members of the middle
class in Germany, in this reading, redirected their hopes and ener-
gies into the realm of cultural production. As a result, educated Germans of the middle class tended to cultivate an ambivalent "aestheticism," which "was partly the expression of their aloofness
from the world in which the 'mind' had proved itself to be power-
less, partly the roundabout way towards the realization of a human
ideal that could not be realized by the direct way of political and
social education."[32]

A defining moment in the aestheticization of intellectual life in
Germany, in this view, was the mid–eighteenth century publication
of Johann Joachim Winckelmann's pioneering study of ancient
Greek art, *Von der Nachahmung der griechischen Werke in der Malery
und Bildhauerkunst* (Reflections on the Imitation of Greek Works in

Painting and Sculpture, 1755). Winckelmann's admiring vision of the full, beautiful humanity of the ancient Greeks—expressing itself in their festivals, sculpture, and athletic competitions—inspired German men of letters from Goethe onward. As counterimage to Germany's perceived political and cultural backwardness, the vision of the ancient polis first propagated by Winckelmann then supplemented by his readers allowed middle-class intellectuals to grasp contemplatively a condition of unity and efficacy so apparently lacking in worldly affairs. "Classicism has usually been the product of corporate feeling, but German classicism looked upon it as its mission to call this corporate feeling into existence through art."[33]

In the search for personally vitalizing and politically renovative access to what Hegel called the "beautiful Greek totality," the texts of Greek tragedy were held to be preeminently significant.[34] The historical role of Greek tragedy as a civic spectacle—a "public artwork" produced, enacted, and judged by members of the citizen body in a performance watched by a large proportion of city residents—rendered it especially attractive in an environment conditioned by displaced hopes for political unity and efficacy.[35] A further reason for German philhellenists' predisposition to seek life-giving contact with ancient Greece primarily through the literary relics of Greek tragedy was their sense of the apparent fitness of Greek form to German content; after all, what art form could be better suited than tragedy to thinking through—and, perhaps, acting on—Germany's lamentable situation of internal political division and external political helplessness?

Friedrich Schiller's 1804 affirmation of the robust political promise of a national theater expressed a claim about the political relevance of drama and invoked a historical precedent, Greek drama, that were enduringly resonant in the German literary context.

> I can not here overlook the great influence that a good-standing theater would have on the spirit of the nation. . . . If we experienced having a national theater, so would we also become a nation. What chained Greece so tightly together? What drew the people so unresistingly to their theater? Nothing else but the national content of the

plays, the Greek spirit, and the great overwhelming interest of the
state and of a better humanity.[36]

Even after the unification of Germany in 1871, calls for German
unity from German speakers residing outside the newly set borders
of the Second Reich continued to be couched explicitly in terms of
the aesthetic-political precedent supposedly set by the ancient Greek
sponsors of tragedy. "Wagner found the drama in its ideal purity and
sublimity among the Greeks; here religion and art were joined in a
bond which produced a community . . . that after two thousand
years seems to us like a beautiful dream of humanity."[37]

Friedrich Nietzsche's *Birth of Tragedy* had no small role in making
it a settled belief among German-speaking intellectuals that effectively engaging contemporary cultural and political problems depended, in important part, on understanding Greek tragedy. In the
preface to the original (1872) edition, Nietzsche asserts, in typical
German philhellenist fashion, the preeminent significance of culture
for Germany's fate, implying, for example, that the seemingly momentous events of the Franco-Prussian War and its political aftermath provided a mere backdrop to his consideration of the nature of
Greek tragedy and its meaning for "German hopes."[38] In this, his first
book, Nietzsche held that Greek tragedy in the time of Aeschylus
achieved the highest aim of art: the promotion of a community of individuals in whom the ("Apollonian") impulse to individual self-assertion is tempered in a life-affirming way by the ("Dionysian") apprehension of the fundamental unity of all things existent. Tragedy
did so, according to Nietzsche, by combining choral song and dance
with enactments of the stories of mythic heroes. In witnessing the
agonies of individuation (represented in the spectacle of a mythic
hero's sufferings and death) while receiving a rapturous intimation of
the "oneness of everything existent," through identification with the
singing and dancing chorus, tragic spectators achieved a sort of reflective and redemptive detachment from the struggles of individuated existence. In Nietzsche's reading, the institution of tragic spectatorship thereby permitted Athenians to put their political and
philosophic impulses in creative interplay and be "fiery and contemplative at the same time." In the cultural and political institutions of
Wilhelmine Germany, however, Nietzsche saw little promise of the
formation of true individuals or of a community fit to house them.[39]

Whether the claim is that Greek tragedy or its modern functional equivalents offers an effective means for resolving serious political problems (as Schiller seems to suggest about theater's significance for German unity) or that it liberates people from primary concern with political affairs by indicating the more fundamental cultural issues at stake (as the above reading of *The Birth of Tragedy* holds), the sense of political displacement is equally palpable.

From the perspective afforded by the displacement thesis of German cultural development, German philhellenism in its tragic variant shows two negative faces. On the one hand, engagement with tragedy has been seen as promoting attitudes of political withdrawal and resignation. Jaspers expressed this danger as one of letting "tragedy shrivel to aesthetic detachment." He noted, as one of the signs indicating this condition, a tendency to "see the world in terms of grandiose and tragic interpretations: the world is so made that everything great in it is doomed to perish, and it is made for the delight of the unconcerned spectator."[40]

If a concern with Greek tragedy—and with tragedy in general—can inappropriately lend itself to a stance of politically resigned aesthetic detachment, it can also, in what Jaspers considered the other pernicious extreme of tragic misuse, become mobilized in the service of highly irresponsible forms of action. If, in the former case, consciousness of suffering is transformed through contact with tragedy into an object of contemplative pleasure *merely*, in the latter, contact with tragedy is felt to give license to an active intensification of suffering. It is this latter possibility that Jaspers apparently has in mind in a passage that implicitly condemns the Nazi misappropriation of Greek tragedy:

> Wherever a total lack of faith seeks to parade as form, it finds the philosophy of nothing-but-tragedy well suited as a camouflage for nothingness. Tragic grandeur is the prop whereby the arrogant nihilist can elevate himself to the pathos of feeling himself a hero. . . . The racial past, the sagas, and Greek tragedy are all invoked. Yet what had then been the reality of faith becomes now a deliberate and dishonest substitute for nothingness. . . . Such perversion of tragic philosophy then sets free the turmoil of dark impulses: the delight . . . in destruction for its own sake, in the raging hatred against the world and man coupled with the raging hatred against one's own despised existence.[41]

Jaspers's approving comments about the tragic nature of Arendt's *On Revolution* confirm that he placed her envisioning of revolution as tragedy at neither of the two extremes, both of which he considered inappropriate. He does not explicitly locate her work in a specifically German tradition of concern with the tragic, and this may be because he conceptualized this tradition narrowly, including in it the work of tragic playwrights only—"Lessing; tragedy representing the ideals of German culture: Schiller and, subsequently, the nineteenth century." However, as Jaspers himself implicitly recognized, the specifically German search for tragic insight and release has occupied philosophers such as Hegel and Nietzsche, as well as playwrights such as Lessing and Schiller.[42]

Arendt shows herself partaking in this search in her engagement with the *Poetics* of Aristotle. German men of letters tended to "take issue . . . with the classic theory of tragedy propounded in Aristotle's *Poetics*," establishing the legitimacy of their reinterpretations and appropriations of Greek tragedy.[43] Although Arendt does not explicitly "take issue" with Aristotle's analysis of Greek tragedy, she does draw on it selectively, interpreting the *Poetics* in accordance with one of the main imperatives of her own theoretical project, the recovery of the true nature and meaning of political freedom.

Arendt's various resorts to Aristotelian notions of tragedy are effected through the mediation of notable theorists of tragedy from the German tradition, including Hegel and Lessing. Several references make this clear. Take, for example, Arendt's conflation in at least two instances (one cited above) of Hegel's notion of "reconciliation with reality" with Aristotle's notion of catharsis. Reconciliation, a central concept of Hegel's philosophical praxis, was identified by him as a characteristic effect of Greek tragedy. Hegel's affirmation of reconciliation as Greek tragedy's proper aim was based on his apprehension of tragic content as the unfolding of a collision of ethical rights that have found expression in the words and deeds of individual agents.

Hegel held that the principal forms of tragic collision were of two kinds. First and preeminently, there were tragedies such as the *Orestiae* trilogy of Aeschylus and the *Antigone* of Sophocles, centered on "the opposition . . . between ethical life in its social universality and the family as the natural ground of moral relations."[44] A second category of tragic collision originated in the tendency of human action

to have unintended consequences; of this type of collision "Sophocles . . . left . . . the most complete example in his *Oedipus Rex* and
Oedipus at Colonus" (*On Tragedy* 69). The revelation of the particularity or "one-sidedness" of both parties to the tragic conflict constituted the basic ground for the reconciliation that followed in the
plot of the tragedy.

> The *tragic* destruction of figures whose ethical life is on the highest
> plane can interest and elevate us and reconcile us to its occurrence
> only in so far as they come on the scene in opposition to one another
> together with equally justified but different ethical powers which have
> come into collision through misfortune, because the result is that then
> these figures acquire guilt through their opposition to an ethical law.
> Out of this situation there arises the right and wrong of both parties
> and therefore the true ethical Idea, which, purified and in triumph
> over this one-sidedness, is thereby reconciled in *us*. (237)

What had first appeared as irreconcilable and contradictory ethical
claims come to be revealed through tragedy's "vision of eternal justice" as "fundamentally and essentially concordant" aspects of a
more objective reality (51). Hegel offers, as an example of this revelation, the conclusion of the *Eumenides*, when Athene's tie-breaking
vote "frees Orestes" from liability for his act of matricide, "and at the
same time promises altars and a cult to the Eumenides [the defenders of maternal right]" (74).

Hegel suggests that, from the point of view of our modern sensibilities, the reconciliation effected in the "ever admirable" *Oedipus at
Colonus* is particularly compelling (*On Tragedy* 75). *Oedipus at Colonus*
recommends itself to modern audiences because the tragic reconciliation appears to play itself out more in the internal domain of Oedipus's spirit than in external action undertaken by the Olympian gods
to restore order and justice. It is Oedipus "who extinguishes all the
disruption in himself and who purifies himself in his own soul" (75).

Hegel's reinterpretation of the essential content of Greek tragedy
as the unfolding conflict or collision of ethical rights and his conceptualization of the tragic effect as one of reconciliation stand as
original, influential contributions to modern theories of tragedy.
Hegel himself was to suggest more than once that his notion of
tragic reconciliation supplemented, if not surpassed, Aristotle's idea

that genuine tragedy depends for its effect on exciting fear and pity in the audience. "Over and above mere fear and tragic sympathy we have . . . the feeling of *reconciliation*" (*On Tragedy* 51; also 123).

It might be taken as a sign of Arendt's acceptance of Hegel's gloss on Aristotle's *Poetics* that, in the two instances where she explicitly refers to Aristotle's notion of catharsis, she equates that notion with Hegel's "reconciliation with reality":

> The scene where Ulysses listens to the story of his own life is paradig-
> matic for both history and poetry; the "reconciliation with reality," the
> catharsis, which according to Aristotle was the essence of tragedy, and
> according to Hegel, was the ultimate purpose of history, came about
> through the tears of remembrance. The deepest human motive for his-
> tory and poetry appears here in unparalleled purity . . . listener, actor,
> and sufferer are the same person. ("The Concept of History," *BPF* 45)[45]

Hegel's emphasis in his theory of Greek tragedy on conflict between agents who put forth claims that are opposite but equally
principled and deserving of fulfillment would seem to recommend
him to a political theorist as concerned as Arendt was to affirm plurality as a basic condition of human affairs. However, in apparently
conflating Hegelian and Aristotelian notions of tragedy, Arendt puts
the theoretical coherence of her tragic partisanship for political freedom at some risk. For (as she was at pains to emphasize in numerous
other instances in her work), Hegel's "reconciliation with reality"
does little if anything to promote the active disposition of the virtuous citizen. To the contrary, insofar as Hegel's reconciliation partakes
of that comforting vision of a "pseudo-kingdom of disembodied spirits working behind men's backs" (*LM:W* 157), it serves to veil the basic contingency of human affairs, lending itself to an attitude of resignation that is consistent with an inappropriate renunciation of
action and freedom.[46] To put the problem in terms of the plot categories utilized by White (1987), the preparation for action promised
by Hegelian contact with Greek tragedy is severely compromised by
the Hegelian "sublation" of the tragedy of (individual) human action
into the comic plot of history as the progressive unfolding of *Geist*.[47]

Arendt gives little explicit indication of the terms upon which she
accepts Hegel's gloss on Aristotle's notion of catharsis. She is somewhat more forthcoming in her consideration and inflection of the

theory of tragedy propounded by G. E. Lessing, another influential figure in the German tragic tradition. A contemporary of Winckelmann, Lessing was a pioneering critic of arts and letters and a dramatist in his own right who translated Aristotle's *Poetics* and offered an interpretation of it as a means of promoting the creation of a vital and independent theater life in Germany. Lessing considered it the distinctive promise of theater to engage the passions and intellect of people to a degree and in a manner that they were more aware of their shared humanity and more motivated to act in accordance with it. Fulfilling this promise depended significantly, in Lessing's view, on understanding the true nature and significance of tragedy.

Lessing contended that genuine tragedy ought both to engage and to improve its (German) audience. It does so, he argued, by presenting characters on stage who are more or less like the German middle-class theatergoer, in situations in which he can imagine himself. It is the spectacle of the sufferings of a tragic hero near in character and situation to the German *Bürger* that is supposed to excite, in a profoundly engaging way, those feelings of compassion (for his fellow human being, the tragic hero) and fear (for himself, imagined in the place of the hero) that Aristotle, in Lessing's reading, considered the appropriate objects of tragedy's power.[48]

In addition to exciting compassion and fear in this way, the experience of watching tragic drama, Lessing argued, promised to purify spectators of the inappropriate extremes of these same emotions. Thus, for those given to excessive fear (for one example) or deficient compassion (for another), the experience of tragedy tends to give courage (in the one case) and stimulate fellow feeling (in the other). It was in this sense that Lessing thought about the promise of tragedy to improve its German middle-class audience morally and intellectually.

Arendt's consideration of Lessing was occasioned by the conferment of the Lessing Prize on her by the Hamburg Senate. (Lessing's long and manifold association with the city and its people included a stint as drama critic for the short-lived Hamburg National Theater.) In her acceptance address, Arendt approached the question of Lessing's significance from the perspective of what she considered one of the major crises of her time, the spreading indifference in the West toward political freedom. Lessing emerges in her presentation as a man who could teach by the example of his work and life that, even in politically inauspicious times, when opportunities for acting directly in politics with others are rare, ways of thinking and writing in support of freedom remain available. What Lessing's activity as critic of arts, letters, and life particularly reveals, according to Arendt, is the sensibility of one who cares that plural perspectives exist, and who takes care that they continue to exist:

> Criticism, in Lessing's sense, is always taking sides for the world's sake, understanding and judging everything in terms of its position in the world at any given time. Such a mentality can never give rise to a definite world view which, once adopted, is immune to further experiences in the world because it has hitched itself firmly to one possible perspective. ("On Humanity in Dark Times: Thoughts about Lessing," *MDT* 7–8)

In the course of arguing that Lessing's critical activity constituted a politically relevant form of "partisanship for the world," Arendt explicitly refers several times to his theory of tragedy. These references serve Arendt primarily as illustrations of what she takes to be Lessing's praiseworthy and politically beneficial tendency to judge things in relation to their reality as aspects of a shared world. Thus, for example, Arendt notes Lessing's Aristotelian approach to evaluating poetry in terms of its effect on the audience. "Lessing was not at all concerned with 'the perfection of art in itself.'. . . Rather—and here he is in agreement with Aristotle—he was concerned with the effect upon the spectator" (*MDT* 6–7). Lessing's worldliness is also apparent to Arendt in the reality-affirming view of the passions underlying his notion of "tragic pleasure": "'all passions . . . are pleasant' because 'they make us feel . . . more conscious of our existence, they make us feel more real'" (*MDT* 6).

In addition to serving as a fund of illustrative examples, Lessing's theory of tragedy provides Arendt with a conceptual framework for thinking about the nature of tragic storytelling and its relevance to the crisis of politics that, in her view, afflicted contemporary times. Insofar as totalitarian domination, particularly in its Nazi variant, was premised on the elimination of human beings' capacity to live as plural beings and to constitute a shared world of plural discourse and common action, its near success challenges the viability of those basic conditions of freedom, worldliness, and plurality that Lessing's activity as critic supported. "The question is how much reality must be retained even in a world become inhuman if humanity is not to be reduced to an empty phrase or a phantom" (*MDT* 22). Arendt considers the challenge posed by Nazism specifically as one of remembering a burdensome past. How can the past of Nazi atrocities be remembered for what it was without its truth giving the lie to the idea of a mutually constituted world of plural beings? Can such a past ever become a viable part of the shared world of plural discourse? Arendt argues that it can, if it is told in the form of a special kind of story, a story capable of evoking in its listeners a "'tragic effect' or 'tragic pleasure,' the shattering emotion which makes one able to accept the fact that something like this . . . could have happened at all." Tragedy is particularly suited to this purpose, Arendt suggests, because "it more than the other literary forms represents a process of recognition" (*MDT* 20).

> The tragic hero becomes knowledgeable by re-experiencing what has been done in the way of suffering, and in this *pathos*, in resuffering the past, the network of individual acts is transformed into an event, a significant whole. The dramatic climax of tragedy occurs when the actor turns into a sufferer; therein lies its peripeteia, the disclosure of the dénouement. (*MDT* 20)

This "suffering by memory operating retrospectively and perceptively" (*MDT* 21) is presented to the audience of a tragedy in the person of the tragic hero. Presumably, this representation has its effect on the audience through the audience's identification with the tragic hero. As Arendt suggests in another context, we, as tragic spectators, share in the tears Ulysses shed when he listened to the rhapsodes at the court of the Phaeacians sing of his deeds and sufferings ("The Concept of History," *BPF* 45). These tears supposedly indicate that we have both remembered the past and become reconciled to it. "The tragic impact of this repetition in lamentation affects one of the key elements of all action; it establishes its meaning and that permanent significance which then enters into history" (*MDT* 21).

Arendt discontinues her discussion of the reconciliatory promise of storytelling without addressing how that promise might resolve the issue with which she began her discussion—how to make the terrible deeds of Nazism a part of the world of plural discourse. One is left wondering exactly what it would mean to tell the story of Nazism so as to elicit a "tragic effect." For example, who would constitute the tragic hero of these terrible events? And how might the telling of this story as a tragedy promote freedom? If Arendt's references to Hegel's and Lessing's glosses on Aristotle's notion of catharsis can be taken as signs of her treading the well-worn path of the German tragic tradition, the tracks are altogether too slight to reveal adequately the distinctive character and significance of her theorization of tragedy. If Arendt can be seen, like her German forebears, to have drawn on Greek tragedy to resolve a political deficit, her sense of the origins, nature, and resolution of this deficit were presumably substantially different.

A change in approach is called for here, one better able to connect the insight that Arendt's perspective on politics was, in important respects, a *tragic* one with more central issues and concerns of her political theorizing. In the following two chapters, Arendt's multifaceted engagement with tragedy—for example, her citation of Greek tragedy and Homeric epic, her use of the term *tragedy* as descriptive metaphor, her references to the political role of ancient Greek theater—will be considered in the context of some central dilemmas raised by her theory about the nature, significance, and prospects of political freedom in contemporary times. Living in a disenchanted world, burdened by the experience of the Nazi regime's nearly successful program of genocide, Arendt struggled to conceptualize forms of political authority and judgment that would be supportive of political freedom. In her search for a mode of theorizing that would be adequate to the formidable challenges of her time, Arendt made important companions of the Greek tragic heroes of Homer and Sophocles. It will be the task of the following chapters to reveal the theoretical aid and comfort she received from them.

CHAPTER THREE

Tragic Foundations

Promoting Political Freedom in a Post-Authority World

> Until the demise of tragedy the Greeks had felt involuntarily impelled to relate all their experiences immediately to their myths, indeed to understand them only in this relation. Thus even the immediate present had to appear to them right away *sub specie aeterni* and in a certain sense as timeless. But the state no less than art dipped into this current of the timeless to find rest in it from the burden and the greed of the moment. And any people—just as incidentally, also any individual—is worth only as much as it is able to press upon its experiences the stamp of the eternal . . .
>
> —Nietzsche, *The Birth of Tragedy (137)*

"Authority has vanished from the modern world." Hannah Arendt makes this declaration at the start of "What Is Authority?" (BPF 93–141), an essay in which she proposes to "reconsider what authority was historically and the sources of its strength and meaning" (*BPF* 91).[1] Arendt begins the essay by offering several examples of the loss of authority in modern times, which serve to point up both the pervasiveness and the profundity of the crisis we purportedly face in contemporary times. Arendt evokes the pervasiveness of the crisis by indicating its manifestations in various spheres of life. In her view, the crisis is linguistically manifest in a deepening lack of consensus about the meaning of the term. The crisis is politically manifest in the "more or less general, more or less dramatic breakdown of all traditional authorities" in the face of emerging totalitarian movements (*BPF* 91). The "most significant symptom of the crisis" Arendt identifies as the proliferation of challenges to authority in "prepolitical areas such as child-rearing and education, where authority in the widest sense has always been accepted as a natural necessity" (*BPF* 92).

In addition to being pervasive, the crisis of authority, as Arendt presents it, is consequential. Authority endowed the perishable human world with "permanence and durability." Its disappearance is "tantamount to the loss of the groundwork of the world," threatening to impose a condition of uncontrollable and chaotic flux on human civilization. Since the loss of authority, "the world has begun to shift, to change and transform itself with ever-increasing rapidity from one shape into another, as though we were living and struggling with a Protean universe where everything at any moment can become almost anything else" (BPF 95).

Running parallel with Arendt's declarations of the pervasive and profoundly consequential loss of authority in modern times are her numerous assertions of the indispensability of authority for the promotion and maintenance of freedom, the element of politics that she values most highly. Arendt repeatedly describes the relationship between freedom and authority as one of necessary complementariness. For example, in "What Was Authority?" she argues that it is a mistake to subscribe to the liberal truism that authority is antithetical to freedom. Where "liberal theory postulat[es] that each loss of authority is compensated by a newly won measure of freedom," experience has shown her that the "progressive loss of authority is accompanied by at least an equal threat to freedom" (83).

In the essay "Ideology and Terror," in the course of distinguishing totalitarian domination from traditional authoritarianism, Arendt describes authority as a limiting condition—rather than as a negation—of freedom.[2] "Quite apart from its origin in Roman history, authority, no matter in what form, always is meant to restrict or limit freedom, but never to abolish it" (OT 405). In other passages, Arendt does not explicitly refer to freedom and authority, but she does evoke the necessary complementariness of the human capacities for initiating change and maintaining stability. For instance, in "Civil Disobedience," she states: "Man's urge for change and his need for stability have always balanced and checked each other."[3] In her book On Revolution, she envisions successful revolution as achieving a balance between two apparently contradictory elements: "To the extent that the greatest event in every revolution is the act of foundation, the spirit of revolution contains two elements which to us seem irreconcilable and even contradictory." One element is associated with stability: "The act of founding the new body politics, of devising the new form of government involves the grave concern with the stability and durability of the new structure." The other element is associated with change: "The experience . . . which those who are engaged in this grave business are bound to have is the exhilarating awareness of the human capacity of beginning, the high spirits which have always attended the birth of something new on earth" (OR 223; also 126).

Viewed against the backdrop of her high valuation of political freedom, Arendt's conceptualization of authority as a necessary limiting factor of political freedom invites an obvious question: Why does Arendt affirm the necessity of limiting the very thing that she values most? If political freedom is a mode of being with uniquely life-affirming potential, what need is there to apply limits to its practice? To answer these questions, let us consider how Arendt defines the nature and significance of authority.

Authority, for Arendt, is based neither on force nor on persuasion: "The authoritarian relation between the one who commands and the one who obeys rests neither on common reason nor on the power of the one who commands." The exercise of authority presupposes a structure of beliefs and practices whose validity is unquestioned: "what they [the leader and the follower] have in common is the hierarchy itself, whose rightness and legitimacy both recognize and where both have their predetermined stable place" (BPF 93). The significance of authority lies primarily in its endowing human relations with stability. This is evident in her choice of metaphors describing the political role of authority:

> Authority, resting on a foundation in the past as its unshaken corner-stone, gave the world the permanence and durability which human beings need precisely because they are mortals—the most unstable and futile beings we know of. Its loss is tantamount to the loss of the groundwork of the world. . . . But the loss of worldly permanence and reliability—which politically is identical with the loss of authority— does not entail, at least not necessarily, the loss of the human capacity for building, preserving, and caring for a world that can survive us and remain a place fit to live in for those who come after us. (BPF 95)

In this passage, which concludes the introductory section of "What Is Authority?" and in the numerous passages quoted above, Arendt

emphasizes the stabilizing aspect of authority. She imagines authority as endowing the world with "permanence" and "durability." It is
like a building that firmly rests on a "cornerstone." Acting as a kind
of "groundwork" of the world, authority is related to the human capacity to "build," "preserve," and "care for" the world (*BPF* 95).

Arendt construes authority as a necessary instrument of stability.
Stability is important because of the "constant influx of newcomers
who are born into the world as strangers" and who are endowed, by
virtue of their being born human, with the capacity to act, to initiate
new things (*HC* 9). The power of human beings to make new beginnings is especially manifest in the faculty of action: "action has the
closest connection with the human condition of natality; the new
beginning inherent in birth [which] can make itself felt in the world
only because the newcomer possesses the capacity of beginning
something anew, of acting" (*HC* 9). Action, the faculty of beginning
something new, tends to be a disruptive force in a world whose stability is guaranteed by the survival across time of relationships, practices, and institutions. She describes the disruptive aspect of action
in terms of its tendency to transgress boundaries. "Action . . . always
establishes relationships and therefore has an inherent tendency to
force open all limitations and cut across all boundaries." The "human condition of natality" endows action with a "boundlessness"
that destabilizes human institutions (*HC* 190–91).

Arendt attributes the transgressive quality of action to the fact
that the human capacity to begin something new is conditioned by
plurality, whereby human beings act upon the world according to
different perspectives and intentions. Since "action and speech are
surrounded by and in constant contact with the web of acts and
words of other men," they give rise to "processes whose outcome remains uncertain and unpredictable" (*HC* 184, 231–32). The "innumerable, conflicting wills and intentions" of human actors ensure
that "the strength of the action process is never exhausted in a single deed but, on the contrary, can grow while its consequences multiply" (*HC* 184, 233). For Arendt, the "process" character of action
lends an inherent boundlessness and unpredictability to action.

While the "process" character of action manifests the human capacity to make new beginnings, it also threatens to undermine that
capacity by eliminating the stable context within which action can
take place. "No civilization—the man-made artifact to house succes-

sive generations—would ever have been possible without a frame-work of stability, to provide the wherein for the flux of change" ("Civil Disobedience," *CR* 79). Human institutions such as law, pri-vate property, and territorial boundaries temper the inherent ten-dency of action to give rise to unpredictable and irreversible processes. They stabilize a world in which action can occur:

> The laws hedge in each new beginning and at the same time assure its freedom of movement, the potentiality of something entirely new and unpredictable; the boundaries of positive laws are for the political exis-tence of man what memory is for his historical existence: they guaran-tee the pre-existence of a common world, the reality of some continu-ity which transcends the individual life span of each generation, absorbs all new origins and is nourished by them. (*OT* 465)

Thus action, insofar as it expresses a human being's capacity to be-gin something new, requires a stable context from which to emerge. Similarly, political freedom, which manifests the capacity of human beings to appear to each other and to act in concert, initiating new relationships, practices, and institutions, requires the stabilizing ef-fect of political authority if the polity itself is to survive the inherent productivity of political action.

Arendt's formulation of the relationship between freedom and au-thority raises a second basic question. The many examples in which Arendt formulates authority as a necessary complement to freedom suggest the almost axiomatic way in which she thought of these two elements of politics as belonging together. Her "axiom" of the com-plementary relationship between freedom and authority, however, sits uneasily with her affirmation of the radical loss of authority in modern times. If, in her view, political authority is so necessary for the survival of political freedom, what prospects does her theory hold out for the survival of freedom in a world from which author-ity has vanished?

What lends a special urgency to this question is the preeminent value she places upon political freedom. In holding both that free-dom needs authority and that authority is irrevocably lost, Arendt seemingly undermines one of the central aims of her political the-ory, the promotion of political freedom as a uniquely life-affirming mode of being and the fundamental aim of politics. At the very

least, Arendt renders her theory vulnerable to critics who characterize her as an essentially nostalgic, antimodernist thinker pining for a
republican politics of virtue that never really existed.[4]

The challenge of promoting political freedom in the contemporary world lies at the center of Arendt's engagement with the concept of authority. In the next section, we shall examine Arendt's
analysis of the meaning, origin, and significance of political authority and proceed to a consideration of Arendt's assessment of the consequences of the event of totalitarian domination for authority. As
Jaspers noted, Arendt viewed the prospects for maintaining or promoting authority in the aftermath of totalitarianism as being "almost entirely bleak."[5] This apparent pessimism will be taken as a
starting point, from which to proceed in revealing the significance
of tragic storytelling in her thought: as one of the various resources
available to the contemporary citizen to maintain the "human capacity for building, preserving, and caring for a world that can survive us and remain a fit place to live in" (*BPF* 95).

PLATONIC POLITICAL PHILOSOPHY AND THE ORIGINS, NATURE, AND RUIN OF WESTERN AUTHORITY

The Romans invented authority, according to Arendt, but her
story of the establishment of an authoritative Western tradition begins with Plato. Although Plato's attempts to institute authority in
the Greek polis failed, they did make available a conceptual framework that eventually would be put to use by the Roman Church in
the aftermath of the collapse of the pagan Western empire. This conceptual framework affirmed the notion of "ideas" as universal, objective standards for political action. In Arendt's reading, the notion of
universal, objective ideas as standards for political action became authoritative, first for pagan Romans, then for Christian Romans, and
eventually for the West until the nineteenth and twentieth centuries. What follows is a recapitulation of Arendt's account of the
genesis of this conceptual framework in the journey of Platonic philosophy from fourth-century Athens to Christian Rome.

Plato's political theory emerged in the context of Athenian polis
life: "to live in a *polis* meant that everything was decided through
words and persuasion" (*HC* 26). The final fate of Socrates (to have
been condemned to death by a jury of his peers for not believing in

the city's gods and for corrupting the youth) brought home to Plato the fact that in a decision-making system such as the polis, where community affairs were ostensibly decided upon according to free, open discussion, debate, and voting, the philosophic life was hostage to the outcomes of citizenly persuasion. In Arendt's view, the philosopher's vulnerability to the political decisions of the polis was the proximate cause of Plato's theorizing the rule of philosophers as an alternative mode of ordering community affairs to citizenly persuasion. In the wake of Socrates' death, Plato's search for a principle of political rule reflected his rejection of citizenly persuasion as a reliable political means. "It was after Socrates' death that Plato began to discount persuasion as insufficient for the guidance of men" ("What Is Authority?" *BPF* 107). In his rejection of persuasion, Plato self-consciously put himself at odds with the conventional understanding of his fellow polis citizens. However, in respect of another aspect of Greek polis citizenship, Plato followed convention: he did not endorse "using external means of . . . coercion" to compel citizens (*BPF* 95).

Plato's tendency to liken ideal citizenly relations to various "models of existing relations, such as that between the shepherd and his sheep, between the helmsman of a ship and the passengers, between the physician and the patient, or between the master and the slave," reflected his search for a principle of rule that eschews the "sheer violence" characteristic of tyrannical rule (*BPF* 108, 105). These models of rulership based on superior knowledge or natural inequality prefigure Plato's conceptualization of rule by philosopher-kings. His theoretical solution to the problem of the philosopher's vulnerability in polis affairs was the establishment of rule by philosophers according to the dictates of universal, impersonal, objective reason. "Nowhere else has Greek thinking so closely approached the concept of authority as in Plato's *Republic,* wherein he confronted the reality of the *polis* with a utopian rule of reason in the person of the philosopher-king" (*BPF* 107). His envisioning a form of rulership for the polis based neither on force nor on persuasion fundamentally rests on his transformation of transcendent "ideas" from objects of pure philosophic contemplation to measures of human behavior in the *Republic* (*BPF* 109). By transforming contemplative "truth" into political "correctness" (see *BPF* 291 n. 16), Plato hoped to shift the compulsive element of rule from men to an impersonal standard outside of men.

Arendt argued that, despite his intention to conceptualize a form of political rulership independent of tyrannical coercion, Plato ended up affirming a form of political authority, rule based on philosophical cognition, which implicitly rested on an acceptance of violence as a means of politics. This is best illustrated by Plato's choice of craftsmanship as a master metaphor for understanding how the contemplative truths accessible to the philosophically minded can become "standards" or "yardsticks" applicable to politics:

> For the transformation of the ideas into measures, Plato is helped by an analogy from practical life, where it appears that all arts and crafts are also guided by "ideas," that is, by the "shapes" of objects, visualized by the inner eye of the craftsman, who then reproduces them in reality through imitation. (*BPF* 110)

By likening politics to craftsmanship, Plato suggests that some members of the polis have expertise in public affairs akin to the expertise of a craftsman. Plato's envisioning of politics as something like the manipulation of raw materials according to a predetermined idea implied an acceptance of violence as an appropriate means of politics (*BPF* 111).

The model of rulership provided in Plato's utopian "blueprint" failed to establish itself authoritatively in the polis of his day (*HC* 227), because Plato's political philosophy constituted a rejection of political freedom, the distinctive remedy offered by the polis for the problems of human living-together stemming from the condition of human plurality. The condition of human plurality ensures that any human community will encompass "innumerable, conflicting wills and intentions" (*HC* 184). Accepting persuasion based on equal association as an adequate and appropriate response to human plurality means accepting the burdens of human action. Human plurality renders action unpredictable in outcome and irreversible in effect. The pre-Platonic Greek "remedy" for the "haphazardness and moral irresponsibility inherent in a plurality of agents" (*HC* 196, 220) was to promote political freedom; that is, to create a lasting space of appearance for human action by making the practice of freedom accessible and continuous. In so doing, the polis offered citizens the promise of individual distinction and lasting fame as recompense for the haphazardness and futility of action. "The *polis*—if we trust the famous words of Pericles in the Funeral Oration—gives a guaranty that those who forced every sea and every land to become the scene of their daring will not remain without witness" (*HC* 197).

The appeal of the polis's promise of immortality to those afflicted with the burdens of plurality derived from the Greeks' sense that mortality, the ultimate expression of human plurality, was "the hallmark of human existence" (*BPF* 42). The "one great and painful paradox which contributed . . . to the tragic aspect of Greek culture is that . . . everything is seen and measured against the background of the things that are forever, while . . . true human greatness was understood, at least by the pre-Platonic Greeks, to reside in [perishable] deeds and words" (*BPF* 45). Insofar as the polis credibly promised to provide a space in which a citizen might "show in deed and word who he was in his unique distinctness" and become an object of "organized remembrance," the burdens of acting in a world fundamentally conditioned by plurality might be tolerated (*HC* 197, 199).

By contrast, Plato's conceptualization of rule by philosopher-kings was premised on a rejection of political freedom as a solution to the burdens of human plurality. In response to the fate of Socrates and consistent with his conceit about the absolute superiority of the contemplative life, Plato theorized a form of authority employing philosophic reason to overcome the frailties associated with action in plurality. Plato's utopian conception of the polis promises a "substitute" for human action, an "escape" from human action's uncertainties and contingencies (*HC* 220, 222). In proposing a solution to the frailty of human affairs so at odds with polis life as it was understood and practiced, the rule of philosopher-kings, Plato doomed his project to political irrelevance in the polis life of his time.

Plato's failure to conceptualize a form of effective and appropriate political authority for the Greek polis was due not only to the particular incompatibility of Plato's philosophy with Athenian political practice but also to the antipathy of the Greek polis to any form of political authority. Greek polis life was characterized, in other words, by an "absence of valid political experience on which to base a claim to authoritarian rule" (*BPF* 105). Insofar as the Greek polis defined itself as a realm of citizenly persuasion, it provided no conceptual or institutional purchase for establishing an authority that precluded persuasion as a means of politics. Thus, the Greek polis proved inhospitable to Platonic authority not only because of the particulars of Plato's conception of authority but also because any project aimed at instituting authority would contradict political freedom as Athenians conceived and practiced it.

In light of Arendt's conceptualization of authority as the necessary complement to freedom, her claim of the incompatibility of Greek polis life with political authority raises an appearance of theoretical inconsistency. If "neither the Greek language nor the varied political experiences of Greek history show any knowledge of authority and the kind of rule it implies" (*BPF* 104), does this mean that Arendt envisioned the Greeks as practicing something other than political freedom? Her repeated assertions to the contrary suggest a negative answer. Or, perhaps, she believed the Greeks to have been endowed by virtue of their historical circumstances with a unique capacity of practicing a form of political freedom unmediated by political authority. Another possibility is that she theorized the existence of a functional equivalent of political authority in the Greek polis. (The last of these possibilities will be considered in the following section.)

A failure in the polis context, Plato's theory did become decisive for the later evolution of political thought in the West once it encountered an understanding of politics more compatible with some of its assumptions about the limits of political action. Roman politics, more than Greek, offered practical purchase to Plato's notion that objective and impersonal ideas, accessible to reason, should provide the standard by which to guide and assess political action. Arendt argues that the greater affinity of Roman politics for Plato's notion of the "ruling, measuring, subsuming, and regulating" function of reason rested on the central place held in Roman politics by the notion of foundation (*BPF* 113). Roman politics differed fundamentally from Greek politics in the importance it placed on the act of foundation. "At the heart of Roman politics . . . stands the conviction of the sacredness of foundation, in the sense that once something has been founded it remains binding for all future generations" (*BPF* 120). The foundation of Rome stood as the "central, decisive, unrepeatable beginning of their [Roman citizens'] whole history" and became the guiding principle of their politics. "To be engaged in politics meant first and foremost to preserve the founding of the city of Rome" (*BPF* 120–21).

Arendt notes the derivation of the word *auctoritas* from the verb *augere* (to augment), arguing that the Roman Senate was the institutional bearer of *auctoritas* in Roman political life. "Those endowed with authority were the elders, the Senate or the *patres,* who had obtained it by descent and by transmission (tradition) from those who laid the foundations for all things to come, the ancestors" (*BPF* 122). Arendt's Romans envisioned the role of the senate as one of "augmenting" the city's foundation. The senate's purpose was to transmit the "testimony of the ancestors, who first had witnessed and created the sacred founding and then augmented it by their authority throughout the centuries" (*BPF* 124).

Arendt relates the Romans' distinctive emphasis on foundation to the Romans' distinctive form of ancestor worship, which held that the gods dwelled among men and that the gods took an interest in the city's political fate. The "deeply political content of Roman religion" was mirrored by the piety of Roman politics. For the Romans, "religion literally meant *re-ligare:* to be tied back, obligated, to the enormous, almost superhuman and hence always legendary effort to lay the foundations, to build the cornerstone, to found for eternity" (*BPF* 121). Roman religion buttressed the authority of the Senate by confirming the "deeds of the ancestors" as binding precedents, as "authoritative models for actual behavior . . . [as] moral political standard[s] as such" (*BPF* 123).

Authority formed, with tradition and religion, the "trinity" that structured Roman politics (*BPF* 126). Plato could become authoritative for the Western tradition of political theory because his account of the subsuming function of "ideas" resembled the subsuming function of Roman ancestor (foundation) worship (*BPF* 119–20). The affinity of the Roman practice of basing political authority on the senate's interpretation of ancestral precedents with the subsuming function of Platonic reason raises a question about the extent to which Roman political authority was compatible with political freedom as Arendt defines it. She had, after all, argued that the subsuming function of Platonic reason, insofar as it precluded the use of persuasion and justified rulership in public affairs, contradicted the political freedom institutionalized by the Athenian polis. Does the affinity of Roman *auctoritas maiorum* with Platonic reason imply an analogous incompatibility with political freedom? Did the *auctoritas maiorum* preclude the exercise of political freedom in Roman politics? Did the *auctoritas maiorum* implicitly or explicitly legitimate violence as a mode of (domestic) politics?

Arendt's account of the Romans' foundation of their city as "the founding of their first polis" attests to her desire to preserve ancient Rome as an example of a place where citizens exercised political freedom in a manner similar to the practice prevailing in the Athenian polis (*BPF* 120). The conventional view of classical scholars is that political arrangements and practices restricted popular political participation in Republican Rome to a much greater extent than in the Athenian polis. M. I. Finley has argued that the Roman patrician class managed to exert more control, retain greater privileges, and reap higher material rewards than the aristocratic families of Athens. Among the formal devices of Roman politics that helped "to ensure tight elite control" was the prohibition of discussion at meetings of the three main political assemblies, *comitia curiae, comita centuriata,* and *concilium plebis*. Instead, "there was only a vote to elect from the list presented by the summoning magistrate or to approve or reject the bill he had submitted beforehand."[6] Compared to the constraints faced by the common citizens of Athens in their assembly, the institutions of popular participation in Republican Rome offered, in Finley's view, little scope for citizens to engage in the mutual persuasion that Arendt considers a defining characteristic of politics. His account of Roman political practices raises questions about Arendt's implicit claim that Roman authority complemented political freedom.

Arendt does try to distinguish Roman foundation worship from deductive modes of Platonic reason by arguing that the functioning of Roman authority does not preclude persuasion or imply rulership based on violence, as Platonic philosophical rule would. What prevented the Roman Senate from playing a role analogous to Plato's philosopher-kings and what distinguished the Roman system of senatorial authority from the "Platonic relation between the master who gives orders and the servant who executes them" was the senate's lack of power. "The most conspicuous characteristic of those in authority is that they do not have power." This is best seen, according to Arendt, in the relationship between the Roman Senate and the Roman people. Citing Cicero, Arendt (*BPF* 122) characterizes this relationship as *cum potestas in populo auctoritas in senatu sit* (while power resides in the people, authority rests with the senate).

Arendt accepts Cicero's contention that the Roman Senate did not command the Roman people as much as offer advice ostensibly grounded in the "time-honored standards and models" of the ancestors (*BPF* 124). The classical historian Theodor Mommsen conceptualized senatorial *auctoritas* as "more than advice and less than a command, an advice which one may not safely ignore" (cited in *BPF* 123). This formulation, which Arendt cites approvingly, can be read as preserving a place for freedom in Roman politics in the Roman people's right to choose whether to follow the advice of the Senate.[7] In support of this, one could cite some instances from republican history, recounted by Livy, in which the plebs, by means of demonstrations, riots, or threats to secede and withhold military service, convinced the patrician class to pass, withdraw, or overturn particular measures. However, as Finley notes, popular approval or disapproval, in the few instances where it appeared to make a crucial difference, manifested itself mainly through extrainstitutional, occasionally violent means:

> When candidates or proposals to be voted on were selected and screened by the oligarchy alone, when elections to the consulship and praetorship and declarations of war were in the hands of an assembly, the *comitia centuriata,* in which it was very rare for the lower-class centuries even to be summoned to cast their votes, it would not be far from the truth to say that the Roman *populus* exercised influence not through participation in the formal machinery of government, through its voting power, but by taking to the streets, by agitation, demonstrations and riots, and this long before the days of the gangs and private armies of the civil-war century.[8]

The Ciceronian distinction between power and authority constitutes Arendt's primary means for asserting the compatibility of Roman *auctoritas* with political freedom. In her later work *On Revolution,* Arendt exhibits a diminished interest in Roman *auctoritas* as a model for political authority in modern times, suggesting, perhaps, a rethinking on her part of her earlier view that Roman *auctoritas* was fundamentally compatible with political freedom. (This idea will be further developed in the next section.)

Another way in which Arendt attempts to preserve a place for freedom in Roman politics is by making a distinction between the

influences exercised by Platonic political philosophy in Roman theory and in Roman political practice. Although the Romans "accepted
the great 'ancestors' in Greece as their authorities for theory, philosophy, and poetry" and "decided to take it [Greek political philoso-
phy] over and acknowledge it as their highest authority in all matters of theory and thought," this did not mean that Platonic theory
came to function as an authoritative guide in Roman politics (*BPF*
124, 120).[9] Plato's notion of philosophically apprehended "ideas"
did not unfold its "full *political* effectiveness" (emphasis added) in
Roman life until Roman Christians (who adhered to religious doc-
trines radically devaluing the affairs of the world) found themselves
faced with the task of governance:

> Precisely those parts of the Christian doctrine which would have had
> great difficulty in fitting in and being assimilated to the Roman politi-
> cal structure—namely, the revealed commandments and truths of a
> genuinely transcendent authority which, unlike Plato's, did not stretch
> above but was beyond the earthly realm—could be integrated into the
> Roman foundation legend via Plato. (*BPF* 127)

Western Christianity's adoption of the Roman practice of authority is evident in several ways. Like the pagan Romans, Christians in
the West grounded political authority in an act of foundation; they
"made the death and resurrection of Christ the cornerstone of a new
foundation" (*BPF* 125). The wonder of Western Christianity's successful institution of a durable polity consisted in the discovery—by
proponents of this fundamentally otherworldly and antipolitical
faith—of "something which could be understood as a worldly event
. . . and could be transformed into a new mundane beginning to
which the world was bound back once more *(religare)* in a curious
mixture of new and old religious awe" (*BPF* 126). Besides adopting
the Roman understanding of foundation as the basis for a political
authority transmitted by a religiously sanctioned tradition, Christian
thinkers and actors in late antiquity followed their pagan predecessors in utilizing Greek philosophic notions to conceptualize and cat-
egorize political practice. The most notable and consequential instance of this process was Western Christianity's incorporation of
the Platonic notion of universal, transcendent measures and rules,
discernible by the knowledgeable few.

The notion of transcending measures and rules, derived, Arendt argues, from Plato's belief in the absolute superiority of the contemplative life over the active life and his recognition of the philosopher's political vulnerability, dovetailed with Western Christianity's radical devaluation of worldly affairs. For example, myths of judgment in the afterlife, like the Er-myth of the *Republic*, found their echoes in Christian notions of a transcendent system of rewards and punishments awaiting the souls of the departed. These notions helped both to bolster the authoritative status of the Western church and to elicit the common people's obedience to traditional rulers. In adopting the idea of divine punishment as a sanction for inappropriate worldly conduct, Western religious authority gained additional strength. However, in utilizing the threat of Hell as a means of compelling obedience, the Church "diluted" the Roman concept of authority and "an element of violence was permitted to insinuate itself into both the very structure of Western religious thought and the hierarchy of the Church" (*BPF* 132–33). In claiming divine origin and in deploying the sanction of hellfire to exact obedience, the Western tradition manifested the legacy of Plato's utopian conception of politics with its implied acceptance of violence. Western authority also manifested its Platonic legacy by holding that privileged contact with transcendent or divine realms would result in the revelation of universal, eternal, and transcendent concepts and categories applicable to worldly affairs. The incorporation into the Western tradition of Platonic assumptions about the nature of political authority fostered a form of political judgment that, insofar as it "consisted in applying general rules of conduct to particular cases," conduced to unquestioning and unthinking obedience to those in authority.[10]

> In spite of the numerous misunderstandings concerning the so-called "authoritarian personality," the principle of authority is in all important respects diametrically opposed to that of totalitarian domination. (*OT* 404)

For Arendt, the catastrophic experience of totalitarianism in Nazi Germany and Stalinist Russia bears in two important ways on the task of determining the prospects for instituting a new and viable form of political authority in the West. She holds that the event of totalitarian domination demonstrates, in the first place, the possibility of organizing a lasting and extremely objectionable form of rule premised on the nonexistence of authority. It demonstrates, in the second place, the danger of seeking to replace the traditional authority lost in the West with another authority similarly based upon transcendent, absolute yardsticks.

Political authority, as it is manifested in customs, manners, traditions, and positive laws, serves to stabilize human affairs by providing a framework within which initiative-taking in politics can take place. Insofar as totalitarian regimes aim at the radical abolition of human initiative-taking and the transformation of human beings into passive bearers of superhuman laws of History or Nature, they require the elimination of authority and the stability it promises. The basic incompatibility of totalitarian rule with authority is evident in the "planned shapelessness" and the "complete absence of system" of totalitarian regimes, which Arendt contrasts with the stability and graduated hierarchy characterizing authoritarian regimes (*OT* 402, 395; also 398, 409). For example, she cites the Nazi regime's apparently redundant multiplication of party and state bureaus. "The inhabitant of Hitler's Third Reich lived not only under the simultaneous and often conflicting authorities of competing powers, such as the civil services, the party, the SA, and the SS; he could never be sure and was never explicitly told whose authority he was supposed to place above all others" (*OT* 399).

The proliferation of redundant and apparently unnecessary bureaus might be explained as the consequence of bureau chiefs' successful protection of their administrative turf. Arendt suggests that the multiplication of offices in a totalitarian regime serves instead to increase the dictator's control. The elimination of all "reliable intervening levels" (*OT* 405) of authority releases the dictator from the constraints imposed by a stable hierarchy of offices and creates a disempowering sense among the populace of the regime's unpredictability: "the multiplicity of the transmission belts, [and] the confusion of the hierarchy, secure the dictator's complete independence of all his inferiors and make possible the swift and surprising changes in policy for which totalitarianism has become famous. The body politic . . . is shock-proof because of its shapelessness" (*OT* 409).

The consequences of "planned shapelessness" for the perceptions, expectations, and capacities of bureaucrats and citizens accord with what Arendt considers the overarching purpose and logic of totalitarian rule: the radical abolition of human spontaneity. Insofar as a totalitarian regime aims to transform individuated human beings into passive, replaceable ciphers of superhuman laws, it must destroy all those structures that endow human affairs with stability, a condition crucial to the promotion of action. A pervasive sense of uncertainty about the future is, therefore, propagated among inhabitants of totalitarian regimes.

The totalitarian incompatibility with traditional authority is also evident, for Arendt, in the radically changed meaning of positive law. "From expressing the stability within which human actions and motions can take place," positive law becomes "the expression of the motion itself" (*OT* 464). "In the interpretation of totalitarianism, all laws have become laws of movement" (*OT* 463). In the West, prior to the emergence of totalitarian forms of rule, positive law had traditionally been understood to be an imperfect human translation of the transcendental laws of God or nature or reason. Totalitarian regimes collapsed the distinction between transcendental sources of authority and positive law; totalitarian rule "goes to the sources of authority from which positive laws receive their ultimate legitimation . . . [and proves] quite prepared to sacrifice everybody's vital immediate interests to the execution of what it assumes to be the law of History or the law of Nature" (*OT* 461–62).

One of the totalitarian means for collapsing the distinction between authority and positive laws is terror: "In the body politic of totalitarian government, this place of positive laws is taken by total terror, which is designed to translate into reality the law of movement of history or nature." Totalitarian terror does not merely suppress the public realm as in a tyranny; it destroys all sources of stability that could possibly provide a context for action. "If lawfulness is the essence of non-tyrannical government and lawlessness is the essence of tyranny, then terror is the essence of totalitarian domination" (*OT* 464).

Totalitarianism for Arendt marks a kind of zero point of Western political authority. The coming to power of totalitarian regimes demonstrated that a form of rule aimed at the radical abolition of human spontaneity could be not only instituted but also maintained indefinitely because it had dispensed with the necessity of stabilizing human affairs. Even tyrants, who had substituted rule by decree for the rule of law, had accepted the fundamental premise embodied in the notion of authority, which was that in order to be durable a government must stabilize human affairs. "If this [totalitarian] practice is compared with that of tyranny, it seems as if a way had been found to set the desert itself in motion, to let loose a sand storm that could cover all parts of the inhabited earth" (*OT* 478). The fact that totalitarian regimes could, through the use of terror, so radically dispense with stability demonstrated that the radical elimination of human spontaneity had become possible.

What prospects does Arendt hold out for the survival of political authority after the appearance of totalitarian forms of rule? To begin with, she rules out the specific form of authority formed from the Western church's amalgamation of Roman reverence for political foundation and transcendental Platonic yardsticks. It is irrecoverably lost in the wake of the decline of Christian religious belief and the end of the Western tradition, as had been demonstrated by the almost total inefficacy of Christian hell as a sanction against mass murder.

She further rules out the establishment of authority based upon an alternate source of transcendent, absolute yardsticks. One of the crucial lessons she drew from the experience of Nazism was that reliance on an authority based upon transcendental, absolute yardsticks atrophies the faculties of independent thought and action and raises the potential for political irresponsibility on a mass scale. She counts it as one of the pernicious outcomes of the long practice of traditional authority in the West that when the transcendental source of authority, the Christian God, became generally disbelieved, totalitarian movements could successfully offer an alternative absolute acceptable to people long habituated to obeying authority.

> Nothing perhaps distinguishes modern masses as radically from those of the previous centuries as the loss of faith in a Last Judgment: the worst have lost their fear and the best have lost their hope. Unable as yet to live without fear and hope, these masses are attracted by every effort which seems to promise a man-made fabrication of the Paradise they had longed for and the Hell they had feared. (*OT* 446)

Arendt's observation of the trial of Adolf Eichmann, the Nazi functionary responsible for organizing the mass transport of Jewish populations to concentration camps, further convinced her that it was undesirable to base political authority on a transcendental absolute. As the case of Eichmann amply showed, relations with an absolute authority tend to foster a kind of "automatic" conscience that is capable merely of "applying categories and formulas which are deeply engrained in our mind . . . and whose plausibility resides in their intellectual consistency rather than in their adequacy to actual events." Instituting a form of absolute authority as a replacement for the traditional authority lost to the West is undesirable, not only because it is imprudent but also because it threatens to diminish severely the stature of human beings as initiative-takers, as independent thinkers and actors.[11]

If an increasingly disenchanted world renders improbable the reestablishment of the authority instituted by the Western church, and if the experience of totalitarianism renders undesirable the establishment of an alternative form of transcendentally sanctioned, absolute authority, what sources of political authority remain to us? Arendt claimed to discover in the modern phenomenon of revolution a standard for political authority that is capable of both limiting and fostering political freedom in a post-authority Western world. That standard, as Arendt saw it revealed in Republican Rome in ancient times and in the revolutionary British North American colonies in modern times, is reverence for political foundation. Her most systematic statement on the promise of establishing a viable and appropriate form of political authority through revolution can be found in *On Revolution*, wherein she assesses the promise and dangers of reverence for political foundation as a standard for political authority in modern times.

For Arendt, the unprecedented event of totalitarian domination indicated the breakdown of Western authority and demonstrated the imprudence of seeking an alternative authority based on a transcendentally sanctioned absolute. She did see some cause for hope, however, that it was still possible in contemporary times to institute a form of political authority compatible with freedom. The source of that hope was revolution: "the revolutions of the modern age appear like gigantic attempts to repair these [Roman] foundations [of the political realm] . . . and to restore, through founding new political bodies, what for so many centuries had endowed the affairs of men with some measure of dignity and greatness" ("What Is Authority?" *BPF* 140). In particular, Arendt looked to the American Revolution, which in her view was the only revolution that successfully, albeit incompletely, instituted a form of political authority compatible with freedom.

The American revolutionaries instituted a form of authority compatible with freedom because its sanction derived more from the revelatory potential of an act of political freedom (foundation) than from the compulsion of philosophic reason or divine justice. How the colonial revolutionaries went about establishing a new political authority after decisively breaking with the king and parliament of England illustrates, for Arendt, the difficulty of founding a political authority compatible with freedom. The intellectual legacy of the Western tradition led the colonial revolutionaries to frame their new task as one of discovering an absolute sanction for the new body politic. The revolutionaries' search for an absolute sanction was conditioned by the legacy of the Judeo-Christian notion of God as transcendent lawgiver: "the whole problem of an absolute which would bestow validity upon positive, man-made laws was partly an inheritance from absolutism, which in turn had fallen heir to those long centuries when no secular realm existed in the Occident that was not ultimately rooted in the sanction given to it by the Church" (*OR* 189).

The Roman Church's long-standing role as institution of political authority in the West gave rise to a notion of law as command on the model of the Old Testament commandments of God. Acceptance of this notion meant that secular rulers could attribute to the laws of the kingdom the absolutely compelling force of the commandments of God, as long as they could sustain belief in the divine sanction of their rule. "Only to the extent that we understand by law a commandment to which men owe obedience regardless of their consent and mutual agreements, does the law require a transcendent source of authority for its validity, that is, an origin which must be beyond human power (*OR* 189).

For Arendt, the search for a transcendent authority is misguided because it aims at a form of authority that is not compatible with political freedom. Establishing transcendent authority means, in effect, raising the law above men, which would require the presence of a lawgiver raised above the level of humanity. In an increasingly disenchanted world, the Christian god is less and less available for that role. Additionally, the search for a transcendent authority diminishes the stature of human beings because it denigrates human beings' capacity for action.

The American Founders, by her account, managed to overcome the dilemma of absolute authority because—however much they were in thrall intellectually to Old World concepts and traditions that envisioned political authority as necessarily absolute—they were largely guided in their revolutionary action by their New World political experience. That New World political experience, consisting of long practice in associating as equals with fellow colonists in various institutions of colonial self-government such as town hall meetings, colonial legislatures, and juries, had fostered in the founders an appreciation of the rewards and promise of action in concert. The patrimony of local self-government had further led them to focus on those Old World writings (Montesquieu) and models (Republican Rome) that were best suited to the task of conceptualizing a form of authority compatible with freedom: "it was not tradition that bound them back to the beginnings of Western history but, on the contrary, their own experiences, for which they needed models and precedents" (*OR* 197).

Arendt notes that, although Jefferson felt it necessary to appeal to the transcendent absolutes of "nature's God" and "self-evident" reason to justify the colonists' break with English king and parliament, he also relativized the absolute nature of his appeal to divinely endowed, self-evident rules of reason by circumscribing (in the famous passage from the Declaration of Independence) that appeal within a particular circle of men acting in concert. Thus, the passage reads, "*We hold* these truths to be self-evident" (*OR* 192). What Jefferson's phrasing reflects, in Arendt's view, is the capacity of political actors to authorize their acts of political freedom by reference to the principle inhering in political freedom:

> What saves the act of beginning from its own arbitrariness is that it carries its own principle within itself, or, to be more precise, that beginning and principle, *principium* and principle, are not only related to each other, but are coeval. The absolute from which the beginning is to derive its own validity and which must save it, as it were, from its inherent arbitrariness is the principle which, together with it, makes its appearance in the world. (*OR* 212)

The principle that "makes its appearance" in the act of foundation is the principle of beginning, by which Arendt means the human capacity, through action in concert based on equal association,
to initiate novel practices and institutions. One could formulate
Arendt's point in the following way: as freedom authorizes foundation, so foundation authorizes freedom. In this reading, the Founding Fathers' partial success in establishing an authority compatible
with the exercise of political freedom illustrates how long experience in participating in public affairs better enables citizens to bear
the element of "complete arbitrariness" inherent in political beginnings without having to have recourse to absolutes. Whereas Old
World tradition indicated the need to sanction the authority of the
new body politic by reference to "nature's God" or "self evident
truth," the acting in concert on the basis of mutual persuasion,
which constituted the American founding, carried its own legiti-
mating principle.

In this regard, revolutionary France stands as a negative example.
The lack of a tradition of widespread and relatively autonomous citizen self-government contributed to French revolutionaries' failure
to establish a viable political authority compatible with a free, popular politics. "The rupture between king and parliament [in France]
. . . dissolved automatically the political structure of the country as
well as the bonds among its inhabitants, which had rested not on
mutual promises but on various privileges accorded to each order
and estate of society" (*OR* 180). Whereas the elimination of the absolute authority of crown and church in the English colonies did
not preclude a resort to the self-generating authority of free participatory practices, the overthrow of the king in France sent many of
the Jacobin leaders in search of a new transcendent and absolute
principle of authority.

For Arendt it is no accident that the "great model and precedent"
for the American founding was, "all rhetoric about the glory of
Athens and Greece notwithstanding[,] . . . the Roman republic and
the grandeur of its history" (*OR* 197). Insofar as the political authori-
ity of the American republic was sanctioned by the revelation of
freedom in political foundation, it revealed its kinship with Roman
authority, which was sanctioned by the Romans' intuitive grasp of
the self-legitimating principle foundation. In Arendt's reading, Virgil
served to make this principle explicit when he rewrote Rome's foun-

dation legend in the *Aeneid* as a story about association based on mutual respect and equality. Thus, the war between the refugee Trojans and the native Italians is concluded when "'both nations, unconquered, join treaty forever under equal laws' and settle down together" as "partners . . . or allies" (*OR* 209). And to the extent that American revolutionary authority originated from and periodically rested upon the participation and consent of the people in their ratifying conventions and regular elections, it was consistent with the Roman principle *potestas in populo, auctoritas in senatu*.

In Arendt's account, the American revolutionaries, in their role as founders of authority, clothed themselves in Roman dress. To a great extent, Arendt appears to accept what she presents as the American founders' self-understanding of the nature and significance of political authority. However, for her the example of Roman foundation ultimately proves inadequate as a model for political authority in a world that has experienced the loss of traditional authority. Her invocation of Theseus from Sophocles' *Oedipus at Colonus*, which concludes *On Revolution*, can be seen to suggest that Arendt's notion of an appropriate and viable authority for contemporary times rests on a combination of Roman foundation with Greek tragedy.

SUPPLEMENTING FOUNDATION: THE SIGNIFICANCE OF TRAGEDY IN ARENDT'S NOTION OF POLITICAL AUTHORITY

> Before they were engaged in what turned out to be a revolution, none of the actors had the slightest premonition of what the plot of the new drama was going to be. However, once the [eighteenth-century] revolutions had begun to run their course . . . the novelty of the story and the innermost meaning of its plot became manifest to actors and spectators alike. As to the plot, it was unmistakably the emergence of freedom. (*OR* 28–29)

In a book that virtually apotheosizes the role of American revolutionaries such as John Adams and Thomas Jefferson in enacting and reflecting about political freedom, the appearance of an ancient Athenian hero, in the role given him by Sophocles in *Oedipus at Colonus*, might be considered anomalous. Theseus, "the legendary founder of ancient Athens," might seem to deserve a place in a book about founders, but Arendt had made clear that the American revolutionaries, in their role as founders, had self-consciously donned Roman togas, not Athenian chitons. If Arendt intended to conclude her book by evoking the deeds of an ancient founder of freedom, would not Aeneas have been a more appropriate choice in light of her sympathetic reading of the American founders' fascination with Republic Rome?

It is worth noting at the outset that Theseus appears as a character in *Oedipus at Colonus,* a Sophoclean tragedy noted for its idealization of the virtues of the fifth-century Athenian polis.[12] Written around 409 B.C.E.,[13] at the end of Sophocles' long life and in the midst of the latter years of Athens's bitter conflict with Sparta in the Peloponnesian War, *Oedipus at Colonus* takes up the story of old, blind Oedipus, former king of Thebes, who, after years of wandering as an impoverished outcast from every place of human settlement, comes to the sacred grove of Colonus in the territory of Athens. There, he prevails on the horrified local inhabitants not to drive him away until he is given the chance to speak with Theseus, the king of Athens. When Theseus arrives, Oedipus offers an exchange: if Theseus would permit the burial of Oedipus's body in Athenian territory, Oedipus would promise his spirit's protection to Athens in a future conflict with Thebes. Theseus agrees. But before they can accomplish this, Creon kidnaps the daughters of Oedipus in an effort to force the exiled former king back to the outskirts of Thebes, where his bones can give no advantage to potential enemies of his native city. After Theseus recovers the daughters, there arrives Oedipus's estranged son Polyneices, also a Theban exile, to ask for his father's blessings for a military campaign against Thebes. He receives a curse instead. At play's end, Theseus accompanies Oedipus to his secret place of burial, learns from him the appropriate mystery rites, and finally, witnesses his abrupt disappearance.

One way to resolve the apparent anomaly of Arendt's invocation of Theseus in the coda of *On Revolution* is to consider it a token of her designation of the polis life of Athens as a paradigmatic instance of political freedom. Arendt's choices of Athens as paradigm and of *Oedipus at Colonus* as means to indicate the paradigm make sense for at least three reasons. First, Athens, as Arendt would have it represented to readers by Sophocles, serves to clarify the significance of political or public freedom. Whereas the American founders (and the French revolutionaries) were ambivalent about whether the "happiness" that citizens were to pursue was of a private or a public nature, Sophocles' Theseus is direct and unambiguous: "it was the *polis*, the space of men's free deeds and living words, which could endow life with splendour" (*OR* 281).[14]

Brief consideration of the role played by Theseus in *Oedipus at Colonus* suggests his fitness as spokesman for Athens's free citizenry. He repeatedly expresses in word and in deed what Arendt held to be a defining characteristic of the Athens polis way of life (in particular) and of political freedom (in general): acceptance of persuasion as the appropriate mode of political relations. For example, when Theseus first comes upon Oedipus, he is not swayed by the people's horror to drive the polluted outcast away; he chooses instead to hear him out. Then, after the kidnapping of Oedipus's daughters, Theseus organizes a rescue and, invoking the polis as institution of law and justice, harshly repudiates Creon for his attempt to substitute brute strength for the rule of law.[15] As a third example, Theseus persuades Oedipus to give a hearing to his "hated son," Polyneices, arguing that there is no harm in listening to words, even the words of someone you do not like.[16]

A second aspect of Athenian polis life that Theseus serves to indicate is the relatively wide and relatively continuous availability of opportunities to exercise freedom in its citizen assembly, council, and law courts. The Athenian polis merits the privileged place Arendt gives it because it made the experience of political freedom relatively accessible. It "enabled *ordinary* men, young and old, to bear life's burden" (*OR* 281; emphasis added). As Arendt put it elsewhere (*HC* 197), "the *polis* was supposed to multiply the occasions to win 'immortal fame,' that is, to multiply the chances for everybody to distinguish himself" (not really "everybody," as Arendt herself acknowledges elsewhere [*HC* 72–73], but every male citizen). In addition to making the exercise of political freedom a generally accessible experience, the Greek polis made the exercise of freedom a relatively continuous experience: "it was intended to enable men to do permanently, albeit under certain restrictions, what otherwise had been possible only as an extraordinary and infrequent enterprise" (*HC* 197). What better spokesman for the durability of Athens's public freedom than the city's legendary founder?

For Arendt the fifth-century Athenian polis stands as a convenient, resonant symbol of what political freedom is and what it means. The question about Theseus's appearance in the coda of *On Revolution* remains, however. What can the Greeks teach Arendt's contemporaries about authority that the Romans, those exemplary political founders, cannot? After all, the Greek polis appears in Arendt's thought as a model of a political community that successfully confronted the "elementary problems of human living-together" without the assistance of authority, "without the religious trust in a sacred beginning" ("What Is Authority?" *BPF* 141). The practice of political freedom by Greek citizens was singularly self-sufficient, uniquely independent of the countervailing presence of political authority. (The proposition that fifth-century Athenian polis citizens acted to a great extent unrestrained by reverence for ancestors is borne out by much of the classical scholarship and the testimony of contemporary Athenian observers.)[17]

The appearance of Theseus at the end of *On Revolution* is suggestive about Arendt's notion of revolutionary authority in several ways. Her citation of *Oedipus at Colonus* suggests that Greek tragedy is significant to her analysis of the challenge of establishing authority in the contemporary world. By referring to a Greek tragedy, she may be signaling her intuition of a practice capable of supplanting, or at least supplementing, political authority based on foundation. By invoking Sophocles' Theseus, she raises the possibility that inhabitants of the latter half of the twentieth century may be able, like the Greeks, to face "the elementary problems of human living-together" (*BPF* 141) without authority. Or, Theseus's appearance could signal her belief that revolutionary foundation needs a supplement in order for it to serve in the modern age as a viable basis for authority.

To reveal more fully the resources Arendt indicates for preserving freedom in a world that has lost traditional authority, we must consider her account of the political significance of storytelling. If storytelling is meant by her to serve as an alternative to political authority, it must fulfill the preeminent requirement of her theory: it must serve to promote political freedom as a mode of being that is accessible, continuous, and durable. Political authority based on reverence for foundation had been the Roman means for achieving this aim. Political authority had worked by functioning as a break put on action that was perceived to be inconsistent with or contradictory to the polity's founding act of freedom.

In discussing the significance of storytelling for the promotion of political freedom, Arendt described its effect as being one of reconciliation rather than limitation. If any formulation can serve to distill her view of the reconciliatory significance of storytelling for political freedom, it is her citation of Isak Dinesen—"all sorrows can be borne if you put them into a story or tell a story about them"—deployed, significantly enough, at the head of the chapter on action in *The Human Condition*. Storytelling appears in Arendt's framework, less as an external "fence" or "boundary" that restricts action than as an internal means for reconciling people to the burdens of action (*HC* 191).

Action is conditioned by human plurality. That action "always falls into an already existing web of human relationships, with its innumerable, conflicting wills and intentions" (*HC* 184) guarantees that the consequences of action will be boundless, unpredictable, and irreversible. That action often frustrates human intention and often defeats human expectation lends human life one of its notably burdensome aspects. Action with others burdens human life, but it also provides resources for reconciling human beings to those burdens. It does so by giving rise to life stories.

The "human ability to act" is the ability "to start new unprecedented processes whose outcome remains uncertain and unpredictable" (*HC* 231–32). In political affairs, the process character of action in the context of human plurality imposes limits upon human intention and desire. At the same time, the suffering that follows from the "frailty of human affairs" lends narrative shape to political action. "The disclosure of the 'who' through speech, and the setting of a new beginning through action start a new process which eventually emerges as the unique life story of the newcomer" (*HC* 184).

Political actors and storytellers, in Arendt's view, relate very differently to the narrative aspect of political action. The actor enacts his or her story but is not the "author" or "producer" of it. "Somebody began it [the story] and is its subject in the twofold sense of the word, namely, its actor and sufferer, but nobody is its author" (*HC* 184).[18] The storyteller witnesses actors' enactments of their life stories and fashions stories in the form of oral or written compositions. In a characteristic formulation, Arendt refers to storytellers as "the poets to whom a god has given to say what men suffer and endure" ("Walter Benjamin: 1892–1940," *MDT* 185).

Arendt poses storytelling as a strategy for acknowledging the burdens that action in concert imposes on human affairs without being overwhelmed by them: "storytelling . . . brings about consent and reconciliation with things as they really are" ("Isak Dinesen," *MDT* 105). Her Plato sought to "solve" the burdensome nature of human affairs by establishing the rule of philosophic reason in polis affairs. Rather than abolish action and eliminate the contingency of human affairs, the polis citizen accepted political freedom. One important way he was reconciled to the burdensome consequences of freedom was through a particular kind of storytelling, drama.

While the fashioning of stories may take various forms, according to Arendt, some forms are more capable of expressing the "specific revelatory quality of action and speech" than others. Arendt gives privileged place in this regard to Greek drama or theater. Only drama or theater "reifies" or "represents" the "implicit manifestation of the agent and speaker." This is because theatrical reenactments, more than any other art form, can express the unique identities revealed by the stories that emerge from the "living flux of acting and speaking." "Only the actors and speakers who re-enact the story's plot can convey the full meaning, not so much of the story itself, but of the 'heroes' who reveal themselves in it" (*HC* 187). Thus, theater has a special significance as a form of storytelling.

Action in politics gives rise to unique life stories that can form the basis for various kinds of artistic representation. By revealing how action gives rise to unique identities and fates, storytelling can reconcile human beings to the burdensome outcomes of action in concert. The form of storytelling that best expresses the distinctly revelatory aspects of action and speech in politics is theater, "the political art par excellence" (*HC* 188). In both attributing reconciliatory power to storytelling and identifying Greek-originated tragic drama as the politically most appropriate form of storytelling, Arendt invites us to draw the conclusion that Greek tragedy fostered freedom by reconciling fifth-century Athenian citizens to the burdens of action by transforming these burdens into an object of ritualized performance and spectatorship.

This reading of Arendt fits her squarely into a predominantly German tradition of thought, which contends explicitly that Greek tragedy acted as the foremost institution of political education and spiritual authority in fifth-century Athens. Werner Jaeger, to take one notable example, claims that the "power" of Greek tragedy over fifth-century Athenians was "so vast that they held it responsible for the spirit of the whole state." In another formulation, he suggests that "the Athenians held them [the tragic composers] to be their spiritual leaders, with a responsibility far greater and graver than the constitutional authority of successive political leaders."[19]

Nietzsche, for another example, has been read as trying to show "how Greek tragedy produced the authoritative understanding of what it meant to be Greek." In Tracy Strong's interpretation of Nietzsche's *Birth of Tragedy,* attendance at performances of tragedy during the festival of Dionysus provided an opportunity for spectators to share an intuition into both the basic unjustifiability of human constructions put on the world and the human capacity to take life-affirming pleasure in aesthetic creation and contemplation. "Nietzsche's interest is in tragedy as a medium . . . making politics possible. . . . Tragedy *establishes* the authority of the human sense before the audience in a manner that this sense can be experienced both as something external and found in oneself."[20]

If Arendt holds implicitly that tragedy permitted the ancient Greeks to practice political freedom in the absence of political authority, what implications does she draw from this for the role of storytelling in contemporary times? Does Arendt recommend some form or functional equivalent of tragedy as a contemporary replacement for revolutionary authority based on foundation? One way to answer this question is to establish whether or to what extent she holds foundation to be an inadequate basis for revolutionary authority.

Arendt puts the viability of foundation to the greatest test in her assessment of the foundation of the American republic: "only the American revolution has been successful . . . in found[ing] a completely new body politic without violence and with the help of a constitution" ("What Is Authority?" *BPF* 140). If foundation is an inadequate basis for authority in this, the very best case, one might conclude that Arendt holds out little prospect for instituting a lasting space for the exercise of political freedom through political authority based on foundation. One could then solve the puzzle posed at the beginning of this chapter about the prospects for political freedom in a post-authority world by recognizing storytelling as a fitting replacement for the authority that has been lost in the West.

As it turns out, Arendt poses storytelling not so much as a replacement of but more as a supplement to foundation. This is best seen in her evaluation of the American founding, which is marked by ambivalence. On the one hand, the Founding Fathers are judged to have successfully accomplished the revolutionary task of establishing a lasting polity. On the other hand, they are judged to be failures in the "second task of revolution, to assure the survival of the [revolutionary] spirit out of which the act of foundation sprang" (*OR* 126).[21]

If the French Revolution failed to institute a lasting government founded on public freedom, other failures—the absence of an institutional space for sustained public participation in politics and the forgetfulness concerning the meaning of public freedom—have afflicted the United States. This is so, partly, because party bureaucrats have had a big stake in maintaining the institutions of representative government and, partly, because the vast numbers of poor immigrants to America have understood America's promise of freedom more in terms of economic betterment than in terms of public participation (*OR* 268–69, 139). The problem was compounded by a failure of the bearers of the American tradition properly to remember what actually constituted revolutionary freedom. The revolutionary voices that won out and that shaped the legacy of the American revolutionary tradition did not articulate the true meaning of freedom ("participation in public affairs, or admission to the public realm" [*OR* 32]) but other, incomplete or mistaken, notions of freedom, such as liberation from tyranny or protection of economic affairs from government interference. "From start to finish, Jefferson's drive for a place of public happiness and John Adams' passion for 'emulation' . . . came into conflict with ruthless and fundamentally antipolitical desires to be rid of all public cares and duties" (*OR* 136). Arendt further finds it striking that even such a proponent as Thomas Jefferson who once envisioned the afterlife as a public realm, of sorts, was ambiguous in his single most important public statement about the nature of freedom: "the historical fact is that the Declaration of Independence speaks of 'pursuit of happiness', not of public happiness, and the chances are that Jefferson himself was not very sure in his own mind which kind of happiness he meant when he made its pursuit one of the inalienable rights of man" (*OR* 127).

Arendt places the failure of the American founders in the context of what she variously describes as the "perplexity . . . [which] has haunted all revolutionary thinking ever since" and the "seemingly inevitable flaw in the structure of the republic." She formulates this perplexity or apparent flaw as this: "that the principle of public freedom and public happiness without which no revolution would ever have come to pass should remain the privilege of the generation of founders" (*OR* 233, 232). The problem Arendt is alluding to bedevils all polities in which political authority is based on foundation. Raising the act of foundation to a preeminent political value may serve to stabilize new political institutions but it also threatens inappropriately to circumscribe posterity's exercise of the very activity that created and justified the foundation, political freedom.

Arendt attributes Thomas Jefferson's "occasional, and sometimes violent, antagonism against the Constitution and particularly against those who 'look at constitutions with sanctimonious reverence'" to his recognition of the injury that reverence for foundation does to the dignity of humans as acting beings. Jefferson's endorsement of Shays's rebellion—"'God forbid we should ever be twenty years without such a rebellion'"—reflects the bind that foundation-based political authority has tended to impose on aspiring actors: either renounce initiative in favor of a program of pious but passive political upkeep or exercise initiative through rebellion against the founders' institutions (*OR* 233).[22] Arendt wants to loosen this bind. To reduce the possibilities of action to a stark choice between passivity and rebellion is to misunderstand the true significance of founding for political freedom. The revolutionary foundation should not be venerated, nor should it be dismissed. The point, in Arendt's view, is to recognize that revolutionary foundation originates from exercises of political freedom, not from one superhuman act of political creation. One way that Arendt tries to desacralize foundation is by reserving a role for posterity in foundation.

Let us imagine authority as a process of augmentation, she suggests. That this understanding reflects Roman notions and practice is attested by the etymological derivation of *auctoritas* from the verb *agere*, "augment": "what authority or those in authority constantly augment is the foundation" ("What Is Authority?" *BPF* 121–22). Bonnie Honig (1991) has emphasized how Arendt's interpretation of authority as augmentation or ongoing foundation permits her theoretically to open a space for the exercise of freedom for posterity:

The very concept of Roman authority suggests that the act of foundation inevitably develops its own stability and permanence, and authority in this context is nothing more or less than a kind of necessary
"augmentation" by virtue of which all innovations and changes remained tied back to the foundation which, at the same time, they augment and increase.[23]

It is in the context of her reconceptualization of the American founding as an ongoing event that Arendt invokes Jefferson's famous in-
junction to "divide the counties into wards" and to propose the council system as an alternative to rule by alternating party bureaucracies
(*OR* 248–51). By the council system, she had in mind those autonomous, democratic-participatory societies that are organized locally in times of revolution and that provide forums in which participants can discuss and debate issues of public relevance. As examples
of this phenomenon she cites the political clubs of the American
colonists and of French townfolk during their respective eighteenth-
century revolutions; the "'miniature federal body'" that "formed the
nucleus of the Parisian Commune government in the spring of 1871";
the organization of workers' soviets in 1905 and 1917 in Russia; the
constitution of *Arbeiter-* and *Soldatenräte* across Germany in the years
of revolutionary upheaval immediately following the end of World
War I; and the formation, under revolutionary conditions in Hungary
in autumn 1956, of workers' councils [*OR* 261–62].[24]

This recurring phenomenon of grassroots council organization reflected, in Arendt's view, the native inclination and capacity of people from all walks of life to participate directly in political affairs.
Similarly, her contention that anti–Vietnam War "civil disobedients
are . . . the latest form of voluntary association . . . quite in tune
with the oldest traditions of the country" and her consideration of
the prospects for "incorporating it [civil disobedience] into the
American legal system" both reflect her interpretation of revolutionary authority as augmentation or ongoing foundation ("Civil Disobedience," *CR* 96, 99). In highlighting Arendt's notion of authority
as augmentation of the founding, Honig directs attention to a
promising aspect of Arendt's theory of political authority and reveals
how thinking of political authority as ongoing foundation serves to
expand one's perspective on what is politically possible beyond a
false choice between passivity and rebellion.

Augmentation is only one aspect of Arendt's conceptualization of a form of political authority capable of appropriately limiting political freedom in modern times. A second, significant aspect of her notion of political authority can be inferred from the role played by tragedy, both as metaphor for the outcome of revolution and as source of citation, in her thinking about revolution. We began this section by raising a question about the role of Greece—and, in particular, Attic tragedy—in Arendt's conceptualization of authority. Does the presumably strategic deployment of Sophoclean tragedy signal her intention to supplant foundation with reconciliatory storytelling as the basis for political authority? I suggest that Sophocles' presence on the last page of *On Revolution* does not signal Arendt's rejection of Roman-imaged foundation as augmentation in favor of Greek-imaged reconciliatory storytelling so much as it signals her fusion of the two. Arendt's presentation of Theseus, the mythological founder of Athens, in the guise of a character from Sophoclean tragedy is especially significant in this regard.

The choice of an Athenian founder rather than a Roman one suggests that Roman foundation (even if appropriately understood as augmentation) is, in and of itself, an insufficient model for political authority. Arendt's analysis of the failure of the American revolutionary foundation illustrates this. In her view, the American Founding Fathers failed to provide for a lasting space in which aspiring actors could exercise political freedom in a continuing and accessible way. The Founding Fathers' exercise of political freedom became reified, so to speak, as members of successor generations mostly accepted the post-revolutionary definition of freedom as economic opportunity (freedom from politics) rather than as active participation in public life (freedom through politics): "the machinery of government . . . could not save the people from lethargy and inattention to public business, since the Constitution itself provided a public space *only for the representatives of the people,* and not for the people themselves" (*OR* 238; emphasis added).

In the appearance of Athens in the coda of Arendt's revolution book, one can read an intention to supplement the Roman notion of foundation. By invoking Athens, the paradigmatic instance of political freedom as a continuous, accessible, and highly esteemed activity, Arendt may be indicating her awareness that political authority based solely on foundation tends to distort political freedom by reducing the scope and meaning of action to the preservation of the Founding Fathers' constitution. Unlike Rome, Athens provides the model of a polity relatively free of the need for political authority based on reverence for foundation. Polis citizens "did not count legislating among political activities." For them, "the lawmaker was like the builder of the city wall, someone who had to do and finish his work before political activity could begin" (*HC* 194; also *OR* 186–87).

We have already noted Arendt's approving reference to the Periclean image of polis freedom as providing an intimation of immortality to compensate citizens for the burdens associated with the plurality characteristic of human affairs. Arendt's concluding citation of Sophocles' last drama can be seen to recapitulate this Periclean image, with Theseus replacing Pericles as spokesman and Sophocles' *Oedipus at Colonus* replacing Thucydides' *Peloponnesian War* as text. Thus, Arendt cites the tragic chorus's "famous and frightening" response to the burdensome nature of human existence—"'Not to be born prevails over all meaning uttered in words; by far the second-best for life, once it has appeared, is to go swiftly as possible whence it came.'"[25] The response concludes with a paraphrase indicating what it was that enabled the Athenian citizen to bear the burdens of living: "it was the *polis,* the space of men's free deeds and living words, which could endow life with splendour" (*OR* 281).

It is noteworthy that Arendt articulates this redemptive insight "through the mouth of Theseus, the legendary founder of Athens and hence her spokesman" (*OR* 281). In eliciting the testimony of the founder of the Athenian polis to inspire contemporary citizens to act and exercise public freedom, Arendt seemingly risks propagating the very ancestor worship that she explicitly repudiates. How can Arendt's invocation of Theseus be understood as not partaking of ancestor worship? The answer may have something to do with Sophocles' dramatic gloss on the legendary status of Theseus as founder.

In addition to being celebrated for his defeat of the Minotaur and various other mythical creatures and malefactors, Theseus was celebrated in Sophocles' lifetime as an important founder of the democratic polis of Athens. (It is worth noting that Theseus was also, inadvertently, a patricide.)[26] As legendary king of Athens, he was credited with having "combined the *demes* (townships) of Attica into an Athenian commonwealth and [with having] formalized the city's dominance over Eleusis and Megara." In addition, Theseus was held to have "proved his own good faith by relinquishing . . . some of his own rights as king" to the newly consolidated polis.[27] In Sophocles' last tragedy, Theseus does play the role of a founder, albeit a different kind of founder than that suggested in popular legend.

As Karl Jaspers has noted, *Oedipus at Colonus* is a tragedy about foundation; it is, in fact, the only tragedy about foundation among Sophocles' extant works. "Sophocles' *Oedipus at Colonus* concludes in a manner comparable to Aeschylus, with a conciliatory act of founding a new institution."[28] However, unlike Aeschylus's *Eumenides*, which concludes with Athena's institution of a court of justice (the *Aeropagus*), Sophocles' last play concerns itself with the founding of a hero cult for the purpose of honoring and remembering the dead.[29] At play's end, after the recovery of his daughters, Oedipus declares it to be the appointed time for fulfilling the bargain he made with Theseus, a home for his mortal remains in Athenian territory in exchange for his spirit's blessing on Athens. The home Oedipus has in mind is not merely a patch of earth for his bones, however, but a place in the collective memory of Athens. So, in his last direct utterance, Sophocles' Oedipus unequivocally links the duty of remembrance with the future good fortune of the polis—"O friend most dear to me! may all good fortune / Come to your land, your followers, and you! / *And that your happiness may evermore / Be at its height, remember me, the dead.*"[30]

A prominent line of argument in the literature on the origins of Greek tragedy holds that the institution of tragedy developed from ritual worship of dead heroes. This ritual worship, the argument goes, reflected a deep-seated human need to come to terms with the threat of personal oblivion posed by the condition of mortality. In this reading, "the epic narratives, festivals, and choral chants that ultimately became the first drama are rooted in the transformation of death into a public ceremony."[31] Consideration of tragedy as a ritual form of collective remembrance suggests that the good fortune Oedipus promises to the Athenian polis consists in its making a home for tragedy. "Oedipus' blessings to Athens are the gift of tragedy itself."[32] In the terms suggested by Arendt, one might say that tragedy, by representing the deeds and sufferings of heroes, provides occasion for a consolatory identification with characters who, by virtue of their being in a story, have achieved a sort of immortality.

Whether or not Arendt's selection of Theseus as her final spokesman in *On Revolution* was consciously influenced by a recognition of Sophocles' gloss on Theseus's role as legendary founder, it is clear from at least one passage that she had thought of political foundation in the image of theatrical foundation:

> In order to understand more concretely what it meant to be in authority, it may be useful to notice that the word *auctores* can be used as the very opposite of the *artifices,* the actual builders and makers, and this precisely when the word *auctor* signifies the same thing as our "author." Who, asks Pliny at the occasion of a new theater, should be more admired, the maker or the author, the inventor or the invention—meaning, of course, the latter in both instances. The author in this case is not the builder but the one who inspired the whole enterprise and whose spirit, therefore, much more than the spirit of the actual builder, is represented in the building itself. In distinction to the *artifex,* who only made it, he is the actual "author" of the building, namely its founder; with it he has become an "augmenter" of the city. ("What Is Authority?" *BPF* 122)

This passage is noteworthy in several respects. First, Arendt seeks to evoke the compatibility of authority based on foundation with posterity's exercise of political freedom through the metaphor of theater. Just as a theater is built for the purpose of providing a durable space for the enactment of drama, and not as a monument to the builder's excellence, so a polity is founded for the purpose of providing a durable space for political action, and not as a monument to the founders' political virtuosity.

The passage's second noteworthy aspect, especially in the contrast it provides with the conclusion of Arendt's later book *On Revolution,* is the absence of any reference to Greek tragedy. Here, Arendt can be seen as attempting to counteract the tendency of political foundation to reify into ancestor worship by evoking theater in a purely Roman context ("Who, asks *Pliny* . . ." *BPF* 122). In *On Revolution,* Arendt's resort to Greek tragedy promises to achieve the same purpose of de-reification more effectively because the metaphor of theater as political authority is historically grounded in the role ostensibly played by Greek tragedy in the polis of fifth-century Athens. (In this regard, Arendt's reference, in the same essay, to "the Roman *pathos* for foundation" [*BPF* 140, my emphasis], anticipates the later shift in *On Revolution* to a Greek-imaged notion of foundation.)

The passage's third noteworthy aspect is the way in which it anticipates Arendt's later conceptualization of political authority as the fusion of reconciliatory storytelling with foundation-as-augmentation. Being in authority, she suggests, is like being an author. The distinctive feature of the *auctor* is that he is without power; he "augments" and "confirms" the actions of others. If we extend Arendt's analogy a little, we might say that the one in political authority acts as a playwright does, fashioning stories that preserve the memory of the deeds and sufferings of human agents.

The role of playwright is, in an important sense, the role Arendt can be seen to assume in *On Revolution* (among other places) in order to work through the bind imposed on political actors by foundation worship. The weight of this claim need not rest solely on Arendt's citation of *Oedipus at Colonus* and her invocation of Theseus; there is, more pointedly, her repeated references to the phenomenon of revolution under the rubric of tragedy. For example, she characterizes the 1956 Hungarian Revolution as a "stark and sometimes sublime tragedy."[33] In addition, she declares that "we know [the events of the French Revolution] in the form of a great tragedy." She also refers to Thomas Jefferson's "premonition" of the revolutionary "tragedy" of failing to incorporate New England township democracy into the U.S. Constitution (*OR* 132, 235).

Arendt's consideration of various revolutions under the rubric of tragedy can be seen to operate on at least three levels of meaning. On one level, Arendt's calling a revolution a "tragedy" implicates the American founders in a serious and consequential failure—the failure to provide a lasting site for the exercise of political freedom. In so doing, she raises the prospect of a role for posterity in making good the failure of their predecessors by exercising political freedom. In applying the term *tragedy* to revolution, Arendt can be seen on a second level to evoke more generally the failures of human effort and intention consequent on the condition of human plurality, which the Periclean polis promised to make bearable through the revelatory and memorializing functions of a free citizen body. In this sense of politics as a kind of tragic theater, Arendt's tragic framework serves the aim of promoting political freedom by evoking the life affirming rewards available to those who exercise freedom.

On yet a third level, Arendt's evocation of the tragic theater of revolution—"the tragedy of Western revolutions in the modern age"
("What Is Authority?" *BPF* 140)—can be seen to serve the goal of promoting political freedom. Arendt's evocation of tragedy stands as a
redemptive token of the capacity of human beings to rescue human
deeds from oblivion through storytelling. The fashioning of revolutionary events into a tragic story supports the promise of political
freedom to provide mortals with a life-affirming intimation of immortality by preserving the remembrance of deeds even after the political sites of communal remembrance have disappeared. Even after
the defeat of efforts to found a realm of political freedom, as in the
repeated demobilization or repression of locally based revolutionary
council democracies, there is still a measure of immortality credibly
to be hoped for. Thus, she describes the Hungarian revolutionary
outbreak as a "true event whose stature will *not depend upon victory or
defeat*," because "its greatness is secure in the tragedy it enacted."[34]

The foregoing assessment of the nature and significance of
Arendt's "emplotment" (to borrow a term from White) of revolution
as tragedy rests on the idea of tragedy as a means of redemptive remembrance.[35] In this reading, Arendt's various uses of the term serve
both to indicate the promise of gaining a redemptive intimation of
immortality through acting and to confirm this promise by activat-
ing this redemptive intimation. However, if the role of tragedy is defined exclusively in terms of its promise to compensate human beings for the burdens of plurality by preserving remembrance of
perishable deeds, some questions might legitimately be raised about
the ostensible distinctiveness of tragedy's association with free polities. For example, if it is only a matter of allaying the fear of oblivion
through rituals of remembrance, then relief may be sought in other
institutions or in other genres besides tragedy. And free, non-author-
itarian polities are by no means unique in requiring effective communal means for reconciling their members to suffering and death.

Tragedy, as the Greeks practiced it and as Arendt uses it, must
promise more than a reconciliatory intimation of immortality. What
tragedy additionally promises, at least as far as Arendt's thought indicates, is implied in the other aspect of the Periclean image of the
polis that Arendt marks out for special consideration. In addition to
its role as a reconciliatory institution of organized remembrance, the
Periclean polis also served as a site for citizens' continuous and in-

tensive talking with one another: "In this incessant talk the Greeks discovered that the world we have in common is usually regarded from an infinite number of different standpoints, to which correspond the most diverse points of view" ("The Concept of History," *BPF* 51). To the extent that the polis citizen became accustomed "to look upon the same world from another's standpoint, to see the same in very different and frequently opposing aspects," (*BPF* 51) he developed a capacity that, in Arendt's reading of Pericles' Funeral Oration, gained special mention—along with the achievement of fame—as a distinctive possession of polis citizens: political judgment.

CHAPTER FOUR

Tragic Intuitions

Judgment as an Instance of Political Freedom

> Tragedy . . . is a representation of an action that is worth serious atten-
> tion, complete in itself, and of some amplitude; in language enriched
> by a variety of artistic devices appropriate to the several parts of the
> play; presented in the form of action, not narration; by means of pity
> and fear bringing about the purgation of such emotions.
>
> —Aristotle, *The Poetics*

THE POLITICAL THEORIST AS POLITICAL ANIMAL?

At first look and with even a bare knowledge of the
details of Arendt's life, the seemingly abrupt and lengthy citation of
a Greek tragedy in one of her more influential and controversial
works is not so surprising. Educated according to the humanistic tradition of German *Bildung*, which emphasized the classics, Arendt
more than once explicitly acknowledged her enduring love for ancient Greek literature, particularly Greek verse. "I have always loved
Greek poetry very much. And poetry has played a large role in my
life."[1] It should further come as no surprise that a German Jew who
barely escaped the Nazi campaign of genocide would cite from a literary genre—Greek tragedy—that is distinctively associated with literature's promise to foster a reconciliatory emotional liberation from
the weight of a burdensome past.

Arendt's multilevel use of tragedy in this and other instances is
not without its problematic aspects. One might, for example, justifiably find it curious that the burdensome past to which Arendt, the
survivor of an annihilated people and culture, regularly and explicitly applies the category of tragedy is not the destruction of European Jewry but rather the various failures of revolutionary actors—in
the American, French, and assorted other revolutions—to establish

genuinely free and lasting political institutions. This failure she calls, in a typical formulation, "the tragedy of Western revolutions in the modern age" ("What Is Authority?" *BPF* 140). Even when writing specifically and contemporaneously about the catastrophic fate of European Jewry under Nazi rule, Arendt does not directly refer to that fate as tragic. Rather, she situates the "defeat of the Jewish people" in the context of a "tragic" history of deviation from the revolutionary promise of genuine citizenship.

> The European background against which Jewish history appears is complicated and involved. Sometimes the Jewish thread is lost in the maze but most of the time it is easily recognizable. The general history of Europe, from the French revolution to the beginning of World War I, may be described in its most tragic aspect as the slow but steady transformation of the *citoyen* of the French Revolution into the *bourgeois* of the pre-war period.[2]

It would be wrong to let the foregoing observations be taken to imply that Arendt did not give the fate of European Jewry under Nazi rule considerable and concentrated attention; her publication of *The Origins of Totalitarianism* and *Eichmann in Jerusalem: A Report on the Banality of Evil* testify to the contrary. Nor do they imply that she did not characterize this fate in terms of other, perhaps equally appropriate categories, such as "catastrophe," "annihilation," or "destruction."[3] At the same time, if Arendt's use of tragedy as a source of citation and as descriptive metaphor in these instances is neither casual nor isolated, one might well wonder why she so explicitly considered under the rubric of tragedy the failure of revolutionaries in the modern age to institute enduring realms of political freedom—and not the destruction of European Jewry.

Some readers might suggest the factor that best explains this oversight or disproportion is Arendt's *Bildung*-bred philhellenism, which led her not only to idealize the ancient Greeks but also to project an image of their purported public virtue as a standard for modern politics. Take, for example, the response of one hostile critic who felt himself prompted, after reading *On Revolution*, to attack her view that "one of the main tragedies of the life of most men is that their lives are passed in private, obscure significance." Arendt's promotion of public virtue demonstrated, in this reader's opinion, her entanglement in "a cult of antiquity that emerged in Germany at the end of the eighteenth century" and propagated an image of "the glories of Greco-Roman antiquity juxtaposed to the sad limitations of Hebraism."[4] In this reading, Arendt's misplaced sense of the truly tragic aspects of modern life is of a piece with her uncritical acceptance of a distorted image of the ancient polis.

The seeming oversight in Arendt's explicit application of the tragic might relatedly be construed as evidencing a problematic aestheticism, a tendency to let her love of beauty, particularly the beauty of the cultural achievements of the ancients, distort her judgments about politics. Arguments to this effect in the Arendt literature typically hold that, although her political writings often reach poetic intensity, they often fail to remain either true to the historical facts or relevant to modern political conditions. From this perspective, the problem would be not that she applies tragedy to politics wrongly but that she applies tragedy, especially in its ancient Greek guise, to politics at all. Rather than dismiss her apparently unbalanced resort to tragedy as the sterile product of a wrongheaded philhellenism or aestheticism, however, one can instead let it serve to open up a potentially fruitful line of inquiry into what many of her readers have considered a theoretically illuminating and politically relevant tension in her political thought, a tension framed by her comparative, potentially inconsistent assessments of the respective modes and rewards of political freedom (or action) and understanding (or judgment).

Political freedom served Arendt's theory as a fundamental concept: "freedom . . . is not only one among the many problems and phenomena of the political realm properly speaking, such as justice, power, or equality; freedom is actually the reason that men live together in political organization at all" ("What Is Freedom?" *BPF* 146). In her view, political freedom held a distinctive significance for human life: "when man takes part in public life, he opens up for himself a dimension of human experience that otherwise remains closed to him and that in some way constitutes a part of complete 'happiness'" ("Thoughts on Politics and Revolution," *CR* 203). Few of Arendt's sympathetic readers would deny that she valued political freedom very highly, perhaps above all other modes of human experience, and that she was centrally concerned, as a political theorist, with affirming and promoting political freedom. (Readers' opinions do diverge when it comes to assessing the coherence, evolution, and significance of her concern for this freedom.)

Coeval with her long-standing affirmation and promotion of political freedom as a distinctively, if not preeminently, life-affirming mode of experience was Arendt's deeply felt need both to comprehend the phenomenon of totalitarianism and to reconcile herself and others to a world that had experienced it. She wrote her first book "out of the conviction that it should be possible to discover the hidden mechanics by which all traditional elements of our political and spiritual world were dissolved." And against what she considered an "irresistible temptation to yield to the process of disintegration," Arendt committed herself to the task of "examining and bearing consciously the burden which our century has placed on us." Arendt's close friend, Alfred Kazin, paid tribute to her enduring "conviction that there *has* been a 'break' in human history," in the concluding observation of his review of Elizabeth Young-Bruehl's biography: "That there has been a 'break,' that we live in truly 'dark times,' no one confronted by her [Arendt] was allowed to doubt."[5] The structure and modes of Arendt's theorizing were conditioned as much by her unwavering insistence that her contemporaries recognize the radical centrality of the break ushered in by the event of totalitarian domination as they were conditioned by her commitment to illuminate the nature and rewards of political freedom. She was as much the unflinching witness to and unyielding analyst of the catastrophic consequences of totalitarianism[6] as she was a "partisan of public freedom, a companion of men like de Tocqueville, Jefferson, and Machiavelli."[7]

On first look, the fact that Arendt's political thought encompasses commitments both to affirm the "dream of political freedom," on the one hand, and to comprehend the nightmare of totalitarianism, on the other, is unremarkable. As the canon of political theory amply illustrates, thoughtful people have often envisioned ideal polities in the course of their trying to come to terms with the personal and collective consequences of political catastrophe. What is distinctive about the pairing of the best and the worst in Arendt's political thought is the manner in which this pairing is polarized. Far from posing the best merely as an unattainable but instructive ideal or a decent, practicable alternative, Arendt construes political freedom as a uniquely life-affirming mode of experience that is no less urgently

to be sought after for its rarely being achieved. At the other pole, totalitarianism constitutes not merely another, more pernicious form
of tyranny but a precedent-shattering event, demanding a substantial rethinking of traditional political concepts and categories.

In both affirming the preeminent worth and rare viability of political freedom and assessing totalitarianism's break with past standards of behavior as radical and, therefore, urgently demanding of
both comprehension and defensive precautions, Arendt exposed her
self to the charge of holding out irresponsibly, in the face of what
she construes as an imminent and extreme threat, for an impractica-
ble ideal. These are the terms, for example, in which George Kateb
(1984) criticized her neglect of the merits of liberal politics:

> One would think that a philosopher so intimately and philosophically
> aware of totalitarianism would let her horror pass into her feelings
> about politics in general, or at least lead her to celebrate the decencies
> of liberal politics as the best possible or as the ideally best. Instead, the
> theorist of politics as the deliberate systematization of unspeakable evil
> *(The Origins of Totalitarianism)* or as the unthinking routinization of
> unspeakable evil *(Eichmann in Jerusalem)* reluctantly tolerates liberal
> politics *faute de mieux* while denying that it is the real thing. And she
> goes on to construct an image of true politics that often taunts us in its
> unavailability.[8]

The apparent disjuncture between Arendt's conceptualizations of the
best attainable and the worst possible has provided convenient purchase for commentators interested in tracing the evolving relationship in her thought between the notions of action and thought, political freedom and the life of the mind. The picture that often
emerges is of an Arendt, impelled by the example of the Nazi functionary Adolf Eichmann's thoughtless complicity in mass murder,
coming to question, even repudiate, the position she had presumably taken in such works as *The Human Condition* and *On
Revolution*—"that the *vita activa* can stand on its own, without interference from or judgment by the *vita contemplativa*."[9] Lewis Hinchman and Sandra Hinchman's (1994) investigation of the conflicting
existentialist and classical sources of Arendt's notion of freedom exemplifies the view that has Arendt retreating from her conceptualization of the best (political freedom) as both autonomous and viable

under the burden of understanding and preventing the worst (totalitarianism). They argue that the evolution of Arendt's "ideal of politically responsible engagement" away from "the ancient citizen discoursing in the Assembly or the Senate" toward "the philosopher *qua* public figure" reflects her "retreat" in *Life of the Mind* from an unconditional affirmation of political action as the guarantor of human plurality to an emphasis on the "thinking ego's quest for meaning" as a surer resort against wholesale violations of human plurality.[10]

In Arendt's conceptualization of judgment, another mental faculty, readers such as Beiner (1982) have detected an analogous shift in her basic commitments from promoting political action to emphasizing the rewards of political theory or spectatorship. Basing his extrapolation of the final trajectory of Arendt's theorizing on her lectures on Kant's political philosophy, first delivered at the University of Chicago in 1964, Beiner argues that Arendt finally gave up on the life-affirming rewards of political freedom to favor the more attainable solace promised by judgment, as a backward-looking faculty of reconciliation. Beiner interprets Arendt's turn to retrospective judgment against the backdrop of a "world [that] offers precious little prospect for genuine action and, therefore, for freedom." Arendtian "judging almost becomes a kind of vicarious action, a way of recouping our citizenship in default of a genuine public realm."[11] For Beiner, the misfortune in Arendt's turn to a Kantian-inspired notion of judgment (which he considers too far removed from praxis) is that Arendt fails to develop other notions of judgment, like Aristotelian *phronesis,* which would have been more compatible with, and connected to, political action.

The preceding critiques all work at the tension in Arendt's thought between the potentially competing requirements and rewards of action or political freedom, on one hand, and thought or understanding, on the other. It is a tension that she herself acknowledged only incompletely and ambiguously. There are passages where she suggests that a resolution of the tension—a conjunction or mediation of political freedom and understanding—is possible, even favored, by the interdependence of their respective modalities. In her 1946 essay "The Moral of History," Arendt implies the interdependence of understanding and action, negatively, by likening her contemporaries' failure to understand the origins, nature, and significance of the genocide of European Jewry to their failure to "assume a responsible role in public affairs." "History, in this sense, has its moral, and if our scholars, with their impartial objectivity, are unable to disclose the moral of history, it means only that they are incapable of understanding the world we have created; just like the people who are unable to make use of the very institutions they have produced." The interdependent relationship that she merely implies in 1946 she makes explicit in a 1953 essay entitled (significantly enough) "Understanding and Politics." "If the essence of all, and in particular of political, action is to make a new beginning, then understanding becomes the other side of action, namely that form of cognition . . . by which acting men . . . eventually can come to terms with what irrevocably happened and be reconciled with what unavoidably exists."[12]

On the other hand, there are passages where she appears more sanguine about the convergence of political freedom and understanding. In a 1970 roundtable discussion, she emphasizes some basic differences, even incompatibilities, between the activities of "thinking" and of "commitment and engagement."[13] And in the concluding remarks of her lectures on the faculty of willing (1974), she argues that men of action have historically demonstrated a propensity to evade the challenge of understanding what it means to live in a world where the continuity of history is broken:

> When we directed our attention to men of action, hoping to find in them a notion of freedom purged of the perplexities caused for men's minds by the reflexivity of mental activities . . . we hoped for more than we finally achieved. The abyss of pure spontaneity . . . was covered up by the device typical of the Occidental tradition . . . of understanding the *new* as an improved restatement of the old. (*LM:W* 216)

(Arendt's promise to escape the "impasse"—to close the gap between action and understanding—by considering the faculty of judgment remained unfulfilled. And, if we accept Beiner's interpretation, a fully worked-out Arendtian concept of judgment would not have redeemed its initial promise anyway.)

To the extent that the foregoing passages are consistent with the theses of displacement we have already discussed, which see Arendt shifting her primary commitment from political freedom conceptualized as autonomous, preeminently rewarding and viable, to either the more reliable autonomy of thinking (Hinchman and Hinchman) or the more attainable solace of retrospective judgment (Beiner), one might be tempted to let the matter rest. Worth considering, however, are Arendt's repeated discoveries and affirmations, to the very last years of her life, of nascent and residual forms of public freedom. Such discoveries could be interpreted as testimony of a continuing belief in the supreme worth and viability of political action. For example, in a 1970 interview, Arendt invoked the incentive of what the "eighteenth century" had referred to as "public happiness" to explain the unexpected and (to her) welcome emergence of student movements in the industrialized West.[14] In a 1970 *New Yorker* article, for another example, Arendt, contending that "civil disobedients are nothing but the latest form of voluntary association . . . quite in tune with the oldest traditions of the [United States]," urged that civil disobedience be formally recognized as an institution of American political life. One of her biographers even tells of Arendt's following the latest events of the revolution in Portugal, during the summer before her own death, "with the same intensity she had given twenty years earlier to the revolution in Hungary."[15] It appears that Arendt, to the end of her life, remained a political spectator who praised the rewards of political freedom and who believed these rewards to be attainable, if not urgently necessary for living a completely human life.

Arendt was not unmindful of the appearance of inconsistency she might give as a politically withdrawn theorist singing the praises of political action. For example, in her acceptance speech at the Sonning Prize award ceremony on April 18, 1975, she felt it necessary to deny that her personal inclination "to shy away from the public realm" contradicted her "praise, perhaps glorification, of the public realm as offering the proper space of appearances for political speech and action." She pointed out that, "in matters of theory and understanding it is not uncommon for outsiders and mere spectators to gain a sharper and deeper insight into the actual meaning of what happens to go on before or around them than would be possible for the actual actors or participants."[16]

While one may concede Arendt's point that "it is quite possible to understand and reflect about politics without being a so-called political animal," one may still question why it is so necessary that those who do "understand and reflect about politics" be "political

animals." She implies the necessity of such a conjunction immediately following her defense of the credibility of the "pure" political
spectator, by characterizing her own instinctive disinclination to political action as a "birth defect."[17] A similar ambiguity marked
Arendt's consideration of the tension between theory and action in
a 1972 roundtable discussion. At one point in the discussion, she
switches back and forth and back again between affirming the advantage she gained through her inclination to be withdrawn from
politics and acknowledging the foolhardiness of her political apathy.

> You see, with the political business I had a certain advantage. I, by na-
> ture, am not an actor . . . I never felt the need to commit myself. Until
> finally, *schließlich schlug mir [einer mit einem] Hammer auf den Kopf und
> ich fiel mir auf:* finally somebody beat me over the head and, you can
> say, this awakened me to the realities. But still, I had this advantage to
> look at something from outside.[18]

In pursuing and acknowledging the rewards of theory while praising
the rewards of political freedom, Arendt invites a question from fellow theorists: Why should we do what you say, not what you do?
For their part, so-called political animals might, with justice, ask
Arendt what the urgency is in theorizing, when one can act and
thereby enjoy those rewards she praises so highly.

This chapter shows how Arendt's political thought, particularly
her conceptualization of the faculty of judgment, can be seen to answer these questions, albeit incompletely. It also develops some aspects of her political thought, which she had left undeveloped, to
show how they might more completely answer the issue raised by
these questions, mediating the respective modes and aims of thinking and political freedom. Central to the task of developing further
Arendt's thought is recognizing the under-theorized potential significance of Greek tragic heroes in her writings.

Hannah Arendt never systematically expounded upon what the
legacy of Greek tragedy might contribute to conceptualizing a theory of judgment that would be capable of revealing the necessary interdependence of political action and thinking. From the evidence
of the "Postscriptum" of *Life of the Mind: Thinking* and of lecture
notes on Kant's political philosophy, it seems reasonable to conclude
with Beiner (1980), Young-Bruehl (1982), and others, that Arendt

had definitively settled on Kant (rather than, say, Homer or Sophocles) as her theoretical guide in this task.[19] If Arendt did not systematically consult the Greek tragedians or their tragic precursor Homer on the matter of judgment, she did invoke them, their poetry, their characters, and their media in a variety of contexts and for a variety of purposes. And while dispersed references and theoretically underdeveloped discussions cannot support a claim for the discovery of an alternative notion of Arendtian judgment, they can supplement Arendt's Kantian-inspired theory.

In particular, the pervasive (albeit under-articulated) presence of a theory of tragedy in Arendt's writings offers materials for constructing a conceptual model of the political spectator (the Athenian tragic spectator) that more fully reveals the promise of storytelling to promote appropriately thoughtful action in politics. Developing the best Arendtian response as to why the theorist should also be a political animal requires thinking through (among other things) the implications of the final passage of *On Revolution*. For, on reading this passage, one finds oneself placed, so to speak, on the ascending rows of an ancient Greek theater, witness to a tragic drama of Arendt's own telling.

ASSESSING THE REWARDS OF POLITICAL FREEDOM AND THINKING

In Arendt's telling, the distinctively life-affirming rewards of political freedom are self-evident to those who have acted politically in a genuine public realm. Her writings and interview transcripts are peopled extensively with "witnesses" who "testify" in various ways to the profound and lasting impact of their experience of political freedom. For example, in a 1970 interview, what struck her most about the student movement as a global phenomenon was its "joy in action," a joy that had to do, in her view, with student activists' discovery that "acting is fun" ("Thoughts on Politics and Revolution," *CR* 202). In *On Revolution*, Arendt writes of the intoxicating effect worked on eighteenth-century revolutionaries such as Robespierre by their experience of "public happiness": "Must he not have feared . . . that the new public space would wither away after it had suddenly burst into life and intoxicated them all with the wine of action which, as a matter of fact, is the same as the wine of freedom?" (*OR* 133). The personal impact of political freedom had been intoxicating enough for Thomas Jefferson to contemplate a state of recurring revolution as a means of extending to posterity the rewards of "public happiness" (*OR* 233). French poet and Resistance fighter René Char's temporary experience of freedom had been tantalizing enough for him to lament the postwar loss of his "treasure"—and for Arendt to use his poetic reflections to introduce her collection of "exercises in political thought" ("Preface," *BPF* 5). Sophocles' Theseus and Thucydides' Pericles testify to the preeminent significance of political freedom in classical Athens from the pages of *On Revolution* (281) and *The Human Condition* (197, 205–6, respectively). Even Arendt, who in a 1972 roundtable discussion declared that acting was not her "primary impulse," acknowledged that she had once participated in jury deliberations—"the last remnant of active citizen participation in the republic"—with "great delight and real enthusiasm."[20]

Arendt's "participators" may become political in two ways. Some of them are described as making their entrance into the public realm willfully, intent on satisfying a passion for "emulation" or "immortal fame" (*CR* 202–3; *HC* 197). In Thucydides' Pericles, for example, Arendt finds articulated the aspiration of polis citizens to ensure "everlasting remembrance of their good and their evil deeds" (*HC* 206).[21] And, if we are to credit John Adams as Arendt does, what brought the American colonist to his town assembly and, later, to his revolutionary convention was "'a desire to be seen, heard, talked of, approved and respected by the people about him, and within his knowledge'" (*OR* 119).

Other "participators" appear to become political by force of circumstance. Thus, in assessing the nature and significance of the student activists involved in the civil rights, free speech, and antiwar movements of the 1950s, 1960s, and 1970s, Arendt (presumably referring to the motivating power of moral indignation) emphasizes that the students *"acted almost exclusively from moral motives"* ("Thoughts on Revolution and Politics," *CR* 203). In another instance, she construes René Char's entry into the genuine public realm constituted by the common action of members of the French Resistance as coming about unexpectedly and "probably against [his] conscious inclination" (*BPF* 3). Even Arendt's participation on a jury was undertaken at the behest of the court.

These accidental citizens do not enter politics with the expectations of political beings such as Pericles or John Adams. Once in the political realm, however, they find unexpectedly that they receive a kind of satisfaction formerly unknown to them, a satisfaction whose passing leads some of them to reflect on the nature and significance of their experience of political freedom. From this group, Arendt more than once singled out René Char for his ability to evoke poetically the distinctive and compelling rewards he and his comrades had gained from their common action in the French Resistance. "What was this treasure? As they themselves understood it, it seems to have consisted . . . of two interconnected parts: they had discovered that he who 'joined the Resistance, *found* himself,' that he ceased to be 'in quest of [himself] without mastery.'" The French Resistance fighters discovered another aspect of the "treasure" of political freedom also, the power to change things, to become "'challengers'": "they had taken the initiative upon themselves and therefore, without knowing or even noticing it, had begun to create that public space between themselves where freedom could appear" ("Preface," *BPF* 4).

In evoking Char's reflections on his wartime Resistance activity, Arendt suggests that the distinctive "treasure" of political freedom, which Char discovered quite by accident, was a form of individuation. Through participating in politics, he came both to recognize his power as initiative-taker and to gain a lasting and more vital sense of self. What to Char was a chance discovery—the accomplishment of a rewarding form of individuality through the exercise of political freedom—was, to Arendt's ancient Greek polis dwellers, a way of life:

> In the Greek city-states, to belong to the few "equals" *(homoioi)* meant to be permitted to live among one's peers; but the public realm itself, the *polis,* was permeated by a fiercely agonal spirit, where everybody had constantly to distinguish himself from all others, to show through unique deeds or achievements that he was the best of all *(aien aristeuein).* The public realm, in other words, was reserved for individuality; it was the only place where men could show who they really and inexchangeably were. (*HC* 41)

Whether the case is Resistance fighters in World War II France or polis citizens of ancient Athens, Arendt always discusses individuation as something achieved in the presence, and with the cooperation, of fellow actors: "the actual content of political life [is] the joy and the gratification that arise out of being in company with our peers, out of acting together and appearing in public, out of inserting ourselves into the world by word and deed, thus acquiring and sustaining our personal identity and beginning something entirely new" ("Truth and Politics," *BPF* 263). For Arendt, the individuation promised by public freedom was an individuation that necessarily occurred in the company of one's fellows.[22] (It will, for the remainder of this chapter, go under the title of *public* individuation.)

In the "Action" chapter of *The Human Condition*, Arendt's most systematic analysis of the nature of politics and its significance for human life, she discusses the individuating effects of political action as coming about through the "disclosure of the agent in speech and action" (*HC* 175). Action, she writes, actualizes the "human condition of natality" (*HC* 9), which corresponds to the fact that human beings, by virtue of their being born into the world as uniquely situated newcomers, have the power to take initiative and change the status quo. By means of speech, a human being can express his uniqueness by "announcing what he [as actor] does, has done, and intends to do" (*HC* 179). Speech thus "actualizes the human condition of plurality," the "already existing web of human relationships with its innumerable, conflicting wills and intentions" in which all human beings are suspended (*HC* 184).

Together, action and speech constitute the unique means for human individuation: "In acting and speaking, men show who they are, reveal actively their unique personal identities and thus make their appearance in the human world" (*HC* 179). Arendt does allow that some degree of individuation is possible even outside a genuine public realm. After all, the appearance of human beings through speech and action "rests on . . . an initiative from which no human being can refrain and still be human" (*HC* 176). Thus, even human beings who never experience political freedom are acknowledged by Arendt as having the capacity to achieve some power of initiative and a sense of identity. These achievements are incomplete and subject to reversal, however, because no public realm exists to confirm them. In Arendt's terms, action conducted outside a genuine public realm fails fully to "disclose the agent together with the act" (*HC* 180).

For the full development of human individuation, a public realm is needed to disclose or reveal the agent behind the action. "This revelatory quality of speech and action comes to the fore where people are *with* others and neither for nor against them—that is, in sheer human togetherness" (*HC* 180). This Arendtian state of being "*with* others," of being in "sheer human togetherness" presupposes actors willing to risk self-disclosure, and a space of appearance allowing actors to disclose their unique selves. It presupposes what Arendt, in other contexts, refers to as public or political freedom, that condition of human togetherness in which peers meet and reach decisions about their collective fate by means of persuasion, not violence.

One can think of the connection Arendt implies between the "disclosure of the agent together with the act" and the public individuation promised by political freedom in the following way. Under the conditions of political freedom, the collective outcomes of a political community are made transparent in such a way as to preserve the sense that a given policy has come about as a result of the discrete acts of individual agents—who spoke to the issue and appealed to their fellows from their unique points of view; who were exposed to the views and appeals of their fellows; and, finally, who came to accept what the group collectively decides. The transparency of the public realm thus reveals the plurality of human affairs. It is this transparency or disclosing power of the genuine public realm that enables human beings to recognize their power as initiative-takers: "in the realm of human affairs, we know the author of 'miracles.' It is men who perform them—men who because they have received the twofold gift of freedom and action can establish a reality of their own" ("What Is Freedom?" *BPF* 171).

In opening to view the innumerable interactions of individuals constitutive of collective policy outcomes, a genuine public realm not only fosters a sense of personal efficacy or agency—"the assurance of being able to change things by one's own efforts" ("Thoughts on Revolution and Politics," *CR* 202).[23] It also compensates individual actors for the frustrating limits imposed on their personal efficacy or agency by the promise of achieving a vital and stable sense of identity. Arendt describes the limits imposed on personal efficacy or agency by the condition of human plurality ("the threefold frustration of action") as consisting of "the unpredictability of its outcome, the irreversibility of the process, and the anonymity of its authors" (*HC* 220). In acting into the "web of the acts and words of other men" (*HC* 188), Arendt holds that the initiative-taker cannot expect to remain master of his action because there will inevitably be consequences he could not have predicted and cannot take back. And whereas he may take credit for beginning a chain of events, he cannot claim sole responsibility for any final outcome, since, in Arendt's view, the conditioning effect of the web of human relationships ensures that the outcome is attributable to many agents (*HC* 188–92).

Arendt warns that the inevitable frustration of individual human purpose in the face of the "haphazardness and moral irresponsibility inherent in a plurality of agents" (*HC* 220) tends to foster fundamentally antipolitical desires, to avoid the consequences of action in plurality by withdrawing from the public realm into private life or by seeking to abolish the public realm through the tyrannical imposition of one will. In either case, the renunciation of action in plurality deprives individuals of the distinctive solution that the exercise of political freedom poses to the "calamities of action" (*HC* 220)—a compensatory revelation of the individual as both doer and sufferer. "To do and to suffer are like opposite sides of the same coin, and the story that an act starts is composed of its consequent deeds and sufferings" (*HC* 190). The Arendtian public realm opens to view the stories of those innumerable individual strivings that, to greater and lesser extents, come to grief by running up against the limits that human plurality sets on human purposefulness.

Whether one speaks of the revelatory quality of the public realm or of public individuation as the promise of political freedom, the stakes are clear for Arendt. Action in a genuine public realm wins for the participants the realization of their power as initiative-takers to change the world, and confirmation of a more vital, lasting identity. This is as true for political beings such as Pericles as it is for accidental citizens such as René Char. (That selfish, exploitative, tyrannical action may promise similar rewards raises a question about the self-sufficiency of action that Arendt's consideration of the faculty of judgment was, in part, meant to answer. Her notion of judgment will be considered in the following sections.)

If Pericles' conduct in the ancient Greek polis and René Char's experience in the French Resistance provide Arendt with examples of the life-affirming rewards that human beings may gain by acting in a genuine public realm, the pathological "parvenu"[24] or assimilationist response of German Jewish refugees acts for her as a cautionary example of what human beings stand to lose when they are alienated or expelled from public life and when they pass up or are deprived of opportunities for exercising political freedom. Arendt clearly considers individuation to be the central stake for the politically alienated, as can be seen from the argument of her wartime essay "We Refugees," which postulates a deepening crisis of identity among assimilationist German Jews who had found themselves victims of Nazi policies of denaturalization and expulsion in the prewar years. In this essay, Arendt singles out for consideration one aspect of the typical German Jewish assimilationist response to Nazi policies: the desperate attempt of many of these refugees to remake themselves in the image of whatever country they have been forced by circumstances to take refuge in.

> Mr. Cohn from Berlin had always been a 150% German, a German super-patriot. In 1933, Mr. Cohn found refuge in Prague and very quickly became a convinced Czech patriot. . . . [A]bout 1937, the Czech government, already under some nazi pressure, began to expel its Jewish refugees. . . . Mr. Cohn then went to Vienna; to adjust oneself there a definite Austrian patriotism was required.[25]

Mr. Cohn's behavior exemplifies, for Arendt, the pathology of assimilationism as a strategy for establishing a place in the world. Having found it acceptable in their native country to deny their links with a socially despised group in order to gain individual entry into a pervasively anti-Semitic, bourgeois, Gentile society, assimilationist German Jews in exile adopt a similar approach in their host countries, to little practical effect. The assimilationist or parvenu response to the condition of political exile not only contributes to some Jewish refugees' inability to establish a lasting and vital identity—that is, "their perfect mania for refusing to keep their identity." It also promotes their failure to confront realistically the precariousness of their position.[26]

If the Jewish assimilationist or parvenu response to the condition of political exile inappropriately inhibits individuation, its negative effects are barely comparable to the radical negation of individuation manifested under conditions of totalitarian domination. If political freedom, in Arendt's thought, is the mode of experience distinctively capable of granting human beings the fullest and most rewarding development of their individuality, then the condition of almost total domination in the Nazi extermination camps constitutes the radical negation of political freedom. Arendt attributes the terrible significance of the camps to their unprecedented attempt to "kill man's individuality" (*OT* 454), to "organize the infinite plurality and differentiation of human beings as if all of humanity were just one individual" (*OT* 438). The connection she posits between political freedom and what I refer to as public individuation is perhaps nowhere more evident or more urgently posed than in her imaginative reconstruction of "the destruction of individuality" that was systematically pursued in the Nazi death camps: "to destroy individuality is to destroy spontaneity, man's power to begin something new out of his own resources, something that cannot be explained on the basis of reaction to environment and events. Nothing then remains but ghastly marionettes with human faces, . . . [marionettes] which all react with perfect reliability" (*OT* 455).

The very multiplicity of instances in which Arendt, with no little passion, praises the achievements of individuation under the conditions of political freedom (or laments their absence under conditions of nonfreedom) attests to her high appreciation for what political freedom promises. That this appreciation reflected her unqualified claim for the life-affirming distinctiveness of those rewards promised by public freedom (that is, public individuation) is manifest in her partisan evocation of the eighteenth-century belief in public happiness. To the question of whether political freedom is *uniquely* or *preeminently* life-affirming, Arendt appears to offer only a qualified "yes."

Considered in relation to the other components of what she referred to as the *vita activa*, political freedom takes on unique and preeminent significance. While granting that the activities of labor and work have their appropriate place in the conduct of a human life, Arendt maintains in *The Human Condition* that they lack the power to endow life with real significance. Labor (either one's own or someone else's) provides the biological necessities for each person to prolong life. To the extent that human beings are subject to the necessities of life, their lives are conditioned by nature's unending cycles of growth and decay. This is reflected, for example, in that human beings are periodically subject to the necessities of consuming and eliminating. Insofar as biology impels human beings to labor in response to its imperatives, Arendt holds labor to be the least individuating of the component faculties of the active life. To the extent that the "automatic functioning" elicited by biological need allows any individuality at all, it is only the "individually sensed pain and trouble of living" (*HC* 322).[27] And although the pain and trouble of living may be "sensed" differently by individuals, the range of responses stimulated by this sensation of pain and trouble is, in Arendt's view, narrow.

The political expression of labor's deficient potential for fostering individuation is, for Arendt, social conformism. The "unnatural conformism of a mass society" (*HC* 58) manifests the fact that as laborers, as entities impelled by biological imperatives, human beings are most like each other. When given collective expression, the commonality of human beings' response to biological imperative tends to manifest itself in an overbearing unanimity of opinion: "society expects from each of its members a certain kind of behavior imposing innumerable and various rules, all of which tend to 'normalize' its members, to make them behave, to exclude spontaneous action or outstanding achievement" (*HC* 40).

Against the measure of individuation, work, the second component of the active life, is considered by Arendt to be less deficient than labor but still not up to the standard set by the experience of political freedom. Through work, human beings fabricate use and art objects and thereby construct and maintain a material world. In the process of constructing and maintaining a durable human world, *homo faber*, especially in his role as artist, is capable of achieving some degree of individuality through his production of unique objects. However, the individuality of a person in his or her role as *homo faber* is partial and incomplete, by Arendt's reckoning, because it reflects more the uniqueness of the art object than the expression of personal uniqueness of the artist. Thus, insofar as "a manufacturing society judges men not as persons but as producers, according to the quality of their products" (*HC* 162), it deprives human beings of

the opportunity of expressing the identity of their person, independent of any objects they happen to use or make. "*Who* somebody is
or was we can know only by knowing the story of which he is himself the hero—his biography, in other words; everything else we
know of him, including the work he may have produced and left behind, tells us only *what* he is or was" (*HC* 186).

The fact that Arendt uses the standard of public individuation for
assessing the significance of labor and work attests to her sense of
the unique and preeminent significance of political freedom in the
vita activa. In the context of a full human life, which, for Arendt, includes both the *vita activa* and the *vita contemplativa*, political freedom remains significant for its life-affirming promise, but only distinctively so. The activity of thinking and the wonder at being that
is at the source of thinking provide their own rewards—rewards that
Arendt knew and prized very highly, as, for example, when she referred to the "activity of thinking" as the "highest and perhaps
purest activity of which men are capable" (*HC* 5).

Arendt's appreciation of the distinctive rewards of the *vita contemplativa* did not prevent her from assessing them against the standard
of public individuation set by the partisans of political freedom. *Thaumadzein*, "the wonder at that which is as it is," is seen, by Arendt, as
promoting a form of singularity rather than individuality: "man in
the singular . . . is for one fleeting moment confronted with the
whole of the universe, as he will be confronted again only at the moment of his death." Arendt's use of the term *singular* to describe the
experience of wonder can be contrasted with her ascription of the ad-
jective *unique* in describing the individuated self of the public realm.
It makes sense to talk of the achievement of a unique identity in political affairs, because uniqueness is a measure applied to distinguish
otherwise similar objects. In politics, one gains a unique identity in
relation to other individuating selves. By contrast, in the pathos of
wonder, the sense of singular identity is grounded in the self's perceiv-
ing the totality of everything not of the self: "This wonder at everything that is as it is never relates to any particular thing."[28]

The state of singularity fostered by *thaumadzein* is further distinguished by its inwardness and apparent passivity. The singularity of
the self is experienced only by the self. To others, the "experience of
speechlessness"—manifested, for example, by the "traumatic states
in which Socrates would suddenly, as though seized by a rapture, fall

into complete motionlessness"[29]—is distinguished only by the radical contrast it provides with the apparent activity of other citizens. Thus, in contrast to the unique identity of the political actor, the sense of singularity experienced in the pathos of wonder remains unconfirmed by witnesses. The wondering self foregoes not only the confirmation of identity as conferred by the public realm but also the realization of any capacity to change the world: "the experience of the eternal . . . has no correspondence with and cannot be transformed into any activity whatsoever" (*HC* 20). Initiative-taking is the last thing on the mind of the person who is confronted with the wonder of being.

Between the solitary singularity of wonder and the public individuation of political freedom, the activity of thinking occupies an intermediate position. Like political freedom—and unlike wonder—thinking occurs by means of speech. And even though the speech of thinking is somewhat removed from political action because it occurs internally and silently between "I" and "myself," this dialogue is wholly incompatible with the continuation of the state of wonder. The asking of questions such as What is being? Who is man? What meaning has life? What is death? that in Arendt's view is so characteristic of thought can begin only when "the speechless state of wonder translates itself into words."[30]

To the extent that the activity of thinking presupposes a temporary withdrawal from and temporary passivity in relation to the world of appearances, it contrasts with the worldliness of political action. Insofar as thinking depends on speech (albeit a silent, inner speech), it is capable of having effects for its practitioners akin to the effects of political action. "While engaged in the dialogue of solitude in which I am strictly by myself, I am not altogether separated from that plurality which is the world of men." For Arendt, "men not only exist in the plural . . . but have an indication of this plurality within themselves" because the thinking "I" lives with another self, "myself."[31] In this regard, Arendt finds the duality of the thinking self more akin to the plurality constituted by the acting self in the company of other acting selves than to the singularity of the wondering self. One might say that the thinking self described by Arendt is more unique than singular.

Thinking is also different from wonder and akin to action in its promoting a personal sense of efficacy or initiative (one of the twofold aspects of public individuation). "Wonder at everything that is as it is" implies an attitude of basic acceptance. Insofar as it entails the "capacity to transform sense-objects into images," to make present in our imagination what is absent from our worldly senses, and to make absent in our imagination what is present to our worldly senses, thinking implies a freedom to imagine the world differently than it is. Imagination is, therefore, a prerequisite for intentionally changing the world. "Such change would be impossible if we could not mentally remove ourselves from where we physically are located and *imagine* that things might as well be different from what they actually are" ("Lying in Politics," *CR* 5).

If the activity of thinking prepares human beings for taking initiative by re-presenting the world differently than it actually is, it cannot lead human beings to realize fully their capacity for taking initiative. "Without a politically guaranteed public realm, freedom lacks the worldly space to make its appearance. To be sure it may still dwell in men's hearts as desire or will or hope or yearning; but the human heart, as we all know, is a very dark place, and whatever goes on in its obscurity can hardly be called a demonstrable fact" ("What Is Freedom?" *BPF* 149).

In regard to the formation of a stable self (the other of the twofold aspects of public individuation), thinking also falls substantially short. For Arendt, identity is mainly and most fully formed in the space of appearance constituted by action with one's fellows. "Identity depends on manifestation and manifestation is first of all outside."[32] Action "*changes* the shapeless, chaotic inside in such a way that it becomes fit for appearance, for being seen and heard. By the same token it pins us down, commits us."[33] The identity gained as a result of thinking is not as secure as the unique identity that comes about through action in the company of one's peers: "the self with whom I am together in solitude can never itself assume the same definite and unique shape or distinction which all other people have for me; rather, this self remains always changeable and somewhat equivocal."[34] It was in terms of this inadequacy of the thinking process to stabilize identity fully that Arendt invoked, at the conclusion of *On Revolution,* the reflections of René Char, which "testify to the involuntary self-discourse, to the joys of appearing in word and deed without equivocation and without self-reflection that are inherent in action" (*OR* 281).

Lest one take the foregoing assessment of the nature and rewards of thinking, reconstructed from various Arendt texts, as evidence of a single-minded affirmation of political freedom, one would do well to recall the standard being applied. It should come as no surprise that thinking—set against the twofold measure of public individuation, realization of one's powers of initiative and achievement of a durable and vital identity—falls somewhat short of action. For, after all, the standard of public individuation has its origins in the experiences and preferences of political beings, who are predisposed to seek the rewards of public freedom. To view the significance of thinking solely in terms of its promoting an intermediate form of individuation, preparatory to the achievement in politics of the fullest possible form of individuation, would be to adopt "the perspective of man insofar as he is an acting being" (*LM:T* 213).

Looked at from the perspective of thinkers rather than that of political animals, the activity of thinking comes off rather better than second-best. Arendt, who counted herself in that company ("I can very well live without doing anything. But I cannot live without trying at least to understand whatever happens"), valued thinking as a distinctive means for endowing life with significance.[35] Having deeply and regularly felt the pathos of wonder and the satisfactions of the "search for the meaning of whatever is or occurs" (*LM:T* 166), she held thinking to be a preeminent, if not unique, means for human beings to "reconcile [themselves] to reality, that is, try to be at home in the world."[36]

The satisfactions of thinking and the political misfortunes of her time did not lead Arendt to emulate Plato and his successors who, having "discovered . . . that the political realm did not as a matter of course provide for all of man's higher activities, assumed at once, not that they had found something different in addition to what was already known, but that they had found a higher principle to replace the principle that ruled the *polis*" (*HC* 18). She looked instead to Socrates, who (in contrast to both Plato, his philosophical-minded admirer, and Meletus, his fellow citizen and main accuser) was able fully to enjoy the rewards of thinking and acting. Arendt's Socrates was "a thinker who always remained a man among men, who did not shun the marketplace, who was a citizen among citizens, doing nothing, claiming nothing except what in his opinion every citizen should do and have a right to" (*LM:T* 167). What

Socrates did and claimed a right to do was think out loud in public. This constant and insistent questioning of his fellow citizens about the meaning and worth of the practices and traditions by which they lived constituted for Arendt a kind of actualization of thinking in the public realm. "To Socrates, maieutic [the art of midwifery] was a political activity, a give and take, fundamentally on a basis of strict equality, the fruits of which could not be measured by the result of arriving at this or that general truth."[37]

In defending his conduct as a public gadfly, insistently posing perplexing questions, the Socrates of the *Apology* "claims that the appearance in Athens of thinking and examining represented in himself was the greatest good that ever befell the City" (*LM:T* 173). Nothing, perhaps, indicates Socrates' appreciation of the "good" done to him by thinking than his argument to the Athenian jury that an unexamined life is not worth living. Here is how Arendt distills Socrates' defense: "A life without thinking . . . fails to develop its own essence—it is not merely meaningless; it is not fully alive" (*LM:T* 191).

Socrates' insistence on his right to think testifies to more than his appreciation of the rewards of thinking, however. For, as Arendt notes, thinking as practiced by Socrates was a form of action, and action requires a space of appearance. Presumably, a majority of the jury would have found acceptable a pledge from Socrates to refrain from pursuing his inquiries in public; to retreat to the household of one of his wealthy friends where his discussions, carried out among a well-chosen circle of intimates, would be less threatening to the good order of the polis. In Socrates' stubborn refusal to renounce a public space for manifesting thought, one can detect the deeply felt impulse of the political actor to guard his access to that space of appearance so necessary for attaining the individuating rewards of political freedom. There is, perhaps, no better negative measure of Socrates' having realized his initiative-taking power through action than the coalescence of a political opposition dedicated to limiting his future capacity to act. And, as far as the second of the twofold aspects of public individuation is concerned, Socrates' achievement is no better illustrated than by the fact that, as Arendt puts it, "although we know much less of Socrates, who did not write a single line and left no work behind, than of Plato or Aristotle, we know much better and more intimately who he was, because we know his story, than we know who Aristotle was, about whose opinions we are so much better informed" (*HC* 186).

Although the example of Socrates as "thinker . . . who in his person unified two apparently contradictory passions, for thinking and acting" (*LM:T* 167) may go some of the way in persuading the partisans of thinking on the one hand and the partisans of acting on the other to recognize the distinctive merits of each other's way of life, it ultimately leaves them short of fully appreciating those merits. This is so because thinking, as practiced by Socrates, gives rise to beneficial political outcomes only indirectly and in a fairly narrow range of circumstances; it is, as Arendt notes, "political by implication." The thinking that "dissolves accepted rules of conduct . . . has no political relevance unless special emergencies arise." This is so, Arendt suggests, because the habit of thinking tends to produce a skeptical detachment in people, and skeptical people prefer to stand apart from groups. In times of political emergency, "when everybody is swept away unthinkingly by what everybody else does and believes in," the independence fostered by the habit of thinking manifests itself in a "refusal to join in." To the extent that this refusal is "conspicuous," Socratic thinking becomes, in Arendt's view, "a kind of action" (*LM:T* 192).

It is precisely the special relevance of Socratic thinking in times of emergency that defines the limits of the appeal of that kind of thinking to the political animal. For, as the political animal well knows, politics is about more than resisting evil in times of emergency. It is also and more often about deciding less immediately consequential issues of public concern. And it is in this more mundane political task that Socratic perplexity reveals its limits. It "does not create values . . . it does not confirm but, rather, dissolves accepted rules of conduct" (*LM:T* 192). For their part, the "pure" thinkers can justifiably ask what relevance Socrates' exemplary combination of acting and thinking has for them. If the aim, after all, is to resist complicity in political evil, is not the pure thinkers' long-standing practice of avoiding altogether the public realm as effective a means to this end as political participation in the role of a Socratic gadfly?

Even while acknowledging the justice of these objections, Arendt insisted on holding the thinking person to the standard of political freedom and the acting person to the standard of thinking. She felt it must be possible to mediate the activities of thinking

and acting even despite the structural incompatibilities of their respective prerequisites, modes, and aims. A noteworthy statement of
her faith in this possibility is contained in her 1953 essay "Understanding and Politics," where she postulates the existence of a
mental faculty capable of appropriately mediating the respective
aims of thinking (reconciliation) and action (beginning). "If the
essence of all, and in particular political, action is to make a new
beginning, then understanding becomes the other side of action,
namely that form of cognition . . . by which acting men eventually
can come to terms with what irrevocably happened and be reconciled with what unavoidably exists."[38] Arendt came to envision
that faculty as judgment, "the most political of man's mental abili-
ties" (*LM:T* 192) because it promised to bridge the "intramural warfare" between the respective prerequisites, modes, and aims of
thinking and acting.

THE PHILOSOPHER-STATESMAN: KARL JASPERS
AS EXEMPLARY JUDGE

"When I suggest that the personal element which comes into the
public realm with Jaspers is *humanitas*, I wish to imply that no one
can help us as he can to overcome our distrust of this same public
realm."[39] If anything can be said to have given the major impulse to
Arendt's concern for conceptualizing a faculty capable of mediating
human beings' practices of thinking and acting it was her encounter
with the ruinous novelty of totalitarianism. Arendt consistently and
insistently held that any adequate reckoning of the political and
spiritual consequences of totalitarianism must take into account
that, in addition to its having caused immense human suffering, it
had also destroyed the Western tradition as an authoritative guide
for thinking and acting. "The event of totalitarian domination has
exploded our traditional categories of political thought and the standards of our moral judgment."[40] "To most people today this (Western) culture looks like a field of ruins which, far from being able to
claim any authority, can hardly command their interest" ("Tradition
and the Modern Age," *BPF* 28).

For Arendt, the ruin of Western authority ushered in a new and
pressing set of moral and political questions. Of particular urgency
was the problem of judging in the absence of authoritative

standards—a problem notably manifested by· the insistence of the Jerusalem judges on holding Adolf Eichmann personally responsible for actions undertaken in a "regime [where] there was hardly an act of state which according to normal standards was not criminal."[41] Arendt took the fact of widespread complicity in the monstrously criminal practices of the Nazi regime as an indication of the extent to which people in contemporary Europe had ceased to think and judge for themselves and had instead applied "categories and formulas which [were] deeply engrained in [their] mind but whose basis of experience [had] long been forgotten and whose plausibility reside[d] in their intellectual consistency rather than their adequacy to actual events" ("Responsibility," 187). It was the working of a kind of automatic obedience to directives from above that had facilitated the systematic extermination, "against all military and other utilitarian considerations," of peoples "who were not even potentially dangerous" (205).

Thus, in addition to its legacy of human suffering, the fact of mass complicity in Nazi criminality posed a serious problem of moral and legal judgment. If morality is merely a "set of *mores,* of customs and manners, which could be exchanged for another set" ("Responsibility," 187) depending on a given ruler's will and capacity to enforce compliance, on what basis could a court hold collaborators personally responsible? A guilty verdict would "presuppose an independent human faculty, unsupported by law and public opinion, that judges anew in full spontaneity every deed and intent whenever the occasion arises" (187). In Arendt's view, the existence of such an independent human faculty was implied not only in the survival of a notion of personal responsibility as a juridical standard in the guilty verdicts of the Nuremberg and Jerusalem trials, but also in the capacity of a very few inhabitants of Nazi Germany to resist complicity in the regime's criminal activities, to be, in her words, "non-participants" (205).

> The non-participants, called irresponsible by the majority, were the only ones who dared judge by themselves, and they were capable of doing so not because they disposed of a better system of values or because the old standards of right and wrong were still firmly planted in their mind and conscience but, I would suggest, because their conscience did not function in this, as it were, automatic way—as though

we dispose of a set of learned or innate rules which we then apply to the particular case as it arises, so that every new experience or situation is already prejudged. (205)

In invoking the phenomenon of nonparticipation in Nazi Germany as evidence of the existence of a human faculty of independent judgment, Arendt almost certainly had in mind her former dissertation advisor, intellectual mentor and friend, Karl Jaspers. In the postwar years, she publicly lauded him more than once for his having stood "firm in the midst of catastrophe" ("Karl Jaspers: A Laudatio," MDT 76) and had connected his refusal to become complicit in Nazi crimes to his good judgment. That she considered him a person capable of good judgment is evident not only from her various public statements about his personal conduct during the time of Nazi rule but also from her repeated affirmations of his manner of relating to others and his characteristic mode of philosophizing. For example, Jaspers was more than ordinarily capable of thinking from the standpoint of others, a crucial Arendtian prerequisite for judging. (Because it is "'related closely to the thoughts of others,'" Jaspers's thought "always confirms that Kantian 'enlarged mentality' which is the political mentality par excellence" ["Karl Jaspers: A Laudatio," MDT 79].) This capacity to relate to the thoughts of others conditioned Jaspers's mode of philosophizing, allowing him to establish communication via his imagination with not only his contemporaries but also his predecessors. "In [Jaspers's mode of] universal communication . . . all dogmatic metaphysical contents are dissolved into processes, trains of thought, which . . . leave their fixed historical place in the chain of chronology and enter a realm of the spirit where all are contemporaries" ("Karl Jaspers: Citizen of the World?" MDT 85).

Jaspers's status as exemplar in Arendt's thinking is, perhaps, nowhere more clearly indicated than in the address she gave at his public memorial service. Noting on that occasion that "he wanted to be and could be an example for others," Arendt evoked his significance: "Every so often someone emerges among us who realizes human existence in an exemplary way and is the bodily incarnation of something that we would otherwise know only as a concept or ideal."[42] His exemplary status in her thinking about judgment was neither ad hoc nor theoretically inconsequential, if Elisabeth Young-

Bruehl is accurate in her reconstruction of the aims and structure of the uncompleted third section of Arendt's *The Life of the Mind*. Extrapolating from the "Thinking" and "Willing" sections of Arendt's uncompleted final work, Young-Bruehl argued that "it would be consistent with Arendt's thought movements to turn to a representational figure who can show us a way to the mental activities which their mental manifestations do not provide." Noting that "Arendt wrote two long essays about Karl Jaspers and his 'unerring certainty of judgment,'" Young-Bruehl argues that "we should look at Jaspers as [Arendt's] model practitioner of judgment."[43]

Although we may accept Arendt's contention that Jaspers's steadfastness under emergency conditions and his openness to the thought of others indicated a capacity on his part to exercise good judgment, we can still question whether his having good judgment was dependent on his experiencing political freedom. For, after all, Jaspers lived in politically inauspicious times, substantially lacking opportunities to engage in the public speech and action that are constitutive of political freedom.[44] If Jaspers, handicapped by his lack of political experience, could prove capable of exercising judgment under the most trying of political and moral circumstances, his example would seem to indicate, if anything, the independence rather than the interdependence of good judgment and political freedom, and therefore, the preeminent urgency of educating people in philosophy rather than encouraging them to develop their political virtue in the public realm. Alternatively, Jaspers's example may indicate the independence of good judgment and political freedom in only a select few men and woman of especially high intelligence. For the rest of us, good judgment could be something that would come with experience of political freedom. In dark times, we would be as reliable in our judgment as our exercise of political freedom had been robust.

Of these two possibilities, the former negates the interdependence thesis while the latter negates the significance of Jaspers as a model for those not blessed with extraordinary intelligence. What is revealed by a study of Arendt's four lengthy public statements about Jaspers is her opting for a third possibility; the convergence in Jaspers of good judgment and political virtue. Her attempt to connect his capacity for judgment to his capacity for exercising political freedom is, perhaps, most notably exemplified in her address at his public memorial service, where she goes out of her way to construe the significance of his life in terms of his "basic gift" for politics, not philosophy. On this occasion, Arendt argued that, although Jaspers did not exercise political freedom in the true, ancient sense, it was only because personal and political circumstances (ill health and the accident of German birth) did not allow him to directly manifest his basic (political) impulses.[45] "Since Plato there have not been many philosophers for whom action and politics represented a serious temptation. But Jaspers? He could have said with Kant, 'It is so sweet to think up constitutions.'"[46]

In so conspicuously affirming Jaspers's political rather than philosophical nature, and the political rather than philosophical significance of his achievements at the 1969 ceremony commemorating his life, Arendt merely encapsulated the common substance of her various postwar public statements about Jaspers's life and work. These included "What Is *Existenz* Philosophy?" her 1946 *Partisan Review* essay; "Jaspers as Citizen of the World," her essay contribution to a 1957 volume of the Library of Living Philosophers dedicated to the philosophy of Karl Jaspers; and her 1958 laudatory address on the occasion of Jaspers's acceptance of the German Book Trade's Peace Prize.[47] One of the recurring themes of these statements is the notion that Karl Jaspers was a good citizen in the Arendtian sense of citizenship; that he was, to put it in her words, "born for the ways of a democratic republic, and took the greatest pleasure in human exchange that was conducted in that spirit."[48] Ultimately, Arendt's conspicuous affirmation of Jaspers's political virtue attests to her enduring concern to consider political action and thinking together as interdependent and mutually reinforcing aspects of political freedom.

Arendt affirms Jaspers's exemplary capacity to link his activity as thinker to his activity as political actor in at least two general ways. She emphasizes how Jaspers's break with traditional philosophy presupposes a kind of thinking compatible with the exercise of political freedom. She also seeks to reveal how that compatibility worked in the many instances of Jaspers's own participation in public affairs. She first implies a basic compatibility of Jaspers's philosophic praxis with the exercise of political freedom in her 1946 assessment of Jaspers's contribution to *Existenz* philosophy. In this early essay, Arendt argues that Jaspers's break with traditional philosophy, unlike Heidegger's, aims at a philosophical praxis that is not another "form of Being, but a form of human freedom." Jaspers's alternative to the "very ancient search for an ontology" is his adoption of a "form of 'playful metaphysics,' in the form of a perpetually experimenting, never fixed representation of definite movements of thought, which have at the same time the character of proposals that men can be brought to work with." In adopting this mode of philosophizing, Jaspers's thinking subject strives to reach the limits of the thinkable in confrontation with "extreme situations" like the "incalculability of one's fellow men or the fact that I have not created myself."[49]

Arendt emphasizes two aspects of this striving. First, it is carried out not in solitary contemplation but in communication with others. "Communication is the extraordinary form of philosophic intelligence . . . in communication the philosopher moves among his fellows, to whom he appeals as they in turn appeal to him." Second, if communicability is the fundamental mode of Jaspers's philosophy, then freedom is its fundamental aim. "Existenz is for Jaspers no form of Being, but a form of human freedom and indeed the form in which 'Man as possibility of spontaneity turns against his mere Being-a-result.'" In coming to the limits of thinking in the "extreme situations" posed by living in the world, human beings are readied for transcending these limits by means of acts of freedom. "'Brought into suspense by passing beyond all knowledge of the world which would fix Being, philosophizing sounds the appeal to my freedom and creates space for an unconditioned deed that would invoke transcendence'."[50]

Thus, in rejecting the conceit that human beings can both know Being and express that knowledge of Being in hard-and-fast conceptual categories, Jaspers's mode of philosophizing establishes the life-affirming significance of acts of freedom.

> It is as if with this concept of Being as that which "surrounds" us in fluid contour there were traced an island, on which Man, unmenaced by the dark Unknowable, that in traditional philosophy pervades every existant like an additional quality—can freely rule and choose. The limits of this island of human freedom are traced out in the "extreme situations," in which man experiences the limitations which immediately become the conditions of his activity.[51]

Arendt's account of Jaspers's philosophic praxis as a mode of mutual and inclusive communication whereby human beings may transcend the limits of their existence without pretending to know or control them absolutely parallels in some important respects her own conceptualization of the public nature and life-affirming potential of that individuation promised by political freedom. Just as the authentic self of Jaspers's description requires the company of good listeners and talkers in order both to shift somewhat and to come to terms with the limits of human knowledge and mastery, so the Arendtian citizen depends upon the associated action and public witness of his or her fellows in order both to realize his or her powers of initiative and to achieve the vital sense of identity that compensates the actor for the inevitable limitation of those powers in human plurality.

In her 1946 discussion of Jaspers's philosophy, Arendt limited herself to considering the implications of his distinctive break with Western metaphysics for promoting "human freedom." In later assessments, she strives to show how his conduct as philosopher was conjoined in an interdependent and symbiotic way with his conduct as virtuous political actor. She implicitly and explicitly situates his conjunction of thinking and political freedom in his "unerring certainty of judgment" ("Karl Jaspers: A *Laudatio*," *MDT* 77).

Arendt indicates and enacts these intentions in her assessment of the significance of Jaspers's conduct during the Nazi period. While his nonparticipation in public affairs during that time certainly fits her description of thinking's potential, in times of political emergency, to "become a kind of action," Arendt chooses to inflect differently the significance of his conduct. She poses his refusal to become complicit in Nazi criminality not so much as a manifestation of the inviolability of the "two-in-one" of his thinking as a manifestation of a political virtue nurtured, in significant part, by his distinctive mode of public-oriented philosophizing.

In the darkest times of political isolation, Jaspers was able, through his long practice of philosophy as a mode of communication, to conjure up a imaginary "space" and populate it with representations of human beings, whose "company" verified the basic plurality of human affairs that the Nazi regime was so single-mindedly striving to eliminate. For Arendt, "thought of this sort, always 'related closely to the thoughts of others,' is bound to be political . . . for it always confirms that Kantian 'enlarged mentality' which is the political mentality *par excellence*" ("Karl Jaspers: A *Laudatio*," *MDT* 76, 79). What Jaspers had demonstrated, in other words, was an exemplary capacity to judge or (to put it in other Kantian terms favored by Arendt) both to "'think in the place of everybody else'" and to "anticipate communication with others with whom [one] knows [one] must come to some agreement" ("The Crisis in Culture," *BPF* 220).

Looked at from a perspective that considers one of Arendt's main theoretical challenges to be the revelation of a necessary interdependence between thinking and acting (convincing enough to both the "pure" thinker and the "political animal"), the case of Jaspers's noncomplicity has its limitations. In order to be persuasive, his case would have to show a link, in situations other than collective emergency, between his practice of judging and his capacity for, if not his experience of, political freedom.

That Arendt would have Jaspers's case show precisely this is evident in the way she contextualizes his conduct under the Nazi dictatorship. First, there is her interesting attempt to suggest that his exercise of good judgment in this extreme instance may have been conditioned by his upbringing in a politically virtuous community. Thus, after acknowledging the contribution made by his philosophic "passion for reason" to his capacity to judge (to "populate" the "native region of his thought"), Arendt writes, in a seemingly curious aside: "If we wished to explain this in psychological and biographical terms, we might perhaps think of the home Jaspers came from. His father and mother were still closely linked to the high-spirited and strong-minded Frisian peasantry who possessed a sense of independence quite uncommon in Germany" ("Karl Jaspers: A *Laudatio*," *MDT* 77). The notion that the Frisian people are more independent-minded than their German co-nationals has a long history, but unfortunately, Arendt does not follow the reference up with a clarification of the specific ways in which Jaspers learned political virtue at home.[52]

Second, despite her high praise of Jaspers's good judgment in times of political emergency, Arendt refuses to let it stand as either the only or the most significant politically relevant manifestation of his capacity to judge: "only in the course of the Hitler period and *especially in the years afterward* did he become a public figure in the full sense of the word."[53] Most significant, in regard to this development, was his publication of books such as *The Question of German Guilt* and

The Atom Bomb and the Future of Man, aimed at intervening "directly in political questions of the day."[54]

If political freedom promises aspiring actors the life-affirming rewards of public individuation, then Jaspers's conduct as a public intellectual should have earned him a share of those rewards. So Arendt argues that Jaspers's ventures into the public realm had won him "what the Romans called, *Humanitas*," a unique, stable, and vital identity: "*Humanitas* is never acquired in solitude and never by giving one's work to the public. It can be achieved only by one who has thrown his life and his person into the 'venture into the public realm'—in the course of which he risks revealing something . . . he can neither recognize nor control."[55]

Lest one too quickly conclude that *humanitas* corresponds in a seamless and unproblematic way to the unique "who" or authentic self (René Char) (Preface, *BPF* 4), which Arendt theorized as one of the twofold aspects of the distinctive reward—public individuation—promised by political freedom, it is worth noting that Arendt also describes Jaspers's *humanitas* as having grown "from the native region of his thought."[56] She describes Jaspers's *humanitas* as something "occupying" or "appearing" in a mental "space" and coming into a relationship with the mental representations of the great philosophers: "Jaspers' thought is spatial. . . . his deepest aim is to 'create a space' in which the *humanitas* of man can appear pure and luminous. . . . In order to explore the space of *humanitas* which had become his home, Jaspers needed the great philosophers."[57] Arendt appears in these passages to be emphasizing the exercise of a mental faculty (judgment) more than the exercise of a worldly capacity (action) as a precondition for achieving *humanitas*.

Jaspers's capacity to judge not only wins him a share of the rewards of political freedom, it also gains him superior access to the distinctive rewards of thinking. Insofar as the faculty of judgment enables one mentally to conjure up representations of other subjects, it can facilitate the thinker's attempt to engage past philosophers not as announcers of authoritative answers to the fundamental questions but as partners in a dialogue of fundamental question-asking. Arendt's affirming the positive implications that Jaspers's capacity to judge holds for the conduct of both politics and philosophy can be seen to dovetail with an agenda aimed at persuading political enthusiasts and "pure" thinkers to acknowledge the distinctive merits of each other's activities. On the one hand, the case of Jaspers raises the possibility for those who live for politics that achievement of the rewards of public individuation through action depends, at least in part, on the extent to which such action is informed by good judgment.

On the other hand, the appeal of the case of Jaspers for "pure" thinkers originates in the link Arendt posits between the capacity of thinking to produce meaning and the cultivation of judgment through political action. For Arendt's Jaspers, thinking is significant insofar as it consists in the asking of fundamental questions; that process of question-asking will bear fruit to the extent that it finds adequate partners in dialogue among both the living and the dead. "Only in communication—between contemporaries as well as between the living and the dead—does truth reveal itself."[58] If judgment is the faculty that enables us to imagine the company of those who cannot physically be present, then the aspiring thinker who wishes the company of Socrates or Buddha or Confucius would do best to cultivate his or her judgment. To the extent that a person finds regular occasion for using his or her judgment in encounters with the plural wills and opinions of fellow citizens, the aspiring thinker is offered a high incentive to enter the public realm.

While the case of Jaspers goes a substantial part of the way in exemplifying the capacity of judgment to mediate the respective modes and aims of thinking and action, it has its limits. Jaspers's Existenz philosophy does call the aspiring thinker out of the traditional solitude of the philosopher, but whether this call leads him or her into a public realm of plural wills and opinions or only into an intimate dialogue between thoughtful friends is unclear. Jaspers's observation in a letter to Arendt dated July 20, 1947, that "one has to be opportunistic in politics, of course—but I am never engaged in politics in this sense and would have no talent for it," raises the question as to whether the "limitless communication" endorsed by Jaspers assumes a convergence of aims and sensibilities that does not hold in a true public realm.[59] Questions of this sort seem to have led Arendt, in her final working up of the 1974 lectures on "Willing," to distinguish the condition of plurality necessarily holding in the public realm from Jaspers's notion of dialogue between friends. "An error rather prevalent among modern philosophers who insist on the importance of communication as a guarantee of truth—chiefly Karl Jaspers and Martin Buber—is to believe that the intimacy of the dialogue . . . can be extended and become paradigmatic for the political sphere" (*LM:W* 200).

Although the case of Jaspers might persuade the "pure" thinker and the person who lives for politics of the desirability, even urgency, of developing one's powers of judgment, it would probably fail to convince either of the necessary linkage of that development to citizenship in the "strong" sense. For example, they might reasonably draw quite different conclusions than Arendt does from the fact that Jaspers chose, after the war, to reside "on Swiss soil, in a republic and in a city that is a kind of *polis*."[60] For it would certainly be within the rights of the political enthusiast to wonder whether a younger and healthier Jaspers would have taken advantage of Swiss citizenship and Basel residence to attend the local assembly and there enjoy the individuating rewards of politics. And it would not slip past the notice of the "pure" theorist that the "public intellectual" (*MDT* 72) activities that health and age did allow Jaspers—writing articles and books on political issues, giving public lectures, participating in radio broadcasts—could have been carried out as easily in a liberal nation-state as in a participatory republic.

THE ATHENIAN TRAGIC SPECTATOR IN ARENDT'S WRITINGS

In the last section, we considered the promise and limits of Arendt's conceptualization of Karl Jaspers as representative figure of judgment. The promise of Jaspers's example to show the interdependence of thinking and acting in the practice of judgment was manifest to Arendt in the frequency and character of his interventions in public *intellectual* life and his development of a mode of philosophizing that "could comprehend politics as one of the great human realms of life" ("Karl Jaspers: Citizen of the World?" *MDT* 91). The significance of judgment for the political actor, properly speaking, we can know only indirectly from Jaspers's case, however, unless we choose to share Arendt's view that it was solely due to external factors such as poor health and inauspicious political times that Jaspers did not more fully manifest his political nature.

If the problem with Jaspers as exemplary model of judgment is that he reveals an interdependence between thinking and only a part of political life (namely, the lecturing, radio-broadcasting, arti-cle-writing activities of the public intellectual), then the need arises for a supplementary model, a model of a full-fledged political actor who also practices good judgment. Arendt implicitly makes such a model available in her writings, particularly in her numerous re-marks about the political significance of storytelling and in her dis-cussion of the role of the spectator in "Thinking" (1978). This model is the Athenian citizen who attends the tragic dramas enacted at the annual festival of Dionysus. Insofar as Arendt accepted the tradi-tional view that participatory citizenship and tragic spectatorship ex-isted as interdependent aspects of ancient polis life, she could have referred in a systematic way to the experience of the tragic spectator in Athens, in order to reveal connections between the reconciliatory rewards of thinking and the individuating rewards of political free-dom that the case of Jaspers cannot fully illuminate. In a completed draft of *Judging,* the Athenian tragic spectator could have well served Arendt to supplement Jaspers as a model for persuading "pure" theo-rists and political beings to appreciate the distinctive merits of each other's chosen vocations.

In Kant's theory of taste, Arendt found the framework she needed to formulate a theory of political judgment indicating both the possibility and the urgency for the individual to think *and* to act, to seek the rewards of reconciliation and individuation. Kant's notion of an "enlarged mentality," distinctive for its capacity both to "think in the place of everybody else" and to "anticipate communication with others with whom [one] knows [one] must come to some agreement" (*BPF* 220) crucially aided Arendt in con-ceptualizing a mode of thinking that was more compatible with ac-tion in plurality than "the (Platonic) silent dialogue between me and myself" (*MDT* 10). No less important to Arendt was Kant's affir-mation of the spectator or critic as preeminent interpreter and judge of the beautiful. Kant's conceptualization of "taste" as the fac-ulty uniquely capable of coordinating the creative output of the artist with the perceptions of the spectator—"Kant says explicitly that 'for beautiful art . . . *imagination, intellect, spirit,* and *taste* are re-quired' and adds in a note that 'the three former faculties are united by means of the fourth,' that is, by taste—i.e., by judgment"

("Appendix: Judging," *LM:W* 262)—confirmed Arendt in her sense of the superiority of the judging spectator's vantage point on the meaning of events. The spectator, the one who has withdrawn from "active involvement" to a place from which to contemplate the whole drama, is better able than the actor to exercise the judgment necessary for discovering the drama's meaning. Kant's privileging of the faculty of judgment in the constitution of a world of potentially beautiful objects—"Kant is convinced that the world without man would be a desert, and a world without man meant for him: without spectator" (*LM:W* 261)—and his sympathetic engagement as spectator in the events of the French Revolution thus guided Arendt's conceptualization of judgment as that "faculty of judging particulars" which "realizes thinking, makes it manifest in the world of appearances" (*LM:T* 193).

Lest the person who lives for action in politics be alienated by the denigration of acting presumably implied in Arendt's Kantian-authorized affirmation of the superior capability of the spectator's judgment ("The actor, being part of the whole, must *enact* his part; not only is he a 'part' by definition, he is bound to the particular that finds its ultimate meaning . . . as a constituent of the whole" [*LM:W* 93–94]), Arendt does not neglect to consider the significance of judgment also in the light of the distinctive needs and aims of the political actor. "The public realm is constituted by the critics and the spectators and not by the actors and makers. *And this critic and spectator sits in every actor and fabricator;* without this critical, judging faculty the doer or maker would be so isolated from the spectator that he would not even be perceived" (*LM:W* 262; emphases added).

In thus aligning Kant's elevation of the spectator as preeminent judge with the requirements of action, Arendt effectively preserves a role for judging in the life of the "political animal." In an analogous way, Arendt implicitly relates Kant's elevation of the spectator to one of the basic assumptions of the "pure" theorist, by noting its affinity with ancient Greek philosophy's affirmation of the primacy of contemplation. Aristotle "ascribed the desire to see to all men," while Plato envisioned the "cave-dwellers" of Book VII of his *Republic* to be "content to look at the *eidola* on the screen before them without uttering a single word" (*LM:T* 131).

Where Arendt's "pure" theorist would part ways with Kant would be on where the spectator's gaze is to be directed. In holding human affairs to be as worthy a subject of observation for the thinker as Being, Arendt's Kant contradicts the philosophic tradition that, at least since Plato, had held human affairs to be an unworthy subject of philosophical contemplation—except in those circumstances when the polis threatened to disrupt the very preconditions of philosophical activity. To broaden the gaze of the philosopher so that it might encompass, besides the "Being" of existence, the "becoming" of human affairs, and to establish, in the eyes of the "pure" theorist, the positive worth of a faculty of political judgment, Arendt recurs to the common ancestor of both the Kantian political judge and the Platonic contemplative: the ancient Greek spectator.

In Greek philosophy's affirmation of the pathos of contemplation, Arendt finds the echo of an earlier, pre-philosophical view of the primacy of spectatorship. Indications of that echo are especially present in a fable attributed by ancient chroniclers to Pythagoras: "'life . . . is like a festival; just as some come to the festival to compete, some to ply their trade, but the best people come as spectators *(theatai)*, so in life the slavish men go hunting for fame *(doxa)* or gain, the philosophers for truth'" (*LM:T* 93).[61] As Arendt interprets it, Pythagoras's story constitutes an attempt to reflect the pre-philosophical prestige of the *theatai* upon philosophers. This prestige derived from what was widely supposed to be the earthly spectator's affinity to the deathless Olympian gods, who appeared in the popular imagination as passionate observers, from their mountaintop vantage point, of the affairs of mortal men. "It is in this vein," Arendt writes parenthetically, "that ancient etymology repeatedly derived the key word *'theorein'* and even *'theatron'* from *'theos'*" (*LM:T* 129).

It is worth speculating what Arendt would have made of the common etymological roots and cultural derivation of "theatre" and "theory" in a completed version of *Judging*. Consideration of her brief discussion of judgment and spectatorship in *Life of the Mind: Thinking* ("Thinking and Doing") suggests that Arendt could well have used the close association of the two Greek terms as a starting point for considering what the role of Attic tragedy in Athenian polis life has to teach about the nature of political judgment and the possibility of theorizing about politics in a way that is compatible with political freedom. In "Thinking and Doing," Arendt distinguishes the activities of the festival spectator and the Pythagorean philosopher in several ways. While both occupy themselves with seeing and both require a place removed from action in order to engage in their preferred activity, the judging spectator is neither solitary nor self-sufficient: "the spectator's verdict, while impartial and free from the [actor's] interests of gain or fame, is not independent of the views of others—on the contrary, according to Kant, an 'enlarged mentality' has to take them into account" (LM:T 94).

The fact that plurality conditions spectatorship is decisive for Arendt; it not only distinguishes the activity of spectatorship from the singularity of traditional philosophic contemplation but also constitutes the ground of spectatorship's fundamental compatibility with the spectacle on which it is directed, human affairs. In order to distinguish more concretely the plurality of the judging spectator from the singularity of the contemplative philosopher, Arendt situates the exercise of judgment in historical time and space.

> I have treated the withdrawal of judgment to the spectator's standpoint . . . because I wanted to raise the question first in its simplest, most obvious form by pointing to cases where the region of withdrawal is clearly located within our ordinary world. . . . There they are, in Olympia, on the ascending rows of theater or stadium, carefully separated from the ongoing games; and Kant's "uninvolved public" that followed events in Paris with "disinterested pleasure" and a sympathy "bordering on enthusiasm" was present in every intellectual circle in Europe during the nineties of the eighteenth century. (LM:T 96–97)

Arendt's choice of the Olympic stadium and late-eighteenth-century salons as exemplary sites for spectatorship makes sense in light of the contributions made by Pythagoras's fable and by Kant's musings on the French Revolution to her conceptualization of the spectator as one judge among many other, differently situated judges of human affairs. Her reference to "theater" in the passage cited above is somewhat curious, however, especially considering that theater was an institution traditionally associated with Attica, not with the Peloponnese. (While one can find a stadium at Olympia and the foundations of at least two of its more ancient predecessors, no trace of an ancient theater is to be found.)[62]

More curious still, in the only other evocation of the Pythagorean spectator's place of judgment, explicit reference to Olympia or its stadium has been dropped. "The Roman spectators were no longer situated on the ascending rows of a theater where they could look down godlike on the game of the world; their place was now the secure shore or haven where they could watch, without being endangered, the wild and unpredictable upheavals of the storm-swept sea" (*LM:T* 139–40). This reference to theater occurs in the context of a distinction she makes between early Greek and later Roman thinkers' assessments of the origin and nature of their thinking: in the former case, "admiring wonder at the spectacle into which man is born and for whose appreciation he is so well-equipped in mind and body" (*LM:T* 151); in the latter case, "the awful extremity of having been thrown into a world whose hostility is overwhelming, where fear is predominant, and from which man tries his utmost to escape" (*LM:T* 162).

Arendt's assimilation of what we can reasonably presume to be Attic theatergoers to Pythagoras's Olympic spectators (and late-eighteenth-century intellectuals avidly following the events of the French Revolution) makes sense if one keeps in mind that her explicit general aim in "Thinking" is to investigate the origins, nature, and implications of the faculty of thinking. If thinking is to give way to judging, the thinking subject must widen his or her gaze to encompass, besides Being, the pre-philosophic object of wonder, human affairs. If judging is to lead to action, the judging subject must be both able and willing to engage in open discourse with others about the meaning of human affairs. Thus, Arendt situates the judging spectator "on the ascending rows of theater *or* stadium" rather than in, say, the groves of Plato's Academe or on a dry patch of Roman shore, safely out of the reach of storm-driven waves.

If the Olympic spectator's contrast with the Platonic or Stoic philosopher works effectively to evoke that worldly and world-affirming orientation that Arendt thought so necessary for judgment, his juxtaposition with the Attic theatergoer serves Arendt's purposes less well. Compared with tragic spectatorship, athletic spectatorship is deficient in promoting that combination of reflective distancing and sympathetic engagement so characteristic of the judgment Arendt endorses. This is historically so because education in political judgment was neither a central aim nor an outcome of the institution of the Olympic Games; it was, rather, affirmation of athletic excellence.

The ideal of athletic excellence personified by the Olympic victor originated "in the severely ordered and defined world of the old aristocracy," which existed before the institutionalization of either the (democratic) polis or tragic drama.[63] One might reasonably suppose that a traditional nobleman whose rule was partly rooted in custom and partly based on his monopoly over the implements of violence would have had little opportunity and even less use for developing his capacity to "think in the place of everybody else" and to "anticipate communication with others with whom one knows one must come to some agreement." Those skills, which one might associate with the "art of *community* action" (as one interpreter of theater's significance for political action phrases it),[64] serve a useful purpose less in a nobleman's warrior band or in his circle of household retainers as in a public realm of action constituted by equal citizens. Those skills presumably are developed more by witnessing the agon of human and (particularly) political affairs than by witnessing the athletic agon at Olympia stadium or by hearing Pindar's odes to Olympic victors.[65] Insofar as Arendt holds that the "theater is the political art par excellence" (*HC* 188) she leads us to expect that it is "on the ascending rows of a *theater*" that polis citizens should expect best to cultivate their judgment.

Assuming that there is a historically valid distinction to be made between the respective political consequences of athletic and tragic spectatorship, one would have to assess Arendt's invocation of theatergoing in "Thinking" as being of limited use in illuminating the interdependent relationship of acting and thinking in the faculty of judgment. The relevant passages do not sufficiently establish the distinctive significance of Greek tragedy for the promotion of political action. They do, however, attest implicitly to Arendt's sense of the exemplary status of ancient Greek practices of communal spectatorship. We may have established the probable relevance of these practices for her thinking about the possibilities of mediating thinking and acting, but we have yet to reveal the distinctive role of the fifth-century Athenian theatergoer in her conceptualization of judgment. What we have hitherto lacked in order to address these issues adequately is a clear sense of the theory of tragedy that Arendt drew upon, however unreflectively, in conceptualizing the link between storytelling and political judgment. In the following section, such a theory will be reconstructed by relating the various, scattered instances in Arendt's writings where the tragic spectator makes an appearance. This reconstructive inquiry will begin and conclude with considerations of the instance in which Arendt appears most self-consciously and strategically to invoke Greek tragedy, namely, her extended quotation of *Oedipus at Colonus* at the conclusion of *On Revolution,* an instance that is highly significant.

Sophocles' last tragedy tells the story of how a tragic hero, formerly active but compelled by circumstances to reflect on the sufferings entailed by his past deeds, becomes a blessing to the polis. Old, blind Oedipus's claim is that the blessing he brings to the Athenian polis is the blessing of the gods. Consideration of Arendt's theory of tragedy will allow us to see Oedipus's blessing to the Athenian polis in a different light, not as a blessing of the gods but as the politically relevant blessing that human beings are capable of dispensing to each other through their telling and retelling of the stories of the deeds they have done and the sufferings they have endured.

TRAGIC RECOGNITION: THE KEY TO AN ARENDTIAN THEORY OF TRAGEDY?

> THESEUS: I know you, son of Laius; for long ago / I heard of the bloody act that blinded you, / And I have learned still more from what was told me / As I was coming here. Your clothes, your face, / Scarred and disfigured, show me who you are. / Such misery as yours moves my compassion. / What suit to Athens or to me has brought you / Into our presence, with the unhappy girl / Who stands beside you there? Make known your purpose. / You could not tell me of a fate so fearful / That I would stand aloof—I who remember / That in my childhood I too was an exile, / And that no man has risked his life so often / As I in my encounters in far lands. / I could not turn away from anyone / Like you, a stranger, or refuse help to him. / I know well, being mortal, that my claim / Upon the future is no more than yours.
>
> OEDIPUS: Theseus, the kindness of your words is kingly, / So that I need say little. You spoke the truth / About my name, my parentage, and my country. / Nothing remains for me except to say / What my desire is, and my tale is told.[66]

If our goal is to delineate a theory of tragedy at work in Arendt's political thought, a reasonable way to begin would be to consult those instances in her writings where she distinguishes between tragedy and other storytelling genres for its distinctive potential to foster political freedom. These instances are somewhat rare. When she discusses tragedy as genre or plot type, or when she refers to it implicitly, she aggregates tragedy with other forms of reconciliatory storytelling that appear to have more to do with reconciliation per se than with political freedom. This would be reason enough to incline toward the view offered by Luban and Benhabib, that the reconciliation Arendt aims for in her practice of political theory as storytelling is intended to serve as compensation for the contemporary absence of the rewards of political freedom, were it not also possible to find instances in which Arendt distinguishes tragedy for its distinctive political promise.[67]

One of the earliest of these instances occurs in Arendt's wartime review of Stefan Zweig's autobiography, *The World of Yesterday*. The relevant passage punctuates her critique of those middle-class Jews in fin-de-siècle Germany and Austria who engaged in cultural activities as a means of social climbing.

> It is hard for us to believe that even Hugo von Hofmannsthal . . . fell under the spell of this theatre hysteria, and for many years believed that behind the Viennese absorption in the theatre lay something of the Athenian public spirit. He overlooked the fact that Athenians attended the theatre for the sake of the play, its mythological content and the grandeur of its language, through which they hoped to become masters of their passions and moulders of their national destiny. The Viennese went to the theatre exclusively for the actors. . . . The star system, as the cinema later perfected it, was completely forecast in Vienna. What was in the making there was not a classical renaissance but Hollywood.[68]

For our current purpose of reconstructing Arendt's theory of tragedy, the point to be emphasized here is that the vitality of theater in fin-de-siècle Vienna, far from reflecting Viennese theatregoers' political virtue, expressed and intensified their political alienation. The problem lay in the response of many middle-class Jews to the political mobilization of mass-based anti-Semitic parties in late-nineteenth-century Vienna. Instead of acting politically and collectively in self-defense, by their theatergoing they either adopted or endorsed a parvenu strategy of seeking individual social advancement through the achievement of artistic celebrity.

It is in the context of this emphasis on the politically disempowering effect of fin-de-siècle Viennese theatergoing that Arendt mentions the politically empowering role of Athenian theatergoing. Her reference to Athenian theatre is noteworthy as a compressed iteration of the classical notion of Greek tragedy as politically significant civic institution. In construing Athenian theater as an institution promising its participants a form of emotional "mastery" that enabled them to act effectively in pursuit of collective goals, Arendt implicitly evokes the Aristotelian notion of catharsis. Her formulation in another, later passage (from "Truth and Politics") confirms the influence of Aristotle's *Poetics* on her assessment of tragedy as a politically relevant storytelling form becomes explicit: "We may see, with Aristotle, in the poet's political function the operation of catharsis, a cleansing or purging of all emotions that could prevent men from acting" (*BPF* 262).

If Arendt, on the authority of Aristotle, would have it that the achievement of emotional mastery in theater contributes to the achievement of political efficacy, we still have not established why or how this should be so. Attention to another of the Aristotelian features of the 1943 passage further illuminates this issue. In distinguishing Athenian theater from the "star system" of fin-de-siècle Vienna, Arendt writes, "Athenians attended theatre *for the sake of the play*."[69] What Arendt might mean by contrasting the primacy of the "play" in Athens with the Viennese obsession with star actors becomes clearer in another passage, in *The Human Condition,* where she explicitly and critically engages Aristotle's *Poetics*. At issue in this passage is the meaning and political relevance of mimesis or imitation, "which according to Aristotle prevails in all arts but is actually only appropriate to the *drama,* whose very name (from the Greek verb *dran,* "to act") indicates that play-acting is an imitation of acting" (*HC* 187). The important point of the *Poetics* in this context is that tragedy imitates not the individuals per se but the stories that arise from their actions: "tragedy does not deal with the qualities of men . . . but with whatever happened with respect to them, with their action and life and good or ill fortune. . . . The content of tragedy, therefore, is not what we would call character but action or plot" (*HC* 187).

It is the combination of Greek tragedy's imitation of the stories that arise from action in the plurality of human affairs and its conveyance of the intangible identities of individual characters through stage acting that establishes Greek tragedy and theater generally as "the political art par excellence." Only in theater, Arendt writes, "is the political sphere of human life transposed into art" (*HC* 188). This passage from *The Human Condition* calls our attention to Arendt's sense of the importance of plot in Greek tragedy, but it fails to reveal fully those aspects of plot that serve to foster spectators' related capacities of emotional mastery and political efficacy. As in preceding instances, we are forced to consult another passage, this one from Arendt's acceptance address for the Lessing Prize, for fuller illumination.

In her acceptance address, consideration of German forgetfulness about the Nazi past leads Arendt to distinguish between "mastering" the past and "knowing and enduring" it ("On Humanity in Dark Times," *MDT* 20). To give an idea of how an unmasterable past can come to be known and endured, Arendt refers to William Faulkner's World War I novel *A Fable,* which, in her view, successfully provokes in its readers the "'tragic effect' or the 'tragic pleasure,' the shattering emotion which makes one able to accept the fact that something like this war could have happened at all" (*MDT* 20). Immediately following this assessment, Arendt distinguishes tragedy from other literary forms:

> I deliberately mention tragedy because it more than the other literary forms represents a process of recognition. The tragic hero becomes knowledgeable by re-experiencing what has been done in the way of suffering, and in this *pathos,* in resuffering the past, the network of individual acts is transformed into an event, a significant whole. The dramatic climax of tragedy occurs when the actor turns into a sufferer; therein lies its peripeteia, the disclosure of the dénouement. (*MDT* 20)

The criterion for tragedy's distinctiveness lies in its preeminent capacity to represent a process of "recognition," an English term often used to translate what Aristotle, in the *Poetics,* calls *anagnorisis:* "a change from ignorance to knowledge."[70] The recognition Arendt appears to have in mind is a process whereby a human agent, who has stopped acting, becomes a listener or spectator of stories and experiences, *in imagination,* the suffering entailed by his past deeds. This "resuffering of the past" or "suffering by memory operating retrospectively and perceptively" lends shape and form to the past, constituting from it "an event, a significant whole" (*MDT* 20–21). Although Arendt does not explicitly say as much in this passage, her sense seems to be that tragedy's preeminent capacity to represent the tragic hero's experience of recognition enables it to provoke an analogous experience of recognition in tragic spectators. Why that might be so may have something to do with the tragic hero's availability as a model for imitation. In other passages, she explicitly refers to heroes as figures who invite imitation: "the examples [of Achilles, Jesus of Nazareth, or St. Francis] teach or persuade by inspiration, so that whenever we try to perform a deed of courage or of goodness it is as though we imitated someone else" ("Truth and Politics," *BPF* 248).[71]

Notwithstanding its Aristotelian echoes and its singling out of tragedy as a literary form distinctively able to represent the process of recognition, the passage from the Lessing address nevertheless falls short as a clear indicator of the political relevance of Greek tragedy in Arendt's thought. For one thing, tragedy's distinctiveness is seen here in terms of its capacity to foster reconciliation, not action. Why ought the reconciliation provoked by our imaginative resuffering of the consequences of the tragic hero's deeds inspire us to take action ourselves? Why not respond to the experience of tragic recognition with resignation?

A second and related problem with Arendt's account of the reconciliatory promise of tragic recognition is her apparent choice, to exemplify it, of a hero from Homeric epic rather than from Greek tragedy proper. "The scene where Ulysses listens to the story of his own life is paradigmatic for both history and poetry; the 'reconciliation with reality,' which, according to Aristotle, was the essence of tragedy . . . came about through the tears of remembrance" ("The Concept of History," *BPF* 45). If Greek tragedy or tragic drama were the paradigm for Arendt's conceptualization of the tragic hero's process of recognition, why choose as exemplary hero a figure from a storytelling genre associated with the rule of aristocratic warriors, a pre-polis, pre-participatory form of decision-making? Tragic heroes are not lacking in Greek tragedy; for example, one could not hope for a better candidate to exemplify what Arendt describes as this pathos-engendering confrontation with the consequences of one's past deeds than Sophocles' Oedipus—as Aristotle himself noted.[72]

In light of these objections (and others one might cite concerning the ambiguity and rarity of instances in Arendt's prodigious output in which tragedy is singled out from other reconciliatory storytelling forms for its distinctive role in fostering political freedom),[73] one might reasonably question whether the resources exist in Arendt's work for reconstructing a theory of Greek tragedy that adequately delineates the interdependent relationship between tragic spectator-ship and political action. Why not remain with Luban and Ben-habib, and perhaps Beiner, on the less exposed ground of claiming reconciliation per se as the aim of Arendtian storytelling, rather than try to establish links between her storytelling and political virtue? If there is a place in Arendt's writings where she self-consciously ex-ploits a theory of tragedy, and where we might best hope to see the distinctive relevance of the reconciliatory storytelling form of tragedy for political virtue, it would be in the coda of *On Revolution*. For here, Arendt does not quote one or another dramatic passage merely as a means to illustrate some discrete aspect of politics or Greek culture; nor does she invoke tragedy as one of several equally suitable forms of reconciliatory storytelling.

We know this because of her explicit consideration and rejection, in the book's final pages, of another politically promising instance of storytelling—French Resistance fighter René Char's poetic reflections on the post-Liberation disappearance of his public space of freedom. "These reflections are significant enough. . . . And yet they are per-haps too 'modern,' too self-centred to hit in pure precision the cen-tre of that 'inheritance which was left to us by no testament'" (*OR* 281). Arendt's extended quotation, in ancient Greek script (accom-panied by both English translation and paraphrase) of key passages from Sophocles' *Oedipus at Colonus* does more; it implicates the reader in the spectacle of a tragic drama. That Arendt provokes this dramatic reading experience in the concluding passage of *On Revolu-tion*—a book that has been variously described as her "principal in-quiry into the possibilities of politics today," "an ideal for practice," even a "Handbook for Revolutionaries"—should give us reason to expect that examination of the passage will yield important insights into her understanding of the potential of tragic storytelling to pro-mote political freedom.[74]

Among the more obvious questions one might ask about this passage is why the choice of a Greek tragedy, *Oedipus at Colonus*? It is Arendt's explicit claim that this particular example of poetry best indicates the revelatory nature and life-affirming significance of political freedom. She gives an illustration by juxtaposing the tragic chorus's "famous and frightening" assertion of the fundamental inadequacy of human existence with her paraphrase of Theseus's affirmation of political freedom as the distinctive life-affirming promise of polis membership (*OR* 281).

Oedipus makes no appearance in Arendt's compressed retelling of Sophocles' last play. This absence is noteworthy, not least because he is the play's main protagonist and it is the spectacle of his plight that provokes the chorus to utter its tragic wisdom. From the perspective we have gained as a result of our reconstructive inquiry into Arendt's theory of tragedy, his absence from Arendt's staging of *Oedipus of Colonus* is curious because it calls to mind another notable absence, this one from Arendt's account, in the acceptance speech for the Lessing prize, of that process of tragic recognition by which the hero, as spectator, "resuffers" the consequences of his past deeds. Oedipus's preeminent suitability as exemplary tragic hero, as exemplary *re*-sufferer, in this former instance has been noted. What importance does this suitability have in light of Arendt's dramatic retelling of *Oedipus at Colonus*? In my view, attention to Oedipus's role as tragic hero in Sophocles' last play serves to illuminate a link between thinking and acting, theory and political freedom, that is only partially exploited in her compressed retelling of *Oedipus at Colonus* and only incompletely theorized in her political thought as a whole. This link between thinking and acting is the link constituted by her notion of tragic recognition as that occasion whereby spectators of tragedy develop their capacity to look at the world from the point of view of one who has acted and suffered.

Our reconstruction of Arendt's theory of tragedy, particularly her notion of tragic recognition, allows the possibility of interpreting in somewhat different terms the conditions of the bargain between Oedipus and Theseus, and the fulfillment of those conditions in the creation of a hero cult. In the agreement of Oedipus and Theseus— the former reduced by his sufferings, especially his self-imposed blindness, to a life of thinking remembrance; the latter an active man taking a leading role in the affairs of his polis[75]—we may see poetically expressed the fulfillment of tragic storytelling's promise to mediate thinking and acting through the fostering of tragic recognition in the spectator. Provisionally, we can construe this fulfillment in the following theoretical terms; Oedipus, as bearer of a story of deeds and sufferings, occasions a moment of tragic recognition on the part of Theseus: "You could not tell me of a fate so fearful / That I would stand aloof—I who remember / That in my childhood I too was an exile, / And that no man has risked his life so often / As I in my encounters in far lands."[76] Reflection on the suffering consequent on Oedipus's past deeds provokes the "suffering by memory" that both reconciles the political actor (Theseus) to what has happened and prepares him to act and change what is. In this sense, Oedipus's significance derives from his role as proponent of the view that the telling and retelling of his story and others like it promises substantial benefits to the political community.[77]

In his last direct utterance, Sophocles' Oedipus is unequivocal about the necessary link between remembrance and the future good fortune of the polis—"O friend most dear to me! may all good fortune / Come to your land, your followers, and you! / *And that your happiness may evermore / Be at its height, remember me, the dead.*"[78] What the specific content of that good fortune is, Oedipus has already indicated: Athens's protection against future Theban aggression.[79]

In the previous chapter we read in Oedipus's parting words an evocation of Greek tragedy's political significance as a medium of remembrance. In this reading, tragic spectatorship fostered an affirming sense of the meaning of human life both by indicating the Periclean promise of gaining a redemptive intimation of immortality through acting in the polis and by confirming this promise through the presentation of characters whose actions have been immortalized in story form. One thing that tragedy taught, in other words, was that, if citizens act, their deeds may become the subject of stories that will outlast their mortal lives. To use the terms suggested by Arendt's conceptualization of the respective rewards of action and thinking, the intimation of immortality consequent on tragic recognition fosters public individuation.

To construe the promise of the tragic recognition of which Arendt speaks exclusively in terms of the individuating intimation of immortality gained through identification with a tragic hero would, however, slight Arendt's emphasis on the actor's need for political judgment.[80] Action undertaken merely for the sake of being remembered forever can sustain as much a clique of aristocratic warlords as it can a gathering of polis citizens. Such action does not particularly require the medium of Greek tragedy for its representation.

It may be (and our consideration of Arendt's notion of spectatorship in "Thinking" would appear to confirm) that Arendt, on occasion, insufficiently distinguishes Greek tragedy from other institutions of communal spectatorship and storytelling genres in terms of their capacity to cultivate the kind of political judgment needed by citizens in a democratic polis. Nevertheless, our current reconstructive inquiry into Arendt's theory of tragedy suggests the probability that, in terms of political benefit, Arendt expected from tragic storytelling not only the inspiration of glory-seeking publicly individuating heroes but the cultivation of citizens' capacities to see things from the points of view of their fellow citizens. What the preceding interpretation of the bargain between Theseus and Oedipus lacks is an indication of how the story of Oedipus's suffering and death fosters that "'enlarged mentality'" (*BPF* 220) of the judging citizen. Another way of expressing this deficit is to say that, while the interpretation gives an account of the promise of tragic recognition to foster public individuation, it fails to address how tragic recognition fosters the pathos of wonder, the state of singularity that she considered to be the distinctive reward of thinking.

We can begin to address this deficit by recalling Arendt's description of the state of wonder that constitutes the beginning of thought: "man in the singular . . . is for one fleeting moment confronted with the whole of the universe, as he will be confronted again only at the moment of his death."[81] For Arendt, the condition of singularity (an extraordinary state sustainable for limited periods) manifests an important affinity of the philosophical pathos of wonder with the experience of confronting death (*HC* 20; *LM:W* 44). Both kinds of experiences dispose the self to a basic affirmation of everything that is and a release from the perception and desire of particular things characteristic of the willing ego.

Recognizing the affinity between contemplative wonder and confrontation with death allows us to identify a second politically relevant dimension of tragedy implied by Arendt besides its capacity to evoke the promise of political freedom to provide a life-affirming intimation of immortality and to confirm this promise through the presentation of characters whose actions have been immortalized in story form. Let us consider again the bargain between Oedipus and Theseus, paying special attention to another and different role played by Oedipus. At play's end, Oedipus dies or, to put it more precisely, disappears from the world of the living.[82] It is in his role as doomed hero that Sophocles' Oedipus can provide a perspective from which better to see another aspect of the political significance of tragic recognition in Arendt's thought.

What might it mean to identify with the dead? Accepting Arendt's reading of the parallel ways whereby philosophical contemplation and confrontation with impending death provoke states of singularity, we can draw the implication that identification with the hero in a tragedy, who confronts and suffers death, can serve to foster a temporary liberation of the self from the willfulness and partiality consequent on living as an individuated being in a plural world.[83] In looking at things from the standpoint of the dead, one learns "acceptance of things as they are" ("Truth and Politics," *BPF* 262). Arendt finds an exemplary expression of this acceptance in the final ("greatest") words attributed to Pope John XXIII on his deathbed, "Every day is a good day to be born, every day is a good day to die."[84] The political significance of the basic acceptance following on the state of wonder lies in its fostering a capacity to "look with equal eyes upon friend and foe" (*BPF* 263), which capacity finds its paradigmatic expression in Homer's choice to "sing the deeds of the Trojans no less than those of the Achaeans" (*BPF* 262–63). We can read in Arendt's approving reference—"even Achilles set out for Hector's funeral" (*OT* 452)[85]—an implicit acknowledgment of the "cathartic" (*BPF* 262) effect of telling a tragic story, relaxing the imperatives of individuation, and fostering that attitude of basic acceptance necessary for looking impartially upon the affairs of the living. If Arendt did not explicitly acknowledge the promise of old Oedipus in eliciting this effect, Nietzsche, one of her precursors in the German tradition of tragic engagement, did:

> in *Oedipus at Colonus* we encounter the same cheerfulness, but elevated into an infinite transfiguration. The old man, struck by an excess of misery, abandoned solely to *suffer* whatever befalls him, is confronted by the supraterrestrial cheerfulness that descends from the divine sphere and suggests to us that the hero attains his highest activity, ex-

tending far beyond his life, through his purely passive posture, while his conscious deeds and desires, earlier in life, merely led him into passivity. Thus the intricate legal knot of the Oedipus fable that no mortal eye could unravel is gradually disentangled—and the most profound human joy overcomes us at this divine counterpart of the dialectic.[86]

Considering the notion of tragic storytelling as means for provoking a state of singularity together with the notion of tragic storytelling as means for gaining an intimation of immortality, we might formulate an Arendtian theory of the political significance of tragic storytelling in the following way. Telling a tragic story promotes political freedom by fostering the audience's appreciation of the distinctive rewards of acting (individuation) and thinking (acceptance). Tragic storytelling does so by representing a process of recognition whereby a tragic hero reflects on the suffering consequent on his or her past deeds. This representation invites audience members to identify with the hero in his twofold role as immortal and as member of the dead.

Immortality is the possession of the hero by virtue of his having acted and thus having become implicated in a story. Identification with an immortal hero such as Theseus or Achilles fosters audience members' appreciation of the promise of gaining a redemptive intimation of immortality through the individuating effects of political action. Death or doom is the condition of the hero by virtue of his having suffered the consequences of action in a plural world. Identification with a dead or doomed hero such as Oedipus or Achilles facilitates audience members' intuition of the state of world-affirming singularity promised by thinking wonder.[87]

This reading of the twofold effect worked by the process of recognition reveals the distinctive suitability of tragedy as a storytelling genre or institution in a free polity. As counterbalance to the centrifugal and potentially antidemocratic effects of tragedy's implicit invitation to reap the immortalizing reward of individual glory through action, there is tragedy's will-taming provocation of a state of wonder and acceptance. Conversely, lest the wonder provoked by identification with a doomed hero lead to a passive state of aesthetic detachment, the promise embodied in the hero's achievement of immortality provides incentive to act. The middle ground between a ruthless and overmastering heroism at one extreme and a politically resigned aestheticism at the other, which we have staked out in the name of Arendt's notion of tragic recognition, can be vividly evoked by reference to a famous passage from Nietzsche's *Birth of Tragedy:*

> But lest us ask by means of what remedy it was possible for the Greeks during their great period, in spite of the extraordinary strength of their Dionysian and political instincts, not to exhaust themselves in either ecstatic brooding or in a consuming chase after worldly power and worldly honor, but rather to attain that splendid mixture which resembles a noble wine in making one feel fiery and contemplative at the same time. Here we must clearly think of the tremendous power that stimulated, purified, and discharged the whole life of the people: *tragedy*.[88]

The phrase "fiery and contemplative at the same time" serves well as a pithy description of the citizenly disposition called for by Arendt's political theory at its best. Attention to the explicitly tragic aspects of Arendt's multifaceted resorting to a storytelling mode of political thought reveals Arendt not as a politically resigned theorist of reconciliation solely or primarily, *pace* Luban and Benhabib, but as a theorist of reconciliation and initiative-taking, judgment and action.

MAKING A TRAGEDY OF THE NAZI PAST: THE CASE OF EICHMANN

Arendt introduces the notion of recognition in her 1959 address on Lessing in the course of thinking about how to come to terms with Nazi criminality, particularly its radical attempt to abolish the human condition of plurality.[89] The challenge lies in making the experience of Nazi genocidal practices a part of the shared world of plural discourse without, on the one hand, minimizing the terrible injury it represents to the idea of a mutually constituted world of differently situated and opinionated beings or, on the other, wholly discarding the idea of a plural, differentiated humanity.

Unfortunately, in the Lessing address Arendt does not fulfill her promise to show how the process of recognition might serve as a means to come to terms with the burdensome past of Nazi rule. Although she raises the possibility of provoking a reconciliatory process of recognition by telling the story of Nazi rule as a tragedy, she does not adequately specify or exemplify how such a tragedy might be told. This reticence is consistent with Arendt's earlier apparent refusal in her wartime essays and first book, *The Origins of Totalitarianism*, to apply the term *tragedy* explicitly to the phenomenon of Nazism. She applies this term—with its constellation of associated terms (such as *drama, theater*) and citations (such as *Oedipus at Colonus*)—to the phenomenon of revolution. The repeated failure to fulfill the initial promise of revolutionary acts of freedom is for Arendt a tragedy, and therefore a phenomenon to which her contemporaries can be reconciled without losing their disposition to be free. The loss of freedom suffered under totalitarian rule was apparently of a degree and scope that resisted explicit narration as a tragedy.

Totalitarian rule was consistent, in Arendt's view, not merely with the strict prohibition of political freedom and the closing off of opportunities for public individuation, as was the case in revolutionary France under the Terror, but also with a wide-ranging and profound attack on all aspects of the human capacity to act, to take initiative, including the human faculties of fabrication and thought. For the Arendt who wrote the *Origins,* the concentration-camp system manifested an unprecedented, nearly successful attempt to "destroy spontaneity, man's power to begin something new out of his own resources" (*OT* 455). This it did in various ways. The first was by abolishing any sense of personal responsibility through a policy of mass incarceration:

> To the amalgam of politicals and criminals with which concentration camps in Russia and Germany started out, was added at an early date a third element which was soon to constitute the majority of all concentration-camp inmates. This largest group has consisted ever since of people who had done nothing whatsoever that, either in their own consciousness or the consciousness of their tormenters, had any rational connection with their arrest. . . . [Members of this group], innocent in every sense, are the most suitable for thorough experimentation in disenfranchisement and destruction of the juridical person. (*OT* 449)

The second was by depriving death of the meaning remembrance might give it through a policy of mass murder: "When no witnesses are left, there can be no testimony" (*OT* 451). The third was by effecting the most complete surrender of individual will through the systematic brutalization of human bodies: "The triumph of the SS demands that the tortured victim allow himself to be led to the noose without protesting, that he renounce and abandon himself to the point of ceasing to affirm his identity" (*OT* 455).

Consistent with Arendt's sense of the totalitarian success at achieving "a much more radical liquidation of freedom as a political and as a human reality than anything . . . witnessed before," Nazi rule appears in her initial formulations as a catastrophe to be faced up to and resisted.[90] It does not appear as a tragedy capable of provoking, in a mutually interactive way, that intimation of immortality and that state of wondering acceptance from which spring action and judgment supportive of a free polity. It is not until her publication of the controversial book *Eichmann in Jerusalem* that Arendt explicitly attempts to muster some tragic significance from the terrible past of Nazi rule.

What underlay the change in her approach? At an additional ten years' distance from the horrible events of Nazi rule, the sense of outrage and shock had, perhaps, diminished somewhat. With the ascendancy of Krushchev and the initiation of a "detotalitarization process" in the Soviet empire, the sense of imminent threat from Soviet-style totalitarianism had probably also subsided.[91] However, if there was a single decisive factor that provoked Arendt's rethinking of the nature and significance of totalitarianism and of Nazi rule in particular it was, by her own account, the spectacle of Adolf Eichmann's "thoughtlessness" in a Jerusalem courtroom. In the course of observing Eichmann on trial, Arendt came to a new, more hopeful understanding of both the limits of totalitarian domination and the possibility of human freedom. Not coincidentally, this new understanding came to be expressed, in significant part, within a tragic framework.

Adolf Eichmann had been a top administrator in the mass deportation of Jews, organizing and coordinating the transportation of victims to the killing centers. Captured by Israeli agents in Argentina in May 1960, Eichmann was brought to Israel. Arendt covered the subsequent trial as a reporter for the *New Yorker*. Her report—published first in magazine form, then as a book—sparked a fierce controversy in intellectual circles in the United States, Israel, and Western Europe. Critics tended to focus on one or more of the following aspects of Arendt's report. In the first place, there were several passages in which she noted and criticized the role of Jewish councils in the organization of their members for deportation. In the second place, there was Arendt's portrait of Eichmann as an unimaginative organization man and social climber, whose collaboration in the Nazi program of mass killing reflected not an ideologically conditioned hatred of Jews or any native sadism but rather a basic incapacity of judgment. In the third place, there was the emotionally detached tone of her report, with respect both to the suffering of the Jewish victims and to the criminality of the Nazi defendant. Separately or in combination, these features provided the major grist for critics' charges that Arendt had engaged in a perverse exercise of blaming the (Jewish) victims and had minimized the gravity of Eichmann's evil by dismissively portraying him as a banal bureaucrat.[92]

Arendt held that the trial of Eichmann called for an exercise of judgment not only in the strict judicial sense of a verdict bearing on the status of a criminal defendant but also in the politically relevant sense of an assessment arrived at independently of legal precedent and existing legal and moral concepts. The necessity of an act of judgment in this latter sense followed from the monstrously unprecedented nature of Eichmann's crime: his direct and knowing collaboration in a policy of genocide. To judge Eichmann would mean to acknowledge him as a co-inhabitant of a plurally constituted, mutually shared world: "the law presupposes precisely that we have a common humanity with those whom we accuse and judge and condemn."[93] Eichmann presented a special challenge in this regard not only because legal or moral precedents were lacking for judging his kind of crime but also because his crime was of a nature that made it extremely difficult to achieve impartiality. To put this challenge in the terms we have developed from Arendt's notion of recognition, judging Eichmann required both an act of initiative (judging in the absence of precedents) and a basic acceptance of the world as it is (acknowledging Eichmann's genocidal crimes as a fit subject of remembrance and plural discourse in a mutually shared world). Initiative-taking and acceptance are precisely the effects that our reading of Arendt's notion of recognition lead us to expect from tragic spectatorship. It should therefore come as no surprise that, in an attempt to facilitate judgment in this difficult case,

Arendt applies concepts deriving from (or, at least, implied by) the theory of tragic recognition that she first outlined in her 1959 address on Lessing.

Consider, for example, how Arendt (particularly in the first chapter of *Eichmann in Jerusalem*) frames her criticism of the state prosecutor's conduct of the trial with standards drawn from drama. The state's attempt to turn the Eichmann process into a "show trial" benefited from the theatricality inherent in the stagelike setting constituted by the Jerusalem courtroom: "the proceedings happen on a stage before an audience, with the usher's marvelous shout at the beginning of each session producing the effect of a rising curtain. Whoever planned this auditorium . . . had a theater in mind, complete with orchestra and gallery, with proscenium and stage, and with side doors for the actors' entrance" (*Eichmann*, 4). On the other hand, the prosecution's failure to focus the state's case centrally on Eichmann's specific deeds robbed the trial of the kind of impact that a well-fashioned play achieves by keeping the hero and his deeds in the limelight: "A trial resembles a play in that both begin and end with the doer, not with the victim. . . . In the center of a trial can only be the one who did—in this respect, he is like the hero in the play—and if he suffers, he must suffer for what he has done, not for what he has caused others to suffer" (9).

Arendt's sense that a trial, like a play, needs a "hero" (*Eichmann*, 9) leads her to reject the prosecution's attempt to make "the tragedy of Jewry as a whole" (6) the central issue in the Jerusalem court.[94] Arendt's insistence on keeping the doer and not the victims at the center of the trial was provocative. Some readers saw it as evidence of her lack of compassion for her fellow Jews. For others it stemmed from her more general tendency to emphasize the dangers of allowing people to voice their suffering in the public realm.[95]

For Arendt, the insistence on keeping the doer at the center of the trial merely represented a necessary concession to what she considered one of the basic principles of justice, the importance and centrality of the individual. "Justice insists on the importance of Adolf Eichmann. . . . On trial are his deeds, not the sufferings of the Jews, not the German people or mankind, not even anti-Semitism and racism" (*Eichmann*, 5). Examination of her insistence on the priority of the doer, from a standpoint provided by her theory of the political relevance of tragic storytelling, reveals another perspective. Let us consider her juxtaposition of two stories told during the trial of Adolf Eichmann and recorded in her controversial book *Eichmann in Jerusalem.*

Reporting the testimony of prosecution witnesses, Arendt singles out and quotes at length the story told by Zindel Grynszpan, a Polish Jew and a longtime resident of Germany until October 28, 1938, when along with seventeen thousand other Polish Jews he was brutally driven by German police back into Polish territory. Arendt marvels at Grynszpan's ability to tell the story of his ordeal on that and following days: "he spoke clearly and firmly, without embroidery, using a minimum of words" (*Eichmann,* 228). In her view, his achievement reflected "a purity of soul, an unmirrored, unreflected *innocence of heart* and mind that only the righteous possess" (229; emphasis added). Curiously, Arendt follows up her praise of Grynszpan's achievement by explicitly noting one dimension in which it was deficient: "No one could claim that Grynszpan's testimony created anything remotely resembling a 'dramatic moment'" (*Eichmann,* 230). Considering all we have learned about the extent of Arendt's links to a tradition of engagement with Aristotle's theory of tragedy, we might reasonably suspect that in referring to someone's (the quote is unattributed) notion of "'dramatic moment,'" she has in mind the "process of recognition," that "dramatic climax of tragedy [that] occurs when the actor turns into a sufferer" ("Lessing," *MDT* 20). Such suspicions are reinforced by the story Arendt chooses to relate immediately after Grynszpan's, a story that in her view did create a dramatic moment.

The story of Anton Schmidt, a sergeant in the German army, is told in the course of the testimony of a Polish Jew and partisan, Abba Kovner. Kovner relates how Schmidt, in charge of a patrol engaged in rounding up German soldiers cut off from their units by the fighting in Poland, had assisted Jewish partisans for five months, until March 1942, when he was arrested and executed (*Eichmann,* 230). Arendt's description of the effect wrought by Kovner's telling of Schmidt's story is worth quoting at length for it reveals her sense of what kind of story it takes to elicit a tragic effect:

> During the few minutes it took Kovner to tell of the help that had come from a German sergeant, a hush settled over the courtroom; it was as though the crowd had spontaneously decided to observe the

usual two minutes of silence in honor of the man named Anton Schmidt. And in those two minutes, which were like a sudden burst of light in the midst of impenetrable, unfathomable darkness, a single thought stood out clearly, irrefutably, beyond question—how utterly different everything would be today in this courtroom, in Israel, in Germany, in all of Europe, and perhaps in all countries of the world, if only more such stories could have been told. (231)

At least two differences stand out between Arendt's assessment of the impact of Schmidt's story and her assessment of the impact of Grynszpan's. The first is that Schmidt's story is reported to have noticeably hushed the crowd (presumably a sign manifesting the passage of what she refers to as a dramatic moment). The second is her implicit claim for the political significance of this story. If we are right in likening her use of the term *dramatic moment* in her report of the impact of witnesses' testimony at Eichmann's trial to her claim that tragedy is a literary form preeminently capable of representing a process of recognition, we might conclude from the different assessments she makes of these stories that in order for a story to be tragic it needs a hero. And, further, not every retelling of experience reveals a hero; only those experiences in which someone acted, took initiative, and risked something can be formulated as a tragedy. Such an interpretation makes sense of Arendt's contrasting treatments of the two stories told at Eichmann's trial. For her, Grynszpan's story is not tragic because he did not act; rather, he did what he was told. What he suffered, he suffered not because of what he did but because of what others did to him. And since he was (to paraphrase Arendt) an "innocent," the story of his suffering cannot induce the process of recognition in the listener. By contrast, Schmidt took initiative in support of an oppressed minority's attempt at self-defense and risked his life in so doing.[96] The suffering that he endured was, therefore, consequent on his action.

Our interpretation of Arendt's notion of recognition leads us to expect that identification with Schmidt in his twofold role as doer and sufferer, as immortal and doomed hero, will provide both a redemptive intimation of that immortality to be gained through acting and a reconciliatory feeling of basic acceptance. These effects are the grounds for the occurrence of that dramatic moment Arendt describes as having accompanied the telling of Schmidt's story. These effects also form the basis of the promise of tragic storytelling to make a positive difference in politics. In any event, the Schmidt story provides Arendt with an opportunity to express a newfound hope that acts of freedom, no matter how isolated and apparently ineffective, may survive in story form to activate and reconcile potential citizens in future times. "The holes of oblivion do not exist. Nothing human is that perfect, and there are simply too many people in the world to make oblivion possible. One man will always be left alive to tell the story" (*Eichmann*, 232–33).

It almost seems to go without saying that the application of the tragic criteria of doing and suffering would disqualify Eichmann's story as an Arendtian tragedy. For he reveals himself, in Arendt's account, as a man barely capable of any initiative-taking whatsoever, let alone initiative-taking constitutive of political freedom.[97] Even as a sufferer, Eichmann appears in Arendt's account to fall far short of the standards of a tragic hero—as is most notably evidenced by what she interprets as his profound inability, "under the gallows," to face the reality of his own impending death. "It surely cannot be so common that a man facing death, and, moreover, standing beneath the gallows, should be able to think of nothing but what he has heard at funerals all his life, and that these 'lofty words' should completely becloud the reality of his own death" (*Eichmann*, 288).

Although Eichmann on trial proved himself, by his "remoteness from reality" and "thoughtlessness" (*Eichmann*, 288) to be wholly inadequate in playing the role of tragic hero, I would argue that Arendt attempts nevertheless to muster some tragic significance for her story, in the judgment she gives of Eichmann at the conclusion of the epilogue. There, in the form of a direct address from the judges' bench, she retells Eichmann's story, reconfiguring him from an essentially passive instrument of the will of his superiors into an active supporter of their murderous policies. "Let us assume . . . that it was nothing more than a misfortune that made you a willing instrument in the organization of mass murder; there still remains the fact that you have carried out, and therefore actively supported, a policy of mass murder" (279).

In recasting Eichmann as an initiative-taker in the pursuit of an unprecedented crime against the plurality of human communities, Arendt establishes the grounds for his punishment. "And just as you supported and carried out a policy of not wanting to share the earth

with the Jewish people and the people of a number of other nations
. . . we find that no one, that is, no member of the human race, can
be expected to want to share the earth with you. This is the reason,
and the only reason, you must hang" (*Eichmann*, 279). Thus, Eichmann, the doer of deeds becomes a sufferer of those deeds as well.

Arendt's act of bringing Eichmann before her own bench of justice is of no small dramatic significance. In the imaginary courtroom setting she implicitly evokes by directly addressing the defendant, Arendt conjures up an Eichmann not only capable of taking
initiative but also able, through an act of judgment (that is, by looking at his genocidal activities from the point of view of people who
respect the plurality of human communities), to come to some
awareness of the terrible nature of his deeds and their consequences
for others as well for himself. *This* Eichmann, and *not* the Eichmann who stood trial in Jerusalem, can perhaps be a fitting subject
for tragedy. Insofar as the criminal defendant Arendt imagines in
the coda of her epilogue is capable of tragic recognition and therefore comparable to "the hero in [a] play" (*Eichmann*, 9), the telling
of his story, like the telling of Schmidt's, is capable of fostering
tragic recognition in spectators. According to our reconstruction of
Arendt's theory of tragedy, we would also expect the telling of such
a story to promote political freedom. If the telling of Schmidt's
story raises the likelihood that people will oppose criminal policies
under even the most politically unpromising circumstances, the
telling of the imaginary Eichmann's story might aim at raising the
likelihood that people will feel capable of taking up the responsibility of judgment even in a world that has experienced deeds of unprecedented criminality.[98]

It might be objected that resistance against a criminal
regime and judgment of a state-sanctioned perpetrator of criminal
deeds hardly exhaust the content of political freedom. It may be,
however, that no one instance of tragic storytelling can be expected
to promote political freedom in all its dimensions. A comparison of
Arendt's *Eichmann in Jerusalem* with the other book she published in
1963, *On Revolution,* suggests that the effect on the prospects of political freedom that can be expected from an instance of tragic storytelling is constrained both by the nature of the historical material

from which the tragedy is fashioned and by the kind of audience to which the tragedy is addressed. If a tragedy were to be fashioned from the history of revolutions rather than from the history of totalitarianism, and if that tragedy were to be heard or read in a country where republican institutions and traditions effectively persist, then a tragic storyteller might aim to do more for political freedom than persuade people to take up the responsibility of appropriately judging the perpetrators of unprecedented political and human crimes. In this more politically promising context, a tragic storyteller might aim to inspire citizens to exercise other, perhaps more rewarding, dimensions of political freedom.

In Arendt's book on revolution, what is at stake is not the capacity to judge deeds of unprecedented criminality so much as the foundation of enduring public spaces of citizen action. The storytelling mode she adopts to meet those stakes is tragic. This means that Arendt tells the story of revolutions as the story of deeds done and sufferings endured by tragic heroes in their pursuit of the rewards of a life of public freedom. Thus, Arendt's Robespierre appears as a person who well knew the "intoxicating" rewards of the "wine of action" (OR 133), and who probably wished to found a republic that would have made these rewards generally available, but who nevertheless eventually came to pursue (partly, she argues, under the interacting pressures of personal feelings of compassion and of the demand of le peuple malheureux for social justice) a program of terror and intimidation that effectively led to the denial of freedom.

The North American English colonists' relative material prosperity and long practice in the procedures of self-rule contributed significantly to the foundation of a lasting republic, but even this revolutionary story is not lacking in tragic significance for Arendt. The American founders failed to establish the new federal republic as a lasting site for the exercise of true political (public) freedom. In this regard, Thomas Jefferson, especially in his post-revolutionary reflections on the significance of Shays's Rebellion in Massachusetts (OR 233), provides Arendt with a fitting tragic hero. In re-suffering the decidedly mixed consequences of the American revolutionary generation's great deed of republican foundation—"while it had given freedom to the people, [it] had failed to provide a space where this freedom could be exercised" (OR 235)—Arendt's Jefferson provides occasion for an experience of recognition by which American readers might come both to realize the life-affirming rewards of action in a public realm and to act on behalf of this realization.

It is, perhaps, the American revolutionary failure to achieve the most preeminently rewarding content of republican freedom, the founding and sustaining of a public realm of action, that may have led Arendt so explicitly to place the readers of *On Revolution* on the ascending rows of a tragic theater at book's end. For it was Greek tragedy's distinctive and exemplary achievement both to foster the spectator's appreciation of the distinctive rewards promised by the exercise of political freedom and to activate and intensify the actor's capacity to reflect on and become reconciled to past deeds and consequent sufferings through the promotion of tragic recognition. In Arendt's telescoped reenactment of the Sophocles tragedy at the conclusion of *On Revolution,* one can detect the desire to appropriate something of the power of Greek tragedy to make "one feel fiery and contemplative at the same time."[99] One can also perceive here an instance where Arendt's long-standing attempt to promote the exercise of a kind of judgment that is equally relevant to theorist and citizen results in the discovery, perhaps, of a new mode of political theorizing—through the rediscovery of one of the oldest modes.

Mortal Messages

Tragic Theory and Democratic Heroism

> Sometimes history is written in the streets: one of those rare moments
> when conscience defies the Party, when the Leader reads the message
> of mortality on a million faces illuminated by candle light.
>
> —*Indian Express*

I t is no coincidence that Arendt's political thought serves
as an informing if not life-giving presence among contemporary political theorists who have discovered in either the example of Greek
tragedy or the techniques of storytelling the promise of a kind of
theory compatible with democratic engagement. In its narrative
style and method her theory invites sustained reflection on the political relevance of Greek tragedy and other storytelling forms. And
in its central concern to identify forms of authority and judgment
that are compatible with free participatory politics, her theory lends
itself to the contemporary project of finding an appropriate role for
theory in democracy.

In her spirit, if not in her footsteps, these contemporary theorists
link the possibility of independent and active political membership
to the capacity of tragic spectatorship or storytelling to activate intuitions. A latent correspondence between "inside" and "outside" becomes actualized in a personally moving way. To the extent that this
moving correspondence is shared with others, it provides an appropriately consensual basis for action in concert. Where contemporary
theorists have been less forthcoming and where this Arendtian
framework shows its distinctive promise is in specifying what this
"inside" is. Our examination of Arendt's notions of authority and
judgment through the prism of her under-articulated theory of
tragedy suggests that this "inside," this intuitive basis for the tragic

effect, comprises deep-seated and opposite longings for both, on the one hand, reassurance about the power and vitality of the self and, on the other hand, release from the burdens of self-consciousness. These longings are provoked by the encounter with limits on human aspirations and capacities. Notable among these limits is the horizon imposed on experience by consciousness of one's own mortality. In their existentially weighted form, the impulses to assert and negate the self find manifold expression in human action and thought. Arendtian storytelling, in a way analogous to Greek tragedy and Homeric epic in Pericles' day, can be seen to canalize them in support of democratic participatory politics.

If inflecting Arendt's thought in the manner I have proposed complements and extends the insights of storytelling theorists, the relevance of this inflection for wider debates about the nature and meaning of democracy remains to be shown. After all, theorists who understand the nature and significance of political freedom differently that Arendt might well concede that an under-articulated and somewhat unreflected theory of the political relevance of tragedy significantly conditions her thinking. They may still judge this particular theory, and Arendt's thought in general, as mostly irrelevant for thinking about democracy. Conversely, more sympathetic Arendt readers who find her insights worth engaging and appropriating might choose to inflect her thought differently than I have. As it turns out, many readers of Arendt both sympathetic and unsympathetic have criticized her notion of the ancient Greek citizen-hero, accounting it an unfortunate, undemocratic archaism. One might reasonably expect that the reservations of such readers would only be confirmed by the notion of a theory at work in Arendt's thought in which exemplary significance is attributed to the heroic exploits of such tragic characters as Achilles and Odysseus.

As will become clear, an insistence on inflecting Arendt's thought so as to bring its tragic elements into sharp relief carries with it the risk of distorting her best insights about democracy and of encouraging the impression of her as a theorist of an existentialist politics of heroic gesture. This risk is worth running for at least two reasons. In the first place, attention to the theory of tragedy at work in Arendt's thought serves to preserve the novelty and uniqueness of her insights about the nature of freedom and democracy and thereby keeps available her vision as a critical control on competing theoretical traditions. In the second place, the tragedy-centered approach outlined above promises to preserve the possibility of recognizing and giving due attention to aspects of political life in a democracy that might, from other theoretical perspectives, be ignored or dismissed. Taking care to preserve the distinctiveness of Arendt's vision is, as I hope to show, especially advisable in an era of radical political discontinuity such as ours, which is more prone to offer up novel challenges to political thought and practice in both fledgling and mature democracies.

For a keener sense of both the novelty of these challenges and the distinctiveness of Arendt's thought, we will have recourse in this chapter to a different set of Arendt readers than the set considered in the first chapter. For many of the theorists of Greek tragedy or storytelling with whom we began, Arendt served as a pathbreaking guide for the kind of approach to the study of politics upon which they saw themselves embarked. With them, Arendt's promise rested more on the mode of political theorizing that her thought embodied or implied than on any particular mode of political engagement it sponsored. For the task of recovering and reconstructing a theory of tragedy at work in Arendt's thought, which I initially set for myself, consideration of this chorus of sympathetic readers was indispensable. In this final chapter, a different task will be set, one of applying this theory, in its Arendtian variant, to contemporary challenges of founding and sustaining democratic polities. In this latter task, I take as my starting point the critical response of a different chorus of readers, a chorus more centrally concerned with assessing the forms of political action and institutions that Arendt's work seems to sponsor. In the interaction of this latter chorus with Arendt's work, the effect will be more contrapuntal because members of this chorus take serious issue with the kind of participatory politics Arendt appears to recommend. Representative voices of this chorus can be divided into two groups: (1) proponents of participatory democracy and (2) liberal defenders of representative democracy.

Proponents of participatory democracy typically argue that Arendt's affirmation of a kind of agonistic republicanism, apparently resting on the exclusion of the claims of social justice from politics, serves to undermine the prospects for just and effective action in concert. Thus, for example, Jenny Ring (1991) argues that Arendt's notion of "action as display," resting on an image of "Greek political actors as warrior-heroes, fiercely competitive, preoccupied with their reputations," slights the need for community. Seeking an Arendtian notion of individuality that is less anarchic and self-centered, and that is more reflective about and oriented toward community, Ring identifies the "pariah," whose status as outsider provides him or her with both motive and opportunity for thinking about the promise and limits of membership, as an appropriate alternative to the "blustering Greek man of action."[1]

Hanna Pitkin (1981) has also questioned Arendt's philhellenic appeal to political heroism, arguing that the political agenda it implies encompasses too little of the real content of politics. "And about what are citizens to talk, in the public realm, as each tries to distinguish himself. . . . The Greeks deliberated much about war; surely that is not what Arendt recommends for us." For Pitkin, taking Arendt at her best means not giving in to her occasional "appeal to heroism for its own sake"—which appeal implies a citizen body seriously lacking in those virtues of self-discipline and reflectiveness so necessary for just and effective democratic self-rule. "Arendt's citizens begin to resemble posturing little boys clamoring for attention ('Look at me! I'm the greatest!' 'No, look at *me!*') and wanting to be reassured that they are brave, valuable, even real. . . . Though Arendt was female, there is a lot of *machismo* in her vision."[2]

In a recent, more extended analysis Pitkin carries forward her critique of Arendt's reliance on a Greek polis-imaged notion of political freedom, suggesting that it marks an ambivalent attempt to appropriate some of the authority of a German academic tradition whose bearers were disposed to yearn for spiritual fellowship with their patriarchal predecessors of ancient Greece. According to Pitkin, the problem with this appropriation of the Greeks and their "notorious misogyny and competitive heroics," is that it required Arendt to repress those aspects of her experience—her participation in the events of her day as a Jew, a woman, and a refugee—that were the wellsprings of her most true and relevant insights about what freedom in the modern world is and means.[3] In this view, the flip side of Arendt's affirmation of a macho Greek-imaged politics of heroic individuation is her call to ban from political consideration maternally identified aspects of human interdependence having to do with bodily needs and emotional intimacy.

In a similarly critical vein, Sheldon Wolin attacks Arendt's "archaic vision of 'a new polity' that was inspired by the version of pre-Socratic Hellenism associated with Nietzsche and Heidegger," arguing that "its presupposition . . . [of] a small audience of heroes" is fundamentally antidemocratic. The "agonal actor of Homer," which Wolin sees as the primary model for Arendt's notion of the citizen, lacks both the capacity and the inclination to recognize the "common being of human beings" and to act cooperatively with others in accordance with a viable and appropriate notion of the common good. For Wolin and these other participatory democrats, assuring the relevance of Arendt's thought for addressing pressing political problems (public apathy; social injustice; the unavailability of institutional sites for direct, continuous, and effective democratic participation) depends on separating the democratic-communitarian wheat in her thought from the aristocratic-agonistic chaff.[4]

In contrast to participatory democrats' critique of Arendt's vision of politics for its unduly putting community solidarity at risk, liberal theorists' reservations about Arendt focus more centrally on the risks posed by this vision to the individual's freedom to do as he or she pleases within appropriate bounds. That participatory democrats and liberals inflect Arendt's thought according to different sets of values should come as no surprise. What is interesting to note is that, despite their differing views of what value or potentiality is inappropriately placed at risk, participatory democrats and liberals share a notion that what is most problematic about Arendt's vision of politics is its affirmation of the ancient Greek polis as paradigmatic locus of political freedom.

So, for example, George Kateb (1984), a major contemporary theoretical defender of liberal political ideals and practices, worries that Arendt's "Greek conception" of politics, insofar as it puts a premium on agonal struggle and exempts political action from the controlling influence of love, goodness, compassion, pity, and other moral impulses, "can too easily accommodate great substantive evils."[5] Arendt's critique of the instrumentalist attitudes fostered by the procedures of representative government and her claim about the priority of achieving the autotelic rewards promised by participation in council forms of democracy strike Kateb as reflecting insufficient appreciation for the achievements of liberal democracy in promoting and defending viable, even existentially fulfilling, forms of individual autonomy. Although unyielding in his defense of liberal democratic ideals and practices in the face of Arendt's critique, Kateb acknowledges Arendt's work as being significant and rewarding. For him (as for the participatory democratic theorists surveyed above), the point in engaging Arendt's work is to purge it of its more problematic elements, particularly the affirmation of agonistic striving that seems to reach its highest intensities in those instances when she recurs to the ancient Greek polis as backdrop for her vision of political action.

For Patricia Springborg (1989), saving a viable core of Arendtian insights for democratic participation by setting aside her apparent affirmation of a Greek-imaged heroic model of political action is not possible because the warrior-hero is the very core of Arendt's political thought. Intent on debunking a notion of politics "as the panacea for all social ills," which she attributes to republican theory, Springborg situates Arendt's agonistic model of political action in a German tradition of idealizing the classical polis as paradigmatic site for conducting the *bios politikos*. According to Springborg, a close look at the history of the reception of Aristotle's *Politics* and the findings of classical scholars and Max Weber reveals that the emergence of citizenship rights in the Greek polis did not represent the Greeks' discovery and subsequent institutional articulation of an autonomous, uniquely rewarding, and preeminently worthy mode of human interaction. Those vaunted rights of citizenship originated, rather, as the outcome of a somewhat stopgap measure to reward members of the new hoplite class for service rendered in war by providing them with their own communal organization.

> The *oikos* did not need politics, nor did the phratry, the *phule* or the hetairy. It was their very exclusivity that made politics necessary—for the hoplite soldier performed services to the city for which there was no forum in its ready-made structures. Conventional accounts of the reforms of Solon and Cleisthenes readily admit their having been prompted by an attempt to accommodate the disenfranchised demesman and non-citizens who could not be enrolled in the phratries. Solon's genius lay in aligning rights to participation in the assembly and councils, as well as jury service, to military rank.[6]

In this reading, the institutions typically identified with politics in classical Athens (the democratized assembly, councils, and law

courts) appear as organizations that, in their founding purpose, par-
alleled rather than contrasted with traditional tribal institutions of
aristocratic solidarity and influence.

Affirmation of the "political" as a uniquely rewarding realm of
freedom set off against the private realm of physical needs rests, in
Springborg's view, on a misunderstanding of the origins of polis citizenship as a means for incorporating unaffiliated fighting men
into ancient city life. It further rests on a failure to appreciate adequately the origins of modern democratic citizenship in the me-
dieval burgher's winning of the right to pursue his economic activity free of any obligation to serve garrison duty for king or emperor.
If the West's legacy of political freedom is to be traced to anyone,
Springborg suggests, it is to the Calvinist saint soberly and pacifi-
cally working at his calling, not to the citizen-militiaman of the ancient city-state:

> Based on the immunities of the medieval burgher from garrison ser-
> vice, the European town dweller, who undertook the continuous ratio-
> nalizing activity out of which capitalism grew, enjoyed the democrati-
> zation of prestige by economic means. Devotion to one's "calling" and
> the honour of one's profession gave satisfactions less dramatic but
> more lasting than the glories of the battlefield.[7]

Springborg's attempt to debunk republican theorists' strict separation
of a public realm of freedom from a private realm of needs by un-
masking ancient citizenship rights as a form of patronage for a new
class of infantry is provocative. If her image of the ancient citizen as
infantryman dressed in Athenian chiton or Roman toga unsettles
proponents of republican virtue, her inference of an affinity between
civic republicanism and fascism based on a shared descent from the
citizen-militiaman of ancient times invites strong objection.[8]

Sympathetic readers of the civic republican tradition, and of
Arendt's work in particular, might respond to Springborg's denigration of republican conceptions of citizenship and freedom by questioning one of her central assumptions. After all, the argument that
republican notions of freedom are irretrievably compromised by their
derivation from a social context of warrior assemblies rests on a
highly suspect idea that origin determines destiny. Even granting that
polis citizenship originated as a form of group privilege conceded to

hoplites, one can still argue that the meaning and uses of those privileges were not thereafter perpetually fixed. The circumstances of foundation may narrow but they do not eliminate the range of variation in the future purposes to which an institution may be put. This is not, of course, to say that practices and ideals can be made to fit any purpose or context. It is rather to suggest that assessing the fitness of past practices or ideals for contemporary appropriation is best done on a case-by-case basis. Even if the political activities of male warrior-citizens in fifth-century Athens were largely subsidized by the labor of their wives, mothers, daughters, and of male and female slaves and were conducted in a macho spirit, this does not necessarily negate the exemplary value of the democratic gains achieved relative to a less democratic past. Nor does it rule out the promise of extending those gains to categories of people traditionally excluded from politics. By the same reasoning, it would be inappropriate for proponents of Arendtian forms of republican politics to discredit liberal conceptions of freedom merely by calling attention to their origin in the male-defined, male-supervised ascetic discipline of Calvinist saints.

If Arendtian republicans do not have to concede prima facie the superiority of Calvin's Geneva to Pericles' Athens as an exemplary site of democratic governance, they should nonetheless take seriously the claim that republican affirmations of the high existential significance of public life all too often come paired with idealizations of the warrior ethic. Consider the emphasis on military valor and discipline as citizenly virtues to be found in such a central figure of the republican tradition as Machiavelli. It is well worth wondering whether his fervent endorsement of a citizen militia for Florence and his sustained interest in martial affairs (his *Art of War* was the only one of his prose works he chose to publish)[9] had less to do with the military exigencies of his time and more to do with a republican tendency to think the virtues of citizenship and the virtues of military service together on the model of the citizen-militiaman of the Roman Republic or Athenian polis.

Pitkin has attempted to recover what she considers Machiavelli's best insights about the nature and promise of democratic citizenship by separating them from his militarist, even "protofascist," yearning for the disciplining authority of a solitary and distant founder. In her view, this yearning echoes the kind of fantasy of the rescuing father that is typical of male adolescents raised in societies such as Renaissance Florence in which fathers mostly inhabit the public world of work and politics and mothers remain the main, if not exclusive, parenting agent in the home. For Pitkin, the yearning for a founding father that marks Machiavelli's political theory does not invalidate his more basic insight about the significance of what remembrance of past republican foundations can, at best, promise—inspiration for contemporary citizens to act together in the spirit of freedom.[10]

For a contemporary example of a political movement matching the militarist profile applied to civic republicanism by its critics, one need go no further than the newly prominent militia movement in the United States. In their membership appeals, militia groups typically combine calls for the defense of local liberties with affirmations of the virtues of military training and discipline. Their most ominous characteristic is the demonization of those considered to be in the opposition, such as federal government employees, international financiers, U.N. functionaries.[11]

Against this backdrop, it is worth noting Arendt's fervent and active support, during the war years, for the formation of a Jewish army to join the fight against Hitler. The urgent political need for a Jewish army provided the subject of the very first article she wrote as a columnist for the *Aufbau*, a New York–based, Jewish American–sponsored, German-language weekly newspaper. In "The Jewish Army—the Beginning of a Jewish Politics?" (1941) she emphasized the political relevance of fighting in partnership with the Allies, arguing that "the Jewish people needed an army for identity as well as defence."[12]

> Jews today are as though possessed by the fixed idea of their own meaninglessness. Partly they hope thereby to be able to exit once again from the political stage, partly they are truly desperate at belonging to a powerless and apparently de-politicized group. . . . The storm, which the creation of a Jewish army of volunteers from the whole world will unleash in our own ranks, will make clear to the truly desperate that with us . . . there is politics.[13]

One did not have to subscribe to republican ideals to support the formation of a Jewish army as a means of self-defense and as a contribution to the fight against Hitler. Arendt's adoption of such a position

could make sense solely against the background of her experience as
a pariah-turned-refugee. As this experience taught her, being clear-
eyed about the precariousness of one's place in the world (the preeminent achievement of the pariah, according to Arendt) is, in and of
itself, an insufficient defense against a ruthlessly organized and determined enemy. The notion of former pariahs engaged in an effective effort of collective self-defense must surely have functioned to
some degree for her as a compensatory counterimage to her memories of extreme vulnerability as a German Jewish refugee. This said, it
must still be conceded that Arendt's emphasis on the role of voluntary military service in fostering a politically meaningful sense of efficacy and shared identity dovetails with the endorsement of the distinctive civic virtues of military service so saliently present in the
republican tradition.

In light of the ancient polity's practice of linking the privilege of
citizenship with military service, the tendency of certain notable republican theorists to give central place in the pantheon of citizenly
virtues to martial valor and discipline,[14] and Arendt's emphasis on
the identity-forming functions of a Jewish army, the promise of an
Arendtian theory of tragedy for thinking about the nature and
meaning of political authority and judgment might appear more
questionable. As it has been reconstructed, Arendt's theory of
tragedy holds that political freedom can be promoted theoretically
through the telling of stories that, in fostering audience identification with a heroic character in his or her twofold aspect as immortal
doer of deeds and doomed sufferer, encourages, in a mutually informing way, both action and thinking. To a democratic-minded
skeptic, the Homeric provenance of the heroic paradigm upon
which this theory appears significantly based—Achilles, slayer of
Hector but also attendee at his funeral (*OT* 452); Ulysses, brought to
tears upon hearing the account of his quarrel with Achilles (*LM:T*
132)—places this theory in a highly suspect light. What use, after all,
can this archaic-heroic strand of Arendt's political thought—with its
emphasis on self-display and agonistic striving—serve in the promotion of democratic participation?

The heroic dimension of Arendt's thought is precisely the aspect I
have chosen to focus on in this book, arguing that a different understanding of its sources and role can yield relevant insights concerning the nature and promise of democratic freedoms in the contem-

porary world. In so doing, I set myself apart both from those (such as Springborg) who see this element as compromising the integrity and viability of Arendt's thought entirely and from those (such as Pitkin, or Kateb) for whom the excision of this element constitutes a necessary condition for recovering Arendt's best, most worthwhile insights. My claim is not that access to the most worthwhile insights of Arendt's thought can *only* or *best* be achieved through the prism of her Greek-imaged theory of politics. It is rather that there is available in her thought a Greek-imaged theory of the political significance of tragedy that raises new questions about, and suggests new avenues of approaching, significant dimensions of political life. What the use of this prism would promise is access to worthwhile insights that might from other perspectives be obscured, downplayed, or missed altogether.

To assess the relevance of Arendtian heroic storytelling let us step back and consider, at somewhat more remove, the main points of difference between various visions: Arendt's republican vision; a participatory democratic vision generalized from the views of Arendt's sympathetic critics, including Ring and Pitkin; a corporatist vision of democratic participation; and the classical liberal vision Springborg implicitly sets forth as an alternative to Arendt and republican thinkers generally. In the last of these, the promotion of a worthy form of life for human beings, as individuals and as members of communities, is seen to depend centrally on self-mastery through the discipline of work. Under this conception, the primary raison d'être of politics would be the task of ensuring the freedom of individuals to choose and pursue their work. Whatever the substance of this work, political participation does not count as a central or significant source of meaning.

In a participatory democratic vision, the achievement of human dignity is seen centrally to rest on respecting, as a primary value, the mutuality and interdependence of human lives. The same can be said of the vision propounded by corporatist theorists of democracy. In a world characterized by vastly uneven distributions of social power and rewards, this means placing a high priority on social justice and accepting political participation as a primary means of achieving social justice. Not only can conditions more reflective of human mutuality and interdependence effectively be approached through politically enacted egalitarian policies; the very experience

of acting jointly in politics can serve to raise participants' consciousness of, and respect for, the mutually conditioned nature of their
lives. It is perhaps on account of this latter promise that participatory democratic theorists seem more disposed than liberals (and the
corporatist theorists of democracy with whom they share an emphasis on mutuality and interdependence) to concede an intrinsic dignity to politics at the margins.

The promise of politics to affirm life autonomously is central to
the vision of a worthy human life implied in Arendt's republican vision of council forms of democracy, in which citizens discuss, debate, and collectively decide public matters. What is promised by direct democratic participation in the way of intrinsic rewards is the
achievement of a form of "heroic" individuation, which Arendt
claimed was capable of affirming human existence in the face of its
ultimate limits, suffering and mortality. Democratic participation of
the sort Arendt had in mind was seen by her to promote individuation in two distinct but complementary ways. To the extent that institutions of direct democracy permitted citizens to appear before
their peers and express their views and opinions about public affairs,
they could foster each citizen's sense of being an individual, of having a perspective on public matters both distinctive and worthy of
expression. Complimentarily, institutions of direct democracy that
permit the expression of differences in perspective and opinion
might also, in this view, promote tolerance, cooperation, and solidarity, as citizens become more conscious of the plurality of perspectives and opinions and more accepting of the limits this condition
of plurality sets upon each individual's assertiveness.

Underlying Arendt's sense of the promise of council democracy
to promote both a heightened sense of one's own individuality and
an increased respect for the individuality of others is an under-
articulated and mostly unacknowledged theory of the distinctive
role of participatory democratic institutions in the sublimation of
existential impulses of self-assertion and self-negation. According to
this theory, the heightened sense of one's own individuality that is
achieved through participation in council democracy serves to ward
off the potentially self-destructive longing to be free of the burdens
of individual consciousness and existence. At the same time, individuating oneself through participation in council democracy
would permit the expression in an appropriately sublimated way of

the opposing impulse to cling desperately to mortal life by providing the individual with an intimation of personal immortality gained from the acknowledgment of one's words and deeds by fellow political participants.

The implicit theory underlying Arendt's partisanship for council democracy also attributes an existential significance to the other hoped-for effect of direct political participation, an increased respect for the individuality of others. The expectation is that increasing respect for the individuality of others will ward off the potentially tyrannical, longing to live forever by making the future a monument to oneself. At the same time, the tolerance for plurality gained as a result of direct political participation would permit the expression in an appropriately sublimated way of the opposite impulse to be free of the sometimes burdensome consciousness of individuated existence.

Arendt's emphasis on the agonistic aspects of political action clearly contrasts with participatory democrats' concern for promoting political and social solidarity and concerted action in pursuit of social justice. The aversion would be felt as well by democratic proponents of corporatism in places such as Sweden, Norway, and Germany, who see broad-based interest aggregation by means of union, workplace, and parliamentary elections combined with peak-level negotiation over the terms of social redistribution by duly elected officeholders as necessary instruments for maintaining social harmony and political stability. Arendt's identification of politics as the central arena of agonistic striving also sets her vision apart from the liberal notion of the marketplace as competitive arena par excellence.

With their traditional concern to protect individual freedoms such as private property, religious affiliation, and political expression from infringement by officials of the state, liberal theorists have accepted political competition as a necessary means, not an end in itself. Liberals seem unwilling to accept the agonistic and performative politics of Arendt's description because they fear the antilibertarian consequences of making individuality more a condition to be attained through virtuoso action in an agonistic public realm than a pre-political status to be recognized by a bill of rights. The characteristic liberal means for taming the political agon has been to adopt representation as the central, if not exclusive, mode of conducting politics and to envision the appropriate role of representative government as safeguarding the play of competitive relations in the marketplace.[15] In this view, representative government not only serves to tame the political agon by insulating policy-making institutions from the kind of classist passions supposedly promoted by direct democracy. It also encourages participants to conduct themselves politically according to the mores of the marketplace, that is, as strictly self-interested individuals seeking the best value for their vote.

Arendt's republican vision also contrasts with liberalism and democratic-participatory notions in its placing a high premium on self-display in politics. Liberal visions place little value on political display for its own sake, since self-mastery, not self-expression, is their primary concern. In democratic-participatory visions such display is seen as a self-indulgent and potentially divisive distraction from more weighty political tasks such as ensuring adequate and fair access to social resources. In the face of liberal concerns about ensuring the integrity of the individual, and participatory democratic concerns about recognizing human interdependence and supporting mutuality, Arendt's (arguably ambivalent) endorsement of agonistically toned and display-oriented forms of participation as a model of democratic politics does seem problematic. Given their respective assumptions about the nature and meaning of politics, liberals and participatory democrats have good reason either to assimilate her political thought in a very selective manner or to reject it outright. Recognizing the working of a theory of tragedy in Arendt's thought opens, in my view, the possibility of appreciating how her Greek-imaged notion of heroic politics might contribute to a different understanding of some significant challenges of contemporary democratic politics than are currently offered by liberal or participatory-democratic or democratic-corporalist theorists. In particular, her Greek-imaged notion of heroism invites us to take more seriously the existential dimensions of democratic politics.

As a necessary first step in addressing the contemporary promise of Arendt's Greeks, let us consider an alternative reading of her vision of participatory politics, made possible by an Arendtian theory of tragedy. Acknowledging the operation of a theory of tragedy in her work means, in the first place, recognizing an alternative image of Greek politics—one encompassing more than the practices of political deliberation and decision that took place in the assembly, the council, and the juries. Included in this larger compass are the theoretical (understanding this word with its Greek root in mind) practices institutionalized to an extent in the fifth-century Athenian civic festivals of poetic recital (the *Panathenaia*, for example) and theatrical performance (the *Dionysia*, for example). In these practices, the impulse to self-display and agonistic striving are acknowledged and given expression in ways that emphasize their centrality in human experience.

One can presume that it is the acknowledgment and expression of human beings' impulse to self-display and agonistic striving that determined, at least in part, the interest these practices once held for ancient audiences, and which the literary and performative relics of these practices continue to hold for modern audiences. The scholarship on Greek tragedy and an Arendtian political theory of tragedy remind us that the drama of individuation was played out within an institutional and ritual context evoking the communities between audience members. It is of no little significance that the city Dionysia stood as one of the most inclusive of Athenian civic practices; tragic audiences in Athens are thought to have included women, slaves, and prisoners. No less significant is that, before these inclusive theatrical audiences, Athens's most highly prized tragic composers felt free to expose to critical scrutiny the excesses of individuation to which the Athenian political agon sometimes gave rise (and for which liberal and participatory democratic theorists disqualify fifth-century Athens as a model of contemporary political relevance). Consider, for example, how difficult it would be to find a drama matching Sophocles' *Antigone* in its power to provoke reflection on the limits of a public officeholder's power to establish and enforce law or the limits of a dissenter's right to defy public authority.

Of course, acknowledging the potential political benefits of Athenian tragedy in former or present times does not logically require one to accept Athens's direct democracy as a model for contemporary political organization. After all, tragedy was a form of poetic—not political—enactment and its effect on the policy-making processes of the city-state could only have been indirect. The point in noting the contribution of a tradition of theorizing Greek tragedy to Arendt's Greek image of politics is to consider how this contribution puts a new light on aspects of that image. Arendt's reliance on a theory of tragedy suggests that her notion of the life-affirming promise of politics can as easily be read as evincing a clear-eyed, reasonable concern

for mediating the claims of individuality and community in demo-
cratically appropriate ways as it can be read as indicating her entrapment in a patriarchal, illiberal German tradition of longing for spiritual union with aristocratic Greek warrior heroes.

Through the prism of an Arendtian theory of tragedy, the existential weight she gives to politics takes on a different appearance. Previously, it has been enough for critics to discredit her vision of politics by associating it with a morally suspect German tradition of
aestheticism, which, in the wake of Germany's experience of trench
warfare and military defeat in World War I, took on new and more
menacing cultural and political forms. In the different context of a
theory of Greek tragedy, Arendt's notion of an existentially weighted
politics in which engagement in political affairs serves to sublimate
powerful impulses of self-assertion and negation invites a more considered examination of the existential significance of politics. What
role, if any, ought politics to play in the sublimation of existential
impulses? This is a significant question, which Arendt's sponsorship
of a kind of "council system" of direct democracy, seen in its affiliation with a theory of tragedy, can be seen legitimately to raise.

> The short space of threescore years can never content the imagi-
> nation of man; nor can the imperfect joys of this world satisfy
> his heart. Man, alone of all created beings, displays a natural
> contempt of existence, and yet a boundless desire to exist; he
> scorns life, but he dreads annihilation. These different feelings
> incessantly urge his soul to the contemplation of a future state,
> and religion directs his musings thither.[16]

As understood here, existential impulses consist of
those emotional longings or drives that tend to be stimulated when
limits on human hopes, aspirations, and action (notably including
personal mortality) become an urgent object of reflection and concern. In cases where political institutions, practices, and ideals play a
central or distinctive role in the sublimation of these existential impulses, an existentially weighted politics can be said to exist.

In what might be called the typical liberal view, politics neither is
nor ought to be an activity of central or distinctive existential significance. Far from holding out the promise of affirming life, in this

view politics serves as a means of protecting the freedom of the individual to pursue meaning in activities of his or her own personal choosing, such as work or religious devotion, aesthetic creation, or scientific study. Even in cases where liberal proponents of political participation seem inspired by a sense of the intrinsic dignity of politics, this sense is in serious tension with a pronounced instrumentalist orientation. This is notably the case with John Stuart Mill, whose ambivalently toned argument for extending the suffrage in *Representative Government* is premised in significant part on the idea that political participation is primarily of use in fostering the intellectual development of citizens.[17]

Paired with the liberal's instrumentalist view of politics is a deep and abiding concern about the threats posed to individual liberties by officeholders who have the capacity to violate citizens' rights, and who are daily faced with the temptation to do just that. In the liberal view, this temptation becomes well-nigh irresistible when politics is seen and practiced as an end in itself. This view has colored liberal assessments of the nature and meaning of National Socialist and Marxist Leninist regimes. The regime feature that stands out for the liberal analyst (among others) in both of these cases is the monopolization of power by a single party and the direct imposition of that party's ideological framework in nonpolitical areas of life including religion, science, business, and art. Deploring the forced mobilization of individuals that typically accompanies this politicalization of all spheres of human activity, liberals can only reject what they see as the ideological assumption underlying it—that the task of seeking and receiving satisfying answers to life's profoundest questions is fundamentally a political one.

The liberal predisposition against endowing politics with existential significance, against seeing politics as a realm of ultimate experience or truth, can be traced historically to cultural innovations and political developments associated with the events of the Protestant Reformation. These events gave impulse in at least two distinguishable ways to attitudes that arguably contributed to liberals' later aversion to existentially weighted politics. In the first place, accepting Weber's explanation of the origins of modern capitalist entrepreneurship, one could understand the liberal aversion to endowing politics with existential significance, as a religious survival, a relic of the Puritan pursuit of ascetically oriented business activity as "the surest and most evident proof of rebirth and genuine faith."[18] From a perspective that holds systematically organized saving and investment to be of preeminent existential significance, engagement in politics, however necessary, could be seen as a distraction from, if not an obstacle to, the pursuit of one's God-given calling.[19]

A second way of understanding the historical basis of liberals' aversion to existentially weighted politics is as a pragmatic response to a long and bloody history of repressive attempts by state authorities to enforce doctrinal conformity in matters of faith. As Judith Shklar has put it, with her characteristic bluntness: "liberalism was born out of the cruelties of the religious civil wars, which forever rendered the claims of Christian charity a rebuke to all religious institutions and parties. If faith was to survive at all, it would do so privately."[20] Although Shklar's formulation of the liberal principle of freedom of religion lacks any reference to existential impulses as described above, it is not difficult to imagine a connection. For what are matters of faith if not the search and discovery of answers to questions such as What constitutes grace and sin in this life? and What system of rewards and punishments applies in the next life? Such questions, along with the emotional responses they can provoke, typically arise when an individual is led by experience and education to consider or to confront the burdensome facts of physiological mortality, suffering of body and mind, and other limits on human existence. One can say that, seen in this light, the liberal imperative of separating questions of faith from matters of state effectively means that politics is not the realm in which individuals are to confront and come to terms with their existential limits. In this view, engaging and discharging existential impulses is or should be a private matter of the spirit, not a public political matter.

If Shklar does not discuss the liberal principle of separating affairs of religious faith from affairs of state explicitly in terms of existential impulses and their exclusion from political consideration and action, one of her notable theoretical predecessors does. In his early-nineteenth-century analysis of the social influence of Christianity in the United States, Alexis de Tocqueville justifies the principle of church-state separation with reference to fundamental human longings or cravings provoked by the limits of human existence. The genius of the American republic, according to Tocqueville in *Democracy in America,* is the separation of church and state, which detached religion from the flux of politics and assigned it a preeminent role in the formation of morals. As he saw it, Christianity played a crucial role in helping Americans retain their freedom by narrowing the range of opinions and aspirations that found expression in the politics of the young republic. Of primary importance to Tocqueville was that the separation of church and state, along with Christianity's commanding influence in moral life, had the effect of sublimating certain existential emotions in religious rather than in political activity.

Man, Tocqueville writes, lives with a fundamental inner tension, at once despising human life for its limits, its "short space of threescore years," its "imperfect joys," and yet craving life and wishing it would never end.[21] Man is reconciled to this tension through contemplation of an afterlife. What is heaven, after all, but a consoling expression both of man's contempt for the failings of life and of his craving to extend life indefinitely? As long as the separation of church and state in American affairs lasts, and this tension of the human spirit between despising life and craving immortality remains outside the range of political consideration, people will not think to resolve the tension by political means. Sublimation along lines fostered by this institutional separation will thereby serve the true interests of both Christian religion and democratic politics. For Tocqueville, those true interests consist of permanence in the case of religion, and freedom from tyranny in the case of politics.

It is not hard to discern the logic of Tocqueville's argument that religion achieves permanence through its limiting itself to the task of providing consolatory visions of the afterlife. As he has it, the need to be consoled for the pains, disappointments, and fundamental limits of life through belief in an afterlife is a permanent and universal interest. "The instinctive desire of a future life brings the crowd about the altar, and opens the hearts of men to the precepts and consolations of religion" ("Principal Causes," 401). In fulfilling this interest a religion may, in this view, credibly aspire to a kind of permanence. This is not the case, however, when a religion unites with government and finds itself tempted both to pursue political interests of less permanence and universality than existential consolation and to use force rather than appeals of the spirit to gather adherents. The tradeoff in becoming a state religion, according to Tocqueville, is a church's temporary gain in power at the expense of a permanent loss of authority (397).

If, for Tocqueville, having faith in a future state is part of man's true happiness, so also is being free. The American separation of church and state promotes the first condition by allowing religions to respond compellingly to men's deepest existential longings with consolatory visions of an afterlife. On how it promotes the second condition, on how "it facilitates the use of freedom" (390), Tocqueville is somewhat less direct. The general sense is that religious belief in America achieves its good effects in political affairs by circumscribing the range of publicly acceptable opinion. The idea apparently is that American social conformity in professing Christian belief of some kind has the effect of setting limits upon Americans' taste for "debate" and "experiment" in political affairs (389).

> The revolutionists of America are obliged to profess an ostensible respect for Christian morality and equity, which does not permit them to violate wantonly the laws that oppose their designs. . . . Hitherto, no one in the United States has dared to advance the maxim that everything is permissible for the interests of society,—an impious adage, which seems to have been invented in an age of freedom to shelter all future tyrants. Thus, while the law permits the Americans to do what they please, religion prevents them from conceiving, and forbids them to commit, what is rash or unjust. (389)

Tocqueville does not specify here what kind of rashness or injustice one might expect to emerge in American political affairs in the absence of the moral effect of Christianity. In reference to the case of France, however, where Christianity's entanglement in politics had in his view served to rob it of any universal moral authority, Tocqueville foresees the rise of men whose ambition for power and glory will encounter no limiting moral authority: "There are persons in France who look upon republican institutions only as a means of obtaining grandeur; they measure the immense space which separates their vices and misery from power and riches, and they aim to fill up this gulf with ruins, that they may pass over it. These men are the *condottieri* of liberty" (393). In his later reflections on the revolutionary events of 1848 in France, these *condottieri* of liberty appear in the guise of revolutionary socialists, whose political programs prominently feature calls for the redistribution of property to the working class. It seems quite plausible that one of the desirable aspects of

Christianity in its moral effect upon American politics that Tocqueville had in mind as a young traveler in America was its sanctifi-
cation of private property.

In and of itself, a liberal-minded thinker defending Christianity
for its ideological support of property rights is neither surprising nor
theoretically interesting. Even granting that a concern for the security of property rights may inform Tocqueville's claim for the beneficial effects of religion upon American politics, it is still worth considering other possible rationales for his argument. Might not
Tocqueville's worry about the absence of Christianity have to do
with a premonition of the potential dangers posed by the entry into
the political arena of existential cravings for heaven? To the extent
that politics, unlike religion (or, at least, the religion of established
Christianity in the nineteenth-century America posited by Tocqueville), aims at transforming this life rather than contemplating
the next and counts coercion among its available means, the liberal
worry about permitting the unmediated political discharge of existential cravings does not seem baseless.

For Nietzsche (not a liberal, to be sure, but a radical theorist of
individuality sharing with liberal theorists several basic assumptions), the prospects for radical and possibly catastrophic upheavals
in European society due to the breakdown of existing cultural
modes of managing existential impulses had become palpably high
a half-century after the publication of *Democracy in America*. Fore-
seeing the spread of atheism to the "masses," Nietzsche predicted
that existentially charged attitudes would find political expression
with revolutionary results:

> When truth enters into a fight with the lies of millenia, we shall have
> upheavals, a convulsion of earthquakes, a moving of mountains and
> valleys, the like of which has never been dreamed of. The concept of
> politics will have merged with a war of spirits; all power structures of
> the old society will have been exploded.[22]

In Tocqueville's book on America, it is not hard to find similar
though less highly pitched recognitions of the role of religious belief
in warding off "despair" and references to the positive political benefits following therefrom: "if the unbeliever does not admit religion
to be true, he still considers it useful. Regarding religious institutions

in a human point of view, he acknowledges their influence upon manners and legislation. He admits that they may serve to make men live in peace, and prepare them gently for the hour of death" ("Principal Causes," 400).[23]

Although Tocqueville's analysis of the political significance of the separation of church and state reveals a basic sympathy with the project of arranging democracy on a liberal basis, it is untypical of liberal analyses in its formulation of the advantages of that separation explicitly in terms of processes of existential sublimation. Tocqueville's distinctive transparency in this particular respect arguably manifests what can be characterized as the hybrid nature of his political thought, in which a liberal-minded, instrumentalist understanding of politics exists in tension with a republican appreciation of the autotelic rewards promised by direct political participation. (This tension is evident in Tocqueville's *Recollections,* especially in his ambivalent treatment of the political mobilization of French working-class men during the course of the 1848 revolution.) What this transparency reveals more fully is the existential context of liberal politics. Although premised on the exclusion of the task of existential sublimation from political consideration and action, liberal politics nevertheless requires that this task be successfully completed by extra-political means. If the viability of liberal politics rests in significant part on the capacity of nonpolitical institutions (the church, the market, the academy) to sublimate existential impulses, then what are the prospects for liberal politics in cases when these institutions cease to function adequately or at all?

Among the historical cases that can be raised as a challenge to liberal thought along these lines is the case of Germany between the two world wars. Whereas from a liberal standpoint the collapse of the Weimar Republic and the coming to power of the National Socialists taught the danger of infusing political institutions and practices with existential significance, from a standpoint informed by an Arendtian theory of tragedy the phenomenon of totalitarianism, in all its varieties, should teach partisans of democracy the dangers of blocking the political sublimation of existentialist impulses. The liberal insistence on defining existential reconciliation as a task to be fulfilled outside of politics entailed a risk of facilitating the very appearance of that pernicious form of existentially weighted politics that liberals seem so intent on avoiding. This risk became prohibitive in the years after the Great War, according to Arendt, because those nonpolitical institutions such as church or workplace that liberalism had designated for the task of sublimating existential impulses had lost their capacity to do so wholly or in part.

A view of the inadequacy of liberalism's unconditional rejection of existentially weighted politics can be inferred from the argument of Arendt's *The Origins of Totalitarianism,* especially in her discussion of mass society in Part III. The picture Arendt draws is of an interwar Europe where conditions of economic dislocation, mass unemployment, and religious disenchantment had stimulated and intensified people's existential longings to affirm and negate the self, at the same time as they manifested the closing down of conventional means of sublimating those longings. Democratic political institutions and practices, premised as they were on a liberal notion of politics as a means of individual or class interest, could offer existentially burdened individuals no therapeutic discharge either. So people felt drawn to movements of race or class supremacy that appealed to prospective members with promises to discharge existential longings in collectivist forms of politics. So, on one hand, membership in a totalitarian movement could serve to discharge cravings of self-assertion by distributing a share of the collective immortality to be achieved by a race or class conceived in ideological terms as a world historical agent. And so, on the other, membership could serve to discharge cravings of self-negation by relieving the individual of the burdens of personal responsibility and choice.

One does not have to subscribe to an account of the origins of Nazism that emphasizes the inadequacy of liberal institutions in Weimar Germany in carrying out the task of existential sublimation to acknowledge the extent to which the characteristically liberal mode of organizing the discharge of existential impulses (that is, extra-politically) is highly vulnerable to disruption in times of social instability. Put another way, liberal theorists, in shunting the task of existential sublimation to nonpolitical agencies, seem to take social stability as their standard of reference. In times of relative social stability, Arendt's vision of council democracy, with its emphasis on display-oriented and agonistically toned political modes of existential sublimation may well appear irrelevant to, if not disruptive of, the business of protecting individual rights or the task of promoting the solidarity needed for effective coalition politics. It may be, however,

that in times of severe social discontinuity or socially disruptive political discontinuity—when conditions of psychological disorientation and material suffering intensify and spread, and when consensus about the nature and meaning of individual rights or social
justice breaks down—a political vision giving due attention to the
existential possibilities of politics might offer unique conceptual resources to liberal or socially minded participatory partisans of democratic citizenship.

"Great tragedy, Greek as well as modern," Karl Jaspers
writes, "arises in eras of transition; it comes up like a flame from the
fires that consume an epoch."[24] The notion that periods of unusu-
ally significant productivity in the composition and performance of
tragedy coincide with or closely follow upon eras of intense, unsettling, perhaps even highly disruptive, political and social change
has become a settled point among those who consider tragedy, particularly Greek tragedy, in its political and social context.[25] Periods
of accelerated political and social change usually entail substantial
dislocations. Institutions suffer losses in their capacity to meet material and emotional needs they had previously met or they find
themselves pressed to meet new demands beyond their capacity.
Conceptual and institutional boundaries and categories formerly
adhered to with little or no apparent or effective questioning become subject to more consequential challenge and critique. The establishment of tragic drama as civic institution of Athens in the last
third of the sixth century B.C.E. has been associated in the literature with just such a period of accelerated and dispute-ridden political and social change, in which growing popular resentment against
aristocratic rule and internecine power struggles between aristocratic factions fostered the rise, from within the aristocracy's own
ranks, of popular champions or tyrants.[26] An unintended consequence of these aristocratic power struggles was the establishment
of settled procedures by which decision-making for the community
became increasingly public, impersonal, and open to the participation of the common folk.[27]

In Athens's contentious shift from a community organized
mainly according to kinship and custom to one in which human relations became significantly more premised on a consciousness of

the conventionality of human affairs, Greek tragedy is thought by its modern interpreters to have played an important role, fostering critical reflection on community, while at the same time promoting a sense of belonging in community. Central to theorists' understanding of this role is the notion that Greek tragedy, in its novel combination of ritual (choral song and dance) and narrative elements (mythic tales of heroic exertion and doom), could provoke an aesthetic effect that intensified, in a mutually supportive way, theatergoers' dispositions to be both active and reflective, to act *for* one's self without compromising the capacity of detachment *from* one's self that is a condition for acting with others in community. Arendt's political thought can be seen as originating in a historical period no less characterized by conflict and discontinuity than the century or two leading up to and spanning democratic rule in Athens, a period of collapsing liberal regimes, emerging systems of totalitarian rule, genocidal warfare, and widespread devastation. A time of more radical change would be hard to imagine. Considered within this context of momentous social and political transformations, Arendt's partly unacknowledged and not fully systematic reliance on a theory of the political relevance of tragedy might be seen more sympathetically as an appropriate response to the special challenges associated with periods of radical social and political discontinuity. For what typically characterizes such times is the strain and breakdown of many of the institutions, routines, and shared understandings that formerly served to insulate people from more direct and continuous confrontation with the extreme limits of human powers and knowledge. For those with even a minimal stake in an existing set of political, social, and psychological structures, the severe strain or breakdown of such structures usually means exposure, on a broader scale and at higher intensities, to disorientation and suffering, at least in the short term. It is in these terms that Ken Jowitt, borrowing the image of a world "without form and void" from the Book of Genesis, describes the "task" faced by Western liberals in the aftermath of the collapse of Leninism as a globally established way of life, as one of responding "to a world that will be increasingly unfamiliar, perplexing, and threatening; in which existing boundaries are attacked and changed; in which the challenge will be to establish new national/international boundaries and 'name'—identify—the new entities."[28]

In a situation of "extreme contingency" (to borrow a phrase from Claus Offe, another analyst of the post-Communist condition of flux), the task of achieving a workable consensus about the nature and meaning of individuality and community is likely to become a more conscious and urgent challenge.[29] The task is likely to be more conscious because previously unchallenged identities, relationships, and modes of action have lost their traditional, customary, or routine qualities. It is likely to be more urgent because impulses of self-assertion and self-negation that had formerly been channeled by established structures of thought and action find more direct and unrestrained expression in individual behavior.

That crisis conditions tend to call forth forms of self-assertion less integrated with the routines and accepted practices of the larger community has been a common observation of historians. In extreme cases such as the near total breakdown of shared standards, commitments, and practices reported by Thucydides in the Greek polis of Corcyra during the Peloponnesian War, the intensification and spread of narrowly self-regarding behavior can take forms approximating the anarchic struggle evoked by Hobbes as that "warre . . . of every man, against every other man."[30] *Corruption* is the term applied to this syndrome in its less immediately life-endangering manifestations, such as when routine acceptance of publicly sanctioned allocative principles and practices devolves into an opportunistic, unrestrained scramble for increasingly uncertain and scarce resources. This syndrome has come recently to be fixed in Western news stories in the image of a post-Communist version of "primitive accumulation" carried out by the apparatchiks of the old order at the expense of their fellow citizens.[31] In addition to raising the potential for more direct and desperate expressions of self-assertiveness, crisis conditions can also give rise more broadly to cravings for release from anxious concern about one's self and for escape from responsibility for one's self and its actions. In the fatalism that leads some individuals in times of crisis to adopt a stance of politically withdrawn apathy and resignation, and others to enlist in a movement ideologically premised on the surrender of self-concern and individual responsibility, one can see a more intense, unmediated expression of the impulse to self-negation.

A sense of the availability of these impulses (at their highly charged extremes) for political mobilization by destructive movements underlies Arendt's account of the emergence of totalitarian regimes in the interwar period. On one hand she emphasizes the intensification and diffusion of feelings of "superfluousness" in explaining the interwar appeal of totalitarian ideologies of race or class supremacy, which invited individuals to identify themselves wholly with a collectivity. On the other hand, and especially in considering the motivation of the administrators of the Final Solution, Arendt focuses on the self-centered opportunism of the bourgeois family man, who, "for the sake of his pension, his life insurance, the security of his wife and children . . . was prepared to sacrifice his beliefs, his honor, and his human dignity."[32] On this account of Arendt's analysis, the populist basis of totalitarian movements lay in their success at rechanneling formerly de-sublimated impulses of self-assertion and negation into novel and pernicious forms of individuality and community.

When reading Arendt as a theorist of tragic sublimation, the past success of totalitarian movements serves to remind us of how noxious the political outcome may be if highly charged impulses of self-assertion and self-detachment do not find appropriate channels of engagement and discharge. The significance of Arendt's thought lies in its revealing the challenge of democratic foundation as one of getting political sublimation right. This can be seen, in the first place, in the tragic mode of Arendt's thought, which can be understood to serve as a means of theoretical sublimation appropriate to the conditions that typically hold in a "Genesis" environment. To the extent that Arendt's mode of theory foregrounds images of the self driven by impulses of self-assertion and self-detachment, which can reach the life and death extremes of self-immortalizing exertion and self-annihilating doom (see Achilles, or Sergeant Schmidt from *Eichmann*), it purportedly corresponds with what people feel or experience as a result of their being exposed to the conditions of disorientation and intensified suffering that typically accompany crises. While the extent of this correspondence is contingent upon the particulars of a given environment of social and political discontinuity, it is arguably less contingent than the contact achievable by those liberal or corporatist visions of democratic transition that naively assume the universal and intrinsic viability of liberal or corporatist definitions of self and community.

Of course, not all liberal or corporatist theorists of democracy are unmindful of the contingent nature of the ways of life they sponsor.

For example, the aforementioned analysts of post-Communist crisis show themselves amply aware of the prospect that polities undergoing radical social and political change may resist consolidation according to liberal or corporatist forms of democratic identity. Thus, despite his own liberal sympathies, Jowitt takes issue with claims asserting that liberalism stands automatically to inherit the loyalty and commitment of post-Communist peoples. In his view, the appeal of liberalism will depend on the degree of fit between the historically conditioned way of life sponsored by liberalism and the ideological and institutional legacies of those post-Communist countries in which attempts are made to implant liberal attitudes and institutions. Where conditions do not favor the consolidation of liberal identities, the possibility of forming individuals and communities on the basis of ethnicity remains an ever present and foreboding possibility. In any case, Jowitt expects that in the "turbulent" environment of post-Communism, "leaders will count for more than institutions, and charisma for more than political economy."[33]

A robust sense of the risks posed by the post-Communist Genesis environment marks as well the analyses of Claus Offe, a notable theorist of democratic corporatism. Among the major paradoxes characterizing the post-Communist condition, according to Offe, is the challenge of founding democracies and markets simultaneously; while the legitimacy of a fledgling democracy rests upon the political empowerment of the people, the capital accumulation requirements of an emerging market requires the material deprivation of the people, at least in the short term.[34] Of the possible solutions to this post-Communist modernization paradox, Offe is sanguine about the prospects of his preferred model, democratic corporatism, in which individuals' interest demands are primarily mediated by "collective actors" with "representational monopoly" (for example, "associations, federations, trade unions"). Foremost among the reasons he presents for the low prospects of this model is the relatively atomized social structures left behind as a result of the leveling policies of Communist regimes. Hardly more promising (or worthy?) of success, in Offe's view, are the various attempts that have already been made to consolidate forms of identity that are adequate to the modernization paradox, attempts which include neoclassical affirmations of free market individualism and nationalist assertions of ethnic community. To the extent that Offe is willing to project future lines of development, he foresees with some trepidation, "a type of 'charismatic' politics and presidentialist constitution-making unmediated by intermediary structures, in the shadow of which the forces of a civil self-organization . . . [will] hav[e] an exceedingly hard time . . . assert[ing] themselves."[35]

Despite their different theoretical starting points, Jowitt and Offe share a sense of the large difficulties facing liberal or corporatist founders of democracy in the "Genesis" environment of post-Communism. This shared sense of difficulty explains, perhaps, the deflationary tone of their analyses. The advice implicitly conveyed to citizens of the new democracies is to lower their expectations about the pace and extent of democratic consolidation, no matter whether this consolidation is to be attempted on the basis of liberal or corporatist ideals. To the extent that Jowitt and Offe aspire to orient political action, then, they can be seen as promoting a mainly ascetic strategy of self-denial and "patient waiting."[36]

By contrast, in Arendt's theoretical approach one detects an aesthetically oriented appeal, which promises both to meet the reality of a "Genesis" environment and to shape that reality in ways that are conducive to the promotion of democratic citizenship through its presentation of stories of tragic heroism. She seeks to do so by holding out a vision of personal immortality gained through individuating action to those who, under the pressure of crisis conditions, feel increasingly driven to take extreme measures to preserve the self, safeguard its boundaries, and ensure its adequate future provisioning. Such a vision cannot control or negate the expression of those drives, only encourage their reorientation and discharge in ways more conducive to the requirements of democratic civility. Thus, for those beset by a radically heightened sense of self-concern, tragic storytelling provides an enticement to waive resort to more extreme and private modes of self-assertion and, instead, to strive for the greatest prize of all, satisfying intimations of personal immortality. And insofar as the achievement of compelling intimations of personal immortality depends on public witness and judgment, aspiring heroes can be expected more often than not to seek public outlets for expressing their self-assertive impulses. In this respect, theory in a storytelling mode can function as a form of authority, serving to channel existential impulses in ways that are promotive of political freedom.

While the striving for compelling intimations of personal immortality can motivate action directed toward an audience, it does
little if anything to guarantee the cohesion of that audience. After
all, in a competitive scramble for personal glory, the interest of each
is to be the one on the stage while the rest watch and remember. As
several critics of Arendt's philhellenism have noted, this hardly
seems the recipe for a broadly activist or stable democratic politics.
For this, one needs political actors more mindful of the equally
pressing claims of others and capable of reflecting on their own
claims in relation to the plural wills and perspectives present in the
larger community.

To understand the promise of Arendt's mode of tragic storytelling
to foster kinds of heroism compatible with democratic community,
attention should be given to the other dimension of the tragic hero,
his or her role as doomed sufferer. This theory of tragedy raises an
expectation that identification with the hero in this aspect will serve
to train the imagination to achieve a reflective distancing from the
press of need, the pull of desire, the partiality of vision characteristic
of the claimant self. The special circumstances of a "Genesis" environment conspire to make this process of identification with the
tragic hero especially compelling. To the extent that conditions of
disorientation and suffering intensify the disposition to seek escape
from concern with the self, identification with the doomed hero can
provide the occasion for sublimation of this impulse in ways that are
constructive of democracy. The reserves of fatalism and resignation
upon which radically anti-individualist solidary movements so prof-
itably draw in times of crisis are instead partially discharged in
modes of thought such as Kant's "enlarged mentality" or Arendt's
"representative thinking" and in modes of action such as council
democracy, which are promotive of independent thinking and individual initiative-taking.

So central a focus on the role of heroic characters in the tragic
storytelling practice attributed to Arendt might give the impression
that she endorsed a politics of charismatic and heroic leadership.
This would be a wrong impression. What Arendt found most striking and promising about eras of radical political transformation was
the "regular emergence" of local organs of self-government such as
councils, communes, *Räte*, and *soviets* (OR 256), not the rise of
charismatic leaders. In line with her affirmation of council forms of

democracy, Arendt conceptualized a kind of political heroism that had more to do with a citizen's "willingness to act and speak" and "insert [his or her] self into the world" (*HC* 186) than with an aspiring leader's exercise of charismatic influence. If a theory of tragedy is at work in Arendt's writings, it is at work in the service of a specifically democratic sort of political heroism, the practice of which is meant to discharge existential impulses in ways that tend against the surrender of individual initiative by followers of charismatic leaders.

The recurrent phenomenon of local political self-organization greatly impressed Arendt; it revealed, in her view, peoples' unflagging aspiration to live life in a meaningful way and their continuing rediscovery of a form of political engagement well-adapted to respond to that aspiration. Refracted through the prism of an Arendtian theory of tragedy, the council phenomenon can be seen as a distinctively promising organizational response to one of the most pressing challenges raised by the circumstances of radical political and social transformation—the definition and consolidation of vital and viable political identities. The distinctive promise of councils appears, in this view, to consist in their capacity to engage, channel, and discharge impulses of self-assertion and self-detachment in ways that meet the requirements of solidarity and individuality and that, at the same time, also suit conditions of political and social flux. Requiring less in the way of ideological and institutional prerequisites than either liberal or corporatist modes of democracy, council modes of participation appear more available and more appropriate as a means of action in highly contingent environments. And by inviting people to act in public, and thus lay themselves open to having who they are be judged by others, councils have a potential to stimulate at the grassroots level a dynamic of individual and collective self-definition. To the extent that the identities resulting from this dynamic are generated by the people acting on their own initiative, rather than coercively imposed by aspiring founders, these identities are more likely to find ready and lasting purchase in the sensibilities of citizens. No less significant for democratic prospects, by the logic of this view, is the possibility that the more direct modes of participation permitted by councils promotes the discharge of impulses that might otherwise be repressed until they find outlets in anti-democratic modes of discharge.

In arguing for the relevance of an Arendtian theory of tragedy for democratic participation, we initially chose radical political and social discontinuity as our point of reference. We reasoned that episodes of radical discontinuity, marked as they are by significant breakdowns in established patterns of thought and action, make more urgent the task of promoting and consolidating forms of political identity by which impulses to self-assertion and self-detachment are appropriately sublimated. Against the backdrop of this dramatically posed sense of political urgency, a case was made for the distinctive promise of an Arendtian theory of tragedy and council forms of participation.

What of the seemingly less dramatic, more mundane tasks that citizens face in an established democracy? The logic of the foregoing argument would suggest that, in times of stable democratic government, the task of promoting and consolidating viable forms of political identity would have less urgency. This prospect raises, in turn, a question as to the relevance of an Arendtian theory of tragedy in non-extreme conditions. After all, what is so "tragic" about the conditions that hold in a long-standing liberal or corporatist democracy that we would significantly gain in our understanding of these conditions by viewing them through a tragic prism?

It may well be that the task of promoting and consolidating political identities in which impulses of self-assertion and self-detachment are appropriately sublimated is, in important respects, less urgent in a long-standing democracy where established routines serve to channel citizens' impulses in ways that are functional for the system. In such a setting, one would reasonably expect political identities to be relatively stable. They would be less prone to being reconstituted in such ways as to permit the expression of impulses of self-assertion and self-detachment in forms or at extremes that immediately threaten regime viability.

While the routines of a stable democracy are less likely to give way to forms of behavior expressive of pathological extremes of self-assertion and self-negation, they are not without their own pathological tendencies. Political scientists have long noted how the routines of representative democracy can accustom citizens to value politics in ways that undermine the long-term viability of democratic procedures. So, on the one hand, to the extent that liberal or corporatist ideals restrict the meaning of democracy to interest representation, they encourage citizens to approach politics in narrowly instrumental, even opportunistic ways. Margaret Canovan in her recent analysis of the nature and significance of populism (1999) highlights the instrumentalist excesses to which the "pragmatic" ethos of representation can give rise. "If it becomes clear that [voters and politicians] see in democracy nothing but horsetrading, they, and eventually the system itself, are liable to lose their legitimacy."[37] According to Canovan, where pragmatic considerations so dominate political affairs that citizens lose contact with democracy's redemptive promise of collective solidarity and self-rule, the emergence of populist organizations aimed at making citizen participation in democracy more direct, continuous, and effective becomes more likely. A similar sense of the vulnerability of representative institutions of government to disabling declines in civic commitment animates the work of Robert Putnam (1995), a key contributor to the emergent "social capital" literature. He has found that in representative democracies with low densities of voluntary, locally based civic organizations, citizens are less likely to develop social trust and more likely to approach politics opportunistically.[38]

If opportunism lies at one extreme of the pathologies that afflict the functioning of the representative institutions of democracy, apathy lies at the other. While the interest group politics to which the practices of representative democracy give rise can incite citizens to more energetic levels of opportunistic political engagement, it can also at the same time and on the other hand foster in them a sense that they do not count too much in political affairs as individuals. When certain interests are not often enough met or are systematically ignored, citizens can be alienated from politics altogether.

On the recognition, shared by Canovan and Putnam, that the functioning of representative institutions in established democracies is, in and of itself, no proof against the degradation of the capacity of citizens to feel a part of a larger community and work for collective goods, or to feel a sense of their individual efficacy and be engaged in political affairs, one can rest a claim for the relevance of an Arendtian theory of tragedy. For the promise of this theory is to channel impulses of self-assertion and self-detachment in ways that promote a robust and balanced sense in citizens of their being both individuals and members of a community. In presenting tragic heroes in their role as immortal actors, this theory entices citizens, for whom the practices of representation provide inadequate rewards, to strive for compelling intimations of immortality through action in public forums. And as counterbalance to the opportunistic excesses to which citizens in representative democracy are sometimes given, this theory invites identification with tragic heroes in their role as doomed sufferers released from the urgent press of self-interest and graced with a more reflective and impartial view of human affairs.

In addition to its modest promise directly to counteract the pathologies to which the processes of representation can give rise, Arendt's thought, seen in its tragic dimension, casts a new light on the significance of the council phenomenon in established democracies—whether that phenomenon manifests itself in dramatic moments of grassroots protest against the failures of establishment politics or in the more mundane, continuous, and uncontroversial practices of civic association and mutual self-help.[39] Seen in their aspect as theaters of the achievements and failures of citizens, council forms of participation (such as jury deliberation) appear as "vital complements" to the representative institutions that so decisively define the character of modern democratic systems.[40] The scale and complexity of these systems demand that the work of interest aggregation and policy coordination be performed by elected officials and their bureaucratic agents. In the role this process reserves for citizens (voting for representatives at regular intervals), opportunities are lacking for citizens to develop a sense of being different from others with the ability to act effectively on the basis of that difference. Citizens also lack opportunities to be both part of a community and able to act effectively in pursuit of collectively determined goals. For accomplishment of this other, necessary kind of political work, which Canovan considers under the notion of "redemptive politics" and Putnam under the notion of "social capital," citizens have had, and will continue to have, recourse to more direct forms of political or politically relevant engagement.

Notes

ABBREVIATIONS USED

BPF   *Between Past and Future*. New York: Penguin, 1978.

CR   *Crises of the Republic*. New York: Harcourt Brace Jovanovich, 1972.

HC   *The Human Condition*. Chicago: University of Chicago Press, 1958.

LM:T   *The Life of the Mind: Thinking*. New York: Harcourt Brace Jovanovich, 1978.

LM:W   *The Life of the Mind: Willing*. New York: Harcourt Brace Jovanovich, 1978.

MDT   *Men in Dark Times*. New York: Harvest/Harcourt Brace Jovanovich, 1968.

OR   *On Revolution*. New York: Penguin, 1979.

OT   *The Origins of Totalitarianism*. New York: Harvest/Harcourt Brace Jovanovich, 1973.

INTRODUCTION

1. See chapter 4 in Elizabeth Young-Bruehl, *Hannah Arendt: For Love of the World* (New Haven: Yale University Press, 1982).

2. Hannah Arendt, "We Refugees (January 1943)," in *The Jew as Pariah: Jewish Identity and Politics in the Modern Age,* ed. Ron Feldman (New York: Grove Press, 1978), 55–56; hereafter cited in the text as "We Refugees," with page reference.

3. Michael Walzer, *The Company of Critics: Social Criticism and Political Commitment in the Twentieth Century* (New York: Basic Books, 1988), ix, 106.

4. Alasdair MacIntyre *After Virtue* (Notre Dame: University of Notre Dame, 1984); Judith Shklar, *Ordinary Vices* (Cambridge, Mass.: The Belknap Press of Harvard University Press, 1984); and Martha Nussbaum, *Poetic Justice* (1995).

5. For example, Dean Hammer, Jessica Bleiman, and Kenneth Park, "Between Positivism and Postmodernism: Hannah Arendt on the Formation of Policy Judgments," *Policy Studies Review* 16.1 (spring 1999): 148–81.

6. For notable and representative examples of feminist, liberal, and

social democratic criticism see, respectively, Adrienne Rich, "Conditions of Work: The Common World of Women," in *On Lies, Secrets and Silence* (New York: Norton, 1979); Stephen Holmes, "Aristippus in and out of Athens," *American Political Science Review* 73 (March 1979); Sheldon Wolin, "Hannah Arendt: Democracy and the Political," *Salmagundi* 60 (spring–summer 1983).

7. A collection of Arendt writings on topics of particular significance to Jews—*The Jew as Pariah,* edited with an introduction by Ron Feldman—is an indispensable sourcebook for scholars taking this approach. Perhaps more than any other sympathetic commentator, Leon Botstein discounts the classical dimensions of Arendt's thought. See, for example, "Hannah Arendt: The Jewish Question," *New Republic,* October 21, 1978, pp. 32–34.

8. For example, see Hanna Pitkin, *The Attack of the Blob: Hannah Arendt's Concept of the Social* (Chicago: University of Chicago Press, 1998).

9. Hannah Arendt, *On Revolution* (New York: Penguin, 1979), 281; hereafter cited in the text as *OR* with page reference. In the original passage, the citations of *Oedipus at Colonus* appear in the original Greek. Thanks to Professor Glenn Rawson for the transliteration.

1: GREEK TRAGEDY, STORYTELLING, AND POLITICAL THEORY

1. J. Peter Euben, *The Tragedy of Political Theory: The Road Not Taken* (Princeton: Princeton University Press, 1990), 23.

2. Ibid., 29.

3. Tracy Strong, *The Idea of Political Theory: Reflections on the Self in Political Time and Space* (Notre Dame: University of Notre Dame Press, 1990), 40, 70. For discussion of Nietzsche and Greek tragedy, see ibid., pp. 56–60. See also Strong's articles "Nietzsche's Political Aesthetics," in *Nietzsche's New Seas,* ed. Michael Gillespie and Tracy Strong (Chicago: University of Chicago Press, 1988), and "Oedipus as Hero: Family and Family Metaphors in Nietzsche," in *Why Nietzsche Now?* ed. Daniel O'Hara (Bloomington: Indiana University Press, 1981). The quotation is from Strong, "Oedipus as Hero," 329.

4. Strong, "Nietzsche's Political Aesthetics," 158.

5. Ibid., 164.

6. Shklar, *Ordinary Vices,* 230; hereafter cited in the text as *Ordinary Vices,* with page reference.

7. A similar sense of the complementariness of storytelling and more abstract modes of political analysis is expressed by Shklar in the introduction to her book. "This is . . . a ramble through a moral minefield, not a march toward a destination, and these essays ought to be read in that spirit. Each one deals with one of the ordinary vices. The final chapter is a theoretical review and analysis of the whole, designed for those who have a taste for political theory; but the preceding chapters do not depend on it, and can be read sep-

arately" (*Ordinary Vices,* 6).

8. Ronald Beiner, *What's the Matter with Liberalism?* (Berkeley and Los Angeles: University of California Press, 1995), 14, 7 (emphases added).

9. MacIntyre, *After Virtue,* 263.

10. "Anyone who has participated in the various important political movements in Western countries over the last twenty-five years knows what communities were founded and remain resonant from those times." Strong, *Idea of Political Theory,* 62. See also Euben's critique of Allan Bloom's interpretation of student activism in the 1960s in Euben, *Political Theory,* ix–xv.

11. Lisa Disch, *Hannah Arendt and the Limits of Philosophy* (Ithaca: Cornell University Press, 1994), ch. 1.

12. Ibid., 13. Disch proposes, through an examination of Arendt's storytelling practice, "to find a way to speak critically from experience without the dogmatic parochialism that asserts *my* experience as an unquestionable ground of *my* authority, and to find a way to hold various claims to experience open to question without the reluctant skepticism that postpones decision making to the point where it becomes politically paralyzing" (209).

13. Victor Turner, *From Ritual to Theatre: The Human Seriousness of Play* (New York: Performing Arts Journal Publications, 1982), 48.

14. Hannah Arendt, "The Crisis in Culture," in Hannah Arendt, *Between Past and Future* (New York: Penguin, 1978), 223; hereafter cited in the text as *BPF* with page reference. As expressions of Arendt's aesthetic bent go, this is fairly typical.

15. For some examples, see Euben, *Political Theory,* 82, 83, 85, 98, 109, 111, 112; also 7, 10–11, 37, 40, 42.

16. See Strong, "Oedipus as Hero," 321; "Nietzsche's Political Aesthetics," 173; *Idea of Political Theory,* 62–63.

17. Karen Hermassi, *Theatre and Polity in Historical Perspective* (Berkeley and Los Angeles: University of California Press, 1977), 33–34.

18. Beiner, *What's the Matter with Liberalism?* Frederick Dolan, *Allegories of America: Narratives, Metaphysics, Politics* (Ithaca: Cornell University Press, 1994).

19. Within this literature, the following texts will be discussed: David Luban, "Explaining Dark Times: Hannah Arendt's Theory of Theory" (1983), and Seyla Benhabib, "Hannah Arendt and the Redemptive Power of Narrative" (1990), both reprinted in *Hannah Arendt: Critical Essays,* ed. Lewis Hinchman and Sandra Hinchman (Albany: State University of New York Press, 1994); Judith Shklar, "Rethinking the Past," and Elizabeth Young-Bruehl, "Hannah Arendt's Storytelling," both published in *Social Research* 44.1 (1977); Melvyn Hill, "The Fictions of Mankind and the Stories of Men," in *Hannah Arendt: The Recovery of the Public World,* ed. Melvyn Hill (New York: St. Martin's Press, 1979); section 9 of Ronald Beiner's "Interpretive Essay: Hannah Arendt

on Judging," in *Lectures on Kant's Political Philosophy*, ed. Ronald Beiner (Chicago: Chicago University Press, 1989); and Disch, *Limits of Philosophy*.

20. Take, for example, the contrasting responses of literary critic and personal friend Alfred Kazin and political scientist A. James Gregor concerning Arendt's *Origins of Totalitarianism* (New York: Harvest/Harcourt Brace Jovanovich, 1973); hereafter cited in the text as *OT* with page reference. On rereading this work, Kazin wrote that "the harshly brilliant structure she built up in her last chapters . . . seems to me now . . . a stupendous literary idea, like the structure of Dante's Hell." "Woman in Dark Times," *New York Review of Books*, June 24, 1982, p. 1. Gregor, on the other hand, finds serious fault with the book for its "great deal of literary and speculative fill." A. James Gregor, *Interpretations of Fascism*, quoted in Luban, "Explaining Dark Times," 101.

21. Disch, *Limits of Philosophy*, 119–20 (emphasis added).

22. Stephen J. Whitfield, *Into the Dark: Hannah Arendt and Totalitarianism* (Philadelphia: Temple University Press, 1980), 178–79.

23. Luban, "Explaining Dark Times," 100.

24. See the preface (p. viii) to *Men in Dark Times* (New York: Harvest/Harcourt Brace Jovanovich, 1968); hereafter cited in the text as *MDT* with page reference. Luban's analysis is particularly illuminating in "Explaining Dark Times," 80–85, 90–95.

25. Disch, *Limits of Philosophy*, 120.

26. Luban, "Explaining Dark Times," 98.

27. Benhabib, "Redemptive Power of Narrative," 131.

28. Beiner, "Interpretive Essay," 154.

29. Benhabib, "Redemptive Power of Narrative," 125.

30. Ibid.

31. Luban, "Explaining Dark Times," 98.

32. Hayden White, "Interpretation in History," in *Tropics of Discourse: Essays in Cultural Criticism* (Baltimore: Johns Hopkins University Press, 1978), 59. In White's reading, the store of Western *mythoi* from which the great historians of the nineteenth century drew comprised Romance, Comedy, Tragedy, and Satire (70).

33. Shklar, "Rethinking the Past," 89. In this category, Shklar may mean to include Homer with the Greek dramatists (82).

34. Hill, "Fictions of Mankind," 298. In distinguishing poetic from historical truth Aristotle wrote, "It will be clear from what I have said that it is not the poet's function to describe what has actually happened, but the kinds of thing that might happen, that is, that could happen because they are, in the circumstances, either probable or necessary" (ch. 9). Aristotle goes on to emphasize the importance of probability in his discussion of tragic poetry—arguing, for example, that "of all the forms of discovery, the best is

that which is brought about by the incidents themselves, when the startling disclosure results from events that are probable" (ch. 16). See the Bywater-based translation in *Aristotle/Horace/Longinus: Classical Literary Criticism*, trans. T. S. Dorsch (London: Penguin, 1965), 43, 54.

35. Disch, *Limits of Philosophy*, 111–12.

36. Kimberley Curtis, "Aesthetic Foundations of Democratic Politics in the Work of Hannah Arendt," in *Hannah Arendt and the Meaning of Politics*, ed. Craig Calhoun and John McGowan (Minneapolis: University of Minnesota Press, 1997). All quotes p. 28 except the last, p. 32.

37. Shklar, "Rethinking the Past," 88.

38. Hill, "Fictions of Mankind," 295, 291, 297 (the second citation is actually formed from two in the original text).

39. Disch, *Limits of Philosophy*, 19, 210; Curtis, "Aesthetic Foundations," 46.

41. Sheldon Wolin, "Hannah Arendt and the Ordinance of Time," *Social Research* 44.1 (spring 1977): 93, 91. Alfred Kazin, "Woman in Dark Times," *New York Review of Books*, June 24, 1982, quotations from second page of review and last paragraph (emphasis added).

41. Luban, "Explaining Dark Times," 99. Homeric epic first existed as court poetry, sung to an aristocratic audience in palace halls. From around 566 *B.C.E. onward, it was competitively recited to inhabitants of a democratic polis gathered in the open air on the occasion of Athens's quadrennial civic festival, the Panathenaia. The inauguration of the city's festival of Dionysus, at which tragedy was competitively performed, is traditionally dated from 534 *B.C.E. Josef Chytry, *The Aesthetic State: A Quest in Modern German Thought* (Berkeley and Los Angeles: University of California Press, 1989), xxxiv.

42. Luban, "Explaining Dark Times," 99; Benhabib, "Redemptive Power of Narrative," 126.

2: ARENDT'S RESORT TO GREEK TRAGEDY

1. For examples of Jaspers's criticism of Arendt's dissertation, her book on Rahel Varnhagen, and her essay on authority, see (respectively) Jaspers to Arendt, October 10, 1928 (note 1); August 23, 1952; April 12, 1956, in *Hannah Arendt / Karl Jaspers Correspondence, 1926–1969*, ed. Lotte Köhler and Hans Saner, trans. Robert and Rita Kimber (New York: Harcourt Brace Jovanovich, 1992), 689, 192–94, 284; hereafter cited as *Correspondence* with page reference. The fact that, of all Arendt's books, *On Revolution* was the only one dedicated to him and his wife, Gertrude, may go some of the way in explaining the unconditionality of his praise in this case. However, in light of Jaspers's consistently demonstrated commitment to the values of intellectual sobriety, one might reasonably expect that other, less personal factors were behind his

singularly unmodulated praise of *On Revolution*.

2. On January 26, 1949, Jaspers wrote to Arendt with news that Beacon Press intended to publish the "section on tragic knowledge from . . . *Von der Wahrheit*." He followed this news with an expression of gratitude: "Once again you have brought this all about, and it is you I have to thank." Letter 83, *Correspondence*, 128.

3. Karl Jaspers, *Tragedy Is Not Enough*, trans. H. Reiche, H. Moore, and K. Deutsch (1952; Hamden, Conn.: Archon, 1969), 57, 103.

4. Ibid., 28, 34, 72, 101.

5. Hannah Arendt, "Totalitarian Imperialism," *Journal of Politics* 20 (February 1958): 5. Arendt wrote of "the tragic fate of Hungary" and the "dramatic events of the Hungarian Revolution" (23, 43). Hannah Arendt, *The Human Condition*, includes a reference to the tragedy of the Hungarian revolution: "If the tragedy of the Hungarian revolution achieved nothing more than that it showed the world that, all defeats and all appearances notwithstanding, this political élan has not yet died, its sacrifices were not in vain" (Chicago: University of Chicago Press, 1958), 217; hereafter cited in the text as *HC* with page reference. In the German edition of the book, the same reference is made to "die Tragödie der ungarischen Revolution." *Vita Activa* (Munich: Piper, 1989), 211.

6. Arendt, "Totalitarian Imperialism," 7, 5. For freedom as revolutionary motive, see section 2, pp. 21–33.

7. The Greek phrase is in Greek script.

8. Karl Jaspers to Hannah Arendt, May 16, 19, 1963, and Arendt to Jaspers, May 23, 1963, in *Correspondence*, 505, 506, 507.

9. For evidence of Arendt's familiarity with *Von der Wahrheit* (from which Jaspers, *Tragedy Is Not Enough*, was excerpted), see the letter dated October 4, 1950, in which she says she is "reading *Wahrheit*" (*Correspondence*, 156). In a letter dated December 21, 1953, she reports that her husband, Heinrich, had "just made *Tragedy Is Not Enough* obligatory reading for his students" (235).

10. Jaspers read over a German language version of this essay in the February 1956 issue of *Der Monat* (*Correspondence*, 284).

11. Jaspers, *Tragedy Is Not Enough*, 36.

12. Ibid., 60–61.

13. For example, Arendt refers to an episode from the *Odyssey* as a "paradigm" of tragic cartharsis ("The Concept of History," *BPF* 45). She describes Achilles as the "hero par excellence" (*HC* 194). Arendt's reference to Achilles' decision to set out for Hector's funeral (*OT* 452) is also worth noting.

14. Jaspers, *Tragedy Is Not Enough*, 34.

15. In the Loeb Classical Library edition, the verse is translated: "Come, cease your lament and do not arouse it more! For in all ways these

things stand fast." *Sophocles II*, ed. Hugh Lloyd-Jones (Cambridge, Mass.: Harvard University Press, 1994), 599. The utterance is apparently directed at the daughters of Oedipus, who have learned from Theseus that the location of their father's tomb must remain a secret even from them. In the view of noted classicist Cedric Whitman, Heidegger "quotes the closing lines of Sophocles' *Oedipus at Colonus* as a token of what he called the Greeks' 'entry into the mysterious truth of Being'." "Existentialism and the Classic Hero," in *The Heroic Paradox*, ed. C. Segal (Ithaca: Cornell University, 1982), 65.

16. Taken from the verse translation provided in Ralph Manheim's edition of Martin Heidegger's *Introduction to Metaphysics*, of which a section is included in Lionel Abel's anthology *Moderns on Tragedy: An Anthology* (Greenwich: Fawcett, 1967), 299.

17. Heidegger cited in Abel, *Moderns on Tragedy*, 307.

18. Ibid., 311.

19. Ibid., 310.

20. As quoted by Martin Heidegger in "Tragedy, Satyr-Play, and Telling Silence in Nietzsche's Thought of Eternal Recurrence," in O'Hara, *Why Nietzsche Now?* 25.

21. Ibid., 26.

22. In her discussion of the contrasting Roman and Greek notions of culture, Arendt cites the second choral ode of *Antigone* to support her contention that "the Greeks understood (the tilling of the soil) as a daring, violent enterprise in which, year in and year out, the earth, inexhaustible and indefatigable, is disturbed and violated" ("The Crisis in Culture," *BPF* 213). For the citation of *Antigone*, see *BPF* 296 n. 8. Arendt writes, in reference to wind as a metaphor for thought: "We find the same metaphor in Sophocles, who (in the *Antigone*) counts 'wind-swept thought' among the most dubious, 'awe-inspiring' (*deina*) things with which men are blessed or cursed." *The Life of the Mind: Thinking* (New York: Harcourt Brace Jovanovich, 1978), 174; hereafter cited in the text as *LM:T* with page reference.

23. George Steiner, *Antigones* (Oxford: Oxford University Press, 1984), 174.

24. According to Arendt, Heidegger's later work expressed the notion that "solitary thinking in itself constitutes the only relevant action in the factual record of history." *The Life of the Mind: Willing* (Harcourt Brace Jovanovich: New York, 1978), 181; hereafter cited in the text as *LM:W* with page reference. Chytry, in his magisterial study of German philhellenic aestheticism, makes a similar point in direct reference to Heidegger's reflection on the nature and meaning of Greek tragedy: "For all its idiosyncrasies, Heidegger's account of his ideal follows the general pattern of German Hellenism. As aesthetic state, the Heideggerian polis reaches its apogee with the public artwork of tragedy. Here Heidegger secures his standard of a people in the ecstasis of

significant time, orchestrated by poeisis within a site, the theatre, that un-
questionably contained spiritual properties. [However, Heidegger is] unable to
conceive of an active assembly or a vital public body, unable finally to con-
done an artwork committed to the sensuous." Chytry, *Aesthetic State*, 391–92.

25. Dana Villa, *Arendt and Heidegger: The Fate of the Political* (Princeton:
Princeton University Press, 1996), 154.

26. In addition to those cited in this text, see Arendt's reference to the
concluding words of *Antigone*—"But great words, counteracting the great
blows of the overproud, teach understanding in old age"—in support of her
claim for the high value placed by the ancient Greeks on the faculty of
speech (*HC* 25). Michael Denneny mentioned that this was a passage Arendt
would often refer to in discussion. Denneny, "The Privilege of Ourselves:
Hannah Arendt on Judgment," in Hill, *Recovery of the Public World*, 268. See
also Arendt's reference to Sophocles' use of the notion of eudaimonia in
Oedipus Rex (*HC* 193 n. 18) and her references to Antigone and a concept
from *Aischylus* in the preparatory notes for a German-language primer on
politics, published posthumously as *Was ist Politik?: Fragmente aus dem Nachlass*, ed. Ursula Lutz (Munich: Piper, 1993), 48, 118 respectively. In addition,
there are numerous references to Aristotle's notion of catharsis and to the
theater in ancient Athens.

27. M. S. Silk and J. P. Stern, *Nietzsche on Tragedy* (Cambridge, England:
Cambridge University Press, 1987), 297. Their concern is with Nietzsche's relationship to German preoccupation with the tragic.

28. For Margaret Canovan, "The first aspect of Arendt's 'public realm'
is that it is a brilliantly lit stage on which common attention is focused."
Canovan, "Politics and Culture: Hannah Arendt and the Public Realm," in
Hinchman and Hinchman, *Critical Essays*, 180. For Wolin, Arendt's treatment of "the political actor and action" in "dramaturgical terms" obscures
rather than illuminates political phenomena. Wolin, "Democracy and the
Political," 10.

29. See Arendt, "The Concept of History" (*BPF* 45) for another reference to Aristotelian catharsis; and "On Humanity in Dark Times" (*MDT* 20)
for references to pathos, "tragic effect," and "tragic pleasure."

30. Silk and Stern, *Nietzsche on Tragedy*, 1.

31. See, for example, Charles Taylor, *Hegel* (Cambridge, England: Cambridge University Press, 1993), 11.

32. Arnold Hauser, *The Social History of Art*, vol. 3 (New York: Vintage
Books, 1951), 117.

33. Winckelmann cited in Chytry, *Aesthetic State*, 7.

34. Hegel cited in Philippe Lacoue-Labarthe, "The Aestheticization of
Politics," in *Heidegger, Art and Politics: The Fiction of the Political* (London:
Basil Blackwell, 1990), 73.

35. "Politics, economic independence and social emancipation are in different degrees closed to the *Bürgertum*, the German middle classes. Literature and philosophy are to replace them as sources of a prospective political unity and national culture; and among the literary means to this end, drama, being obviously the most public, is the most readily available." Silk and Stern, *Nietzsche on Tragedy*, 299. For the phrase "public artwork," see Chytry: "As aesthetic state, the Heideggerian polis reaches its apogee with the public artwork of tragedy" (*Aesthetic State*, 391).

36. Friedrich Schiller, "Die Schaubühne als eine moralische Anstalt betrachtet," *Schillers Werke in fünf Bänden* (Berlin: BDK, 1981), 1:245–46 (my translation). Acknowledgment of Schiller's sense of the relevance of Greek theater as a historical example of a politically relevant site of aesthetic experience should not obscure his thoroughly ambivalent attitude to the suitability of Greek tragedy as a model for contemporary dramatic production. He was ultimately to conclude that the pure tragic form, developed to its highest perfection by the Athenian playwrights, was not the most promising and potent dramatic form for the contemporary stage. In his view, the dramatic form most appropriate to contemporary times was the historical play.

37. Quotation is from an 1883 article, "Richard Wagner's Significance for the German Nation," published in *Deutsche Worte* and cited in William McGrath, *Dionysian Art and Populist Politics* (Hartford: Yale University Press, 1974), 186.

38. See the "Preface to Richard Wagner," in Friedrich Nietzsche, *The Birth of Tragedy: The Case of Wagner*, ed. and trans. Walter Kaufmann (New York: Vintage, 1967), 31.

39. Ibid., 74, 125.

40. Jaspers, *Tragedy Is Not Enough*, 87, 88.

41. Ibid., 101. Karl Deutsch discusses the political context of this passage in his introduction to the 1969 edition.

42. Ibid., 29 (quotation), 79.

43. Silk and Stern, *Nietzsche on Tragedy*, 1.

44. G. W. F. Hegel, *Hegel on Tragedy*, ed. Anne Paolucci and Henry Paolucci (Garden City: Anchor Books, 1962), 68; hereafter cited in the text as *On Tragedy*, with page reference.

45. The other instance is found in Arendt, "Truth and Politics," *BPF* 262.

46. Arendt implicitly notes Hegel's neglect of action in his notion of reconciliation, in comments she made at a 1972 York University conference. "I cannot live without trying at least to understand whatever happens. And this is somehow the same sense in which you know it from Hegel, namely where I think the central role is reconciliation—reconciliation of man as a *thinking* and *reasonable* being." Hill, *Recovery of the Public World*, 303 (emphases added).

47. The paraphrase is based on Hayden White, *Metahistory* (Baltimore: Johns Hopkins University Press, 1987), 122: "[According to Hegel] the whole series of Pathetic, Epic, and Tragic Dramas contained in the historical record are sublated into a Drama of essentially comic significance, a human Comedy, a theodicy which is a justification not so much of the ways of God to man as of man's own ways to himself."

48. For the connection between Lessing's reinterpretation of catharsis and his notion of the middle-class nature of contemporary theater, see Victor Lange's introduction to G. E. Lessing, *The Hamburg Dramaturgy* (New York: Dover, 1962), xii–xiii. For Lessing's reinterpretation, see 178–94.

3: TRAGIC FOUNDATIONS

1. Further on in the essay, Arendt retreats only slightly from this claim: "Who can deny . . . that the disappearance of practically all traditionally established authorities has been one of the most spectacular characteristics of the modern world?" (*BPF* 100).

2. Hannah Arendt, "Ideology and Terror," was originally published in *Review of Politics* (July 1953) and was then added, in a somewhat revised form, to the second (1958) edition of *Origins of Totalitarianism*.

3. Hannah Arendt, "Civil Disobedience," *Crises of the Republic* (New York: Harcourt Brace Jovanovich, 1972), 79; hereafter cited in the text as *CR* with page reference.

4. Abundant examples are to be found in the critical response to *On Revolution*. A reviewer in the *Times Literary Supplement*, March 12, 1964, suggested that Arendt's revolution book "reveals the inadequacy of the 'classical' mode of political reasoning, which Dr. Arendt adopts, for providing clues to actual political behavior without which our values become irrelevant word-spinning." Irving Horowitz concluded his review in *American Journal of Sociology* (January 1964) with the question, "If massive revolution defines the century, might it not be wiser to reach for new combinations of policy and publics rather than to look with nostalgia upon the Greek city-states and their prudent elitism which rested, after all, on a slave base?" In the *Reporter*, George Steiner partly attributes to Arendt's "classicism" the book's "lack of historical sensibility, of respect for the obstinate chaos and vitality of mere fact." Steiner, "Lafayette, Where Are We?" *Reporter*, May 9, 1963.

5. Letter 184, *Correspondence*, 284.

6. M. I. Finley, *Politics in the Ancient World* (Cambridge, England: Cambridge University Press, 1983), 86.

7. R. D. Cumming offers an interpretation of Cicero's *De Republic* that parallels Arendt's reading. Drawing on Cicero's work and T. Mommsen's history of Rome, Arendt contends that the Roman Senate's practice of *auctoritas*

was compatible with political freedom. Cumming argues that, although Cicero accepted Platonic assumptions about the desirability of good order in both the soul and the state, he imagined differently the mechanism by which the good order of the wise man's soul becomes transmitted to the state. In the case of Socrates' imaginary polity, the well-ordered soul of the philosopher functions as a kind of template according to which transcendent ideas can be translated into politically relevant measures whose acceptance by the populace of the ideal city is predetermined by a program of eugenics and indoctrination. While good order of the soul justifies the Ciceronian statesman's claim that he is capable of ruling well, it is his ability to persuade the people to accept his leadership that is the appropriate means for his gaining and exercising leadership. Cicero, Cumming writes, converts "the wise man's self-control into the political control exercised rhetorically by the ideal statesman." R. D. Cumming, *Human Nature and History: A Study of the Development of Liberal Political Thought,* vol. 1 (Chicago: University of Chicago Press, 1969), 300. Insofar as rhetoric aims at political influence by means of persuasion, rhetoric is compatible with political freedom as practiced in the Athenian polis imagined by Arendt.

8. Finley, *Politics,* 91.

9. Arendt's distinction between the importance of Greek philosophical influence in Roman literature and in Roman political practice finds support in classical scholarship. For example, H. D. Jocylen doubts that "an activity [the study of Greek philosophy] carried on by a tiny minority of the ruling class in restricting physical and social conditions, in a foreign language and in an atmosphere of general antipathy could have had much effect on the behavior of this minority when it participated in the governing of the state." Jocylen, "The Ruling Class of the Roman Republic and Greek Philosophers," *Bulletin of the John Rylands University Library* 59 (1977): 366.

10. Hannah Arendt, "Thinking and Moral Considerations: A Lecture," *Social Research* 38, no. 3 (1971): 434.

11. Hannah Arendt, "Personal Responsibility under Dictatorship," *Listener,* August 6, 1964, pp. 186–87. The model of authority exemplified in the parent-child or teacher-pupil relationship "is based . . . on an absolute superiority such as can never exist among adults and which, from the point of view of human dignity, must never exist" ("The Crisis in Education," *BPF* 191).

12. For a recent analysis, see Mary Whitlock Blundell, "The Ideal of Athens in *Oedipus at Colonus,*" in *Tragedy, Comedy, and the Polis,* ed. Alan H. Sommerstein (Bari: Levante Editori, 1993), 287–306.

13. H. C. Baldry, *The Greek Tragic Theater* (New York: Norton, 1971), 6.

14. Or rather, *Arendt's* Theseus is direct and unambiguous. In the Loeb Classical Library edition, the relevant passage is translated: "I strive to give my life lustre not through words but through actions" (*Sophocles II* 539, ll.

1143–44). The passage occurs in the scene wherein Theseus restores to Oedipus his two daughters, Antigone and Ismene, after their kidnapping by Theban soldiers on Creon's orders. Overcome with joy, Oedipus embraces his daughters and asks them to tell the story of their rescue. Antigone responds that their rescuer, Theseus, should be the one to recount what has happened, upon which Oedipus asks the king's pardon for his inattention. Theseus graciously concedes the appropriateness of Oedipus's show of paternal concern and declares that, anyway, he chooses to gain fame not through the telling of stories but through the doing of deeds.

15. *Sophocles II* ll. 870–81.

16. Ibid., ll. 1131–32. The virtues associated with acting together with others with whom one must come to a mutually acceptable agreement are also not lacking in Theseus's fellow polis inhabitants. The peasant who first discovers Oedipus's trespass on sacred ground declares that he will not act against the intruder "without the *polis.*" Also noteworthy is the chorus's assumption of the role of "citizen jury" in the confrontations between Oedipus and Creon, first, and then between Oedipus and Polyneices. In these encounters the jury provides an audience to whose judgment the disputants alternately appeal. In this sense, the chorus in *Oedipus at Colonus* manifests "the prized democratic ability to evaluate persuasive words." Blundell, "Ideal of Athens," 294, 298, 298.

17. Arendt finds it noteworthy that the Greek historian Dio Cassius, "when writing a history of Rome, found it impossible to translate the word *auctoritas*" (*BPF* 289 n. 3). Philip Slater has described fifth-century Athens as "the most child-oriented civilized society known prior to the modern era." Slater, *The Glory of Hera: Greek Mythology and the Greek Family* (Boston: Beacon Press, 1968), 74. Alvin Gouldner, in his study *Enter Plato: Classical Greece and the Origins of Social Theory* (New York: Basic Books, 1965), links the heavy emphasis on individual fame and honor in Greek polis affairs to what he (following Nietzsche) calls the "Greek contest system," (43) suggesting that the contest system fostered a condition of hypercompetitiveness among male Athenians, not only between contemporaries but also across generations. In his view, the Greek contest system challenged the Athenian citizen to surpass the achievements of ancestors. One might, with reason, suppose that the spirit of innovation and daring attributed to the Athenians as a matter of course by the ancients would not have coexisted easily with the kind of ancestor worship that infused Roman notions of *auctoritas*. The testimony of contemporary Athenian observers further supports the notion that the Athenian polis of the fifth century B.C.E. lacked a form of political authority grounded in the sacredness of political foundation. The matter-of-factness with which Euthyphro goes about prosecuting his father in the Platonic dialogue, *Euthyphro*, speaks to the absence of paternal reverence in Athens.

18. MacIntyre articulates a sense of the narrative shape of human action in very similar terms: in heroic societies, "human life has a determinate form, the form of a certain kind of story. It is not just that poems and sagas narrate what happens to men and women, but that in this narrative form poems and sagas capture a form that was already present in the lives they relate." MacIntyre, *After Virtue*, 124.

19. Werner Jaeger, *Paideia: The Ideals of Greek Culture* (New York: Oxford University Press, 1974), 1:274.

20. Strong, "Nietzsche's Political Aesthetics," 159, 163–64.

21. Arendt is not always consistent in the terms she uses to assess the course and outcome of the American and French Revolutions. Sometimes she rules out judging the outcome in terms of "success" and "failure" (*OR* 68). Sometimes, she sees the "tasks" of revolution differently; for example, in *On Revolution,* chapter 1, the assurance of the revolutionary spirit is the *only* task of revolution.

22. Lincoln's address on November 7, 1837, to the Young Men's Lyceum of Springfield on the "perpetuation of our political institutions" provides a textbook example of a political activist's entrapment in this bind. In this address, the future president invokes the burdens imposed on his generation by the virtuous acts of the founding generation.

23. Honig quotes this Arendt passage in "Declarations of Independence: Arendt and Derrida on the Problem of Founding a Republic," in *American Political Science Review* (March 1991): 109.

24. In a 1970 interview, Arendt insists again on the spontaneous organization of popular councils in times of revolution: "Spontaneous organization of council systems . . . in the French Revolution, with Jefferson in the American revolution, in the Parisian commune, in the Russian revolutions, in the wake of revolutions in Germany and Austria at the end of World War I, finally in the Hungarian revolution . . . never came into being as a result of a conscious revolutionary tradition or theory, but entirely spontaneously, each time as though there had never been anything of the sort before." Arendt, "Thoughts on Politics and Revolution: A Commentary" (*CR* 231).

25. Nietzsche provides some mythic background to this utterance: "There is an ancient story that King Midas hunted in the forest for a long time for the wise Silenus, the companion of Dionysus, without capturing him. When Silenus at last fell into his hands, the king asked him what was the best and most desirable of all things for man. Fixed and immovable, the demigod said not a word, till at last, urged by the king, he gave a shrill laugh and broke out into these words: 'Oh, wretched ephemeral race, children of chance and misery, why do you compel me to tell you what it would be most expedient for you not to hear? What is best of all is utterly beyond your reach: not to be born, not to *be*, to be *nothing*. But the second best for you

is—to die soon'." Nietzsche, *The Birth of Tragedy: The Case of Wagner,* ed. and trans. Walter Kaufmann (New York: Vintage, 1967), 42.

26. One version of legend has it that, before his departure for Crete as presiding member of the annual Athenian delegation of victims to be sacrificed to the Minotaur, Theseus had arranged with his father, King Aigeus, that if he survived his encounter in the Labyrinth and managed to take ship home, he would exchange the vessel's black sails for white ones. On his successful return journey, Theseus apparently forgot this arrangement, and the king, on catching sight of the black sails from his cliff vantage point, flung himself to his death.

27. Edward Tripp, ed., *The Meridian Handbook of Classical Mythology* (New York: New American Library, 1974), 119.

28. Jaspers, *Tragedy Is Not Enough,* 81.

29. In this respect, *Oedipus at Colonus* resembles Euripides' *Hyppolytus,* which concludes with Artemis promising the fatally injured Hyppolytus a hero cult in Troezen that will ensure everlasting remembrance—"they will not forget you, your name will not be left unmentioned"—as a means of "compensation for [his] ills." See *Hyppolytus,* trans. David Grene in *Greek Tragedies VI,* ed. Richmond Lattimore and David Grene (Chicago: University of Chicago Press, 1967), 289–90.

30. Sophocles, *Oedipus at Colonus,* in *Three Theban Plays,* trans. Theodore Howard Banks (Oxford: Oxford University Press, 1956), p. 128, ll. 1488–91 (emphasis added).

31. Hermassi, *Polity and Theatre,* 30, 33.

32. Charles Segal's sense of the tragic promise of Oedipus's blessings is very different from mine. See *Tragedy and Civilization: An Interpretation of Sophocles* (Cambridge, Mass.: Harvard University Press, 1981), 406.

33. Arendt, "Totalitarian Imperialism," 7.

34. Ibid., 5 (emphasis added).

35. White, *Tropics of Discourse,* 70.

4: TRAGIC INTUITIONS

1. Arendt to Günther Gaus in a German television interview on October 28, 1964, printed in Günther Gaus, *Zur Person: Porträts in Frage und Antwort* (Munich: Deutscher Taschenbuch Verlog, 1965), 18. See, in addition, Arendt's comments at a 1972 York University conference: "But because this [God] had disappeared Western humanity was back in the situation in which it had been before it was saved . . . by the good news. . . . And this situation sent them (i.e., the eighteenth century revolutionaries) back scrambling for antiquity. And not as in some cases because you are in love with Greek verse or Greek songs as may be the case in my case." At the same conference she

said, "You see, I went back to Greek and Roman antiquity only half because I liked it so much—I like Greek antiquity but I never liked Roman antiquity." Cited in Young-Bruehl, *For Love of the World,* 313, 330.

2. Arendt, "The Moral of History (January 1946)," in Feldman, *The Jew as Pariah,* 109.

3. Ibid.

4. Benjamin Schwartz, "The Religion of Politics: Reflections on the Thought of Hannah Arendt," *Dissent* (1970): 145, 148, 150.

5. Arendt, "Understanding and Politics," *Partisan Review* 20.4 (July–August 1953): 377. Arendt cited from "Preface to the First Edition," *OT* viii; Alfred Kazin cited from "Woman in Dark Times," *New York Review of Books,* June 24, 1982.

6. Agnes Heller, "An Imaginary Preface to the 1984 Edition of Hannah Arendt's *The Origins of Totalitarianism,*" in *Eastern Left, Western Left: Totalitarianism, Freedom, Democracy,* ed. Ferenc Féher and Agnes Heller (Cambridge, England: Polity Press, 1987), 243.

7. Margaret Canovan, *The Political Thought of Hannah Arendt* (London: Dent and Sons, 1974), 15.

8. George Kateb, *Hannah Arendt: Politics, Conscience, Evil* (Totowa, N.J.: Rowman and Allanheld, 1984), 28.

9. Leah Bradshaw, *Acting and Thinking: The Political Thought of Hannah Arendt* (Toronto: University of Toronto Press, 1989), 7.

10. Lewis P. Hinchman and Sandra K. Hinchman, "Existentialism Politicized: Arendt's Debt to Jaspers," in Hinchman and Hinchman, *Critical Essays,* 169–70. Article originally published in the *Review of Politics* 53.3 (summer 1991).

11. Beiner, "Interpretive Essay," 153.

12. Arendt, "The Moral of History," in Feldman, *Jew as Pariah,* 109–10; Arendt, "Understanding and Politics," 391.

13. Roundtable Discussion, "On Hannah Arendt," in Hill, *Recovery of the Public World,* 308–9, 328.

14. Arendt, "Thoughts on Politics and Revolution: A Commentary," *CR* 203.

15. Arendt, "Civil Disobedience," *CR* 96, reprinted from *New Yorker,* September 12, 1970; Young-Bruehl, *For Love of the World,* 438 (quote), 466.

16. Sonning Prize Address, April 18, 1975 (Library of Congress), 6–7.

17. Ibid., 7–8.

18. Roundtable Discussion, "On Hannah Arendt," 306.

19. Ronald Beiner, "Judging in a World of Appearances: A Commentary on Hannah Arendt's Unwritten Finale," *History of Political Thought* 1.1 (1980); Elizabeth Young-Bruehl, "Reflections on Hannah Arendt's *The Life of the Mind,*" *Political Theory* 10.2 (1982).

20. Roundtable Discussion, "On Hannah Arendt," 304, 317.

21. Arendt's translation of Thucydides' transcription of Pericles' funeral oration.

22. Arendt's appropriation of Char as spokesman for the man of action raises the question of how groups of Resistance fighters, necessarily working in secrecy, could constitute a "*public* space." Arendt apparently has in mind the various spaces formed when Resistance fighters came together: "they . . . had begun to create that public space *between themselves*" (*BPF* 4; emphases added).

23. Arendt is discussing what distinguishes the student activists of the 1960s from the youth activists of other generations. See also "On Violence," in the same volume, where she describes the 1960s generation as characterized by a "no less astounding confidence in the possibility of change" (*CR* 118–19).

24. Arendt, "The Jew as Pariah: A Hidden Tradition," in *The Jew as Pariah,* ed. Ron Feldman (New York: Grove Press, 1978), 68.

25. Arendt, "We Refugees," in Feldman, *Jew as Pariah,* 62–63.

26. Ibid., 64.

27. "But this 'collective nature of labor,' far from establishing a recognizable, identifiable reality for each member of the labor gang, requires on the contrary the actual loss of all awareness of individuality and identity" (*HC* 213).

28. Arendt, "Philosophy and Politics," *Social Research* (spring 1990): 98.

29. Ibid.

30. Ibid.

31. Ibid., 88. See also *LM:T* 185.

32. Arendt to McCarthy, August 9, 1969, in *Between Friends: The Correspondence of Hannah Arendt and Mary McCarthy, 1949–1975,* ed. Carol Brightman (New York: Harcourt Brace, 1995), 242.

33. Ibid.

34. Arendt, "Philosophy and Politics," 88.

35. Roundtable Discussion, "On Hannah Arendt," 303.

36. Arendt, "Understanding and Politics," 377. In a letter dated May 28, 1971, to Mary McCarthy, Arendt describes some of her recent experiences in terms very much like earlier descriptions she gave of the pathos of wonder: "During the last months I have often thought of myself—free like a leaf in the wind. (It is a German idiom: *frei wie ein Blatt im Winde*.) And all the time I also thought: Don't do anything against this, that is the way it is, let no 'autocratic will' interfere" (*Between Friends,* 294).

37. Arendt, "Philosophy and Politics," 81.

38. Arendt, "Understanding and Politics," 391.

39. Arendt, 1958 laudatory address for the German Peace Prize, cited in "Karl Jaspers: *A Laudatio*" (*MDT* 74).

40. Arendt, "Response to Eric Voegelin's review of *The Origins of Totali-*

tarianism," Review of Politics 15 (January 1953): 80. She repeats this assessment in "Understanding and Politics," 379. See also "Tradition and the Modern Age": "Totalitarian domination as an established fact, which in its unprecedentedness cannot be comprehended through the usual categories of political thought, and whose 'crimes' cannot be judged by traditional moral standards or punished within the legal framework of our civilization, has broken the continuity of Occidental history" (*BPF* 26).

41. Arendt, "Personal Responsibility under Dictatorship," *Listener*, August 6, 1964, p. 187; hereafter cited in the text as "Responsibility," with page reference.

42. Arendt, "Memorial Address," *Correspondence*, 684–85.

43. Young-Bruehl, "Reflections on *The Life of the Mind*," in Hinchman and Hinchman, *Critical Essays*, 351, 358.

44. I say "substantially" rather than "wholly" because the possibility of Jaspers's forming a public space of freedom with other opponents of the regime (as Char and his comrades did) was not totally foreclosed. Given the fact that Jaspers was married to a German Jewish woman and had come under the suspicion of the Nazi authorities for his obvious lack of sympathy with the regime, active participation in an organized resistance would have required extraordinary courage, if not foolhardiness.

45. Jaspers testifies to such an impulse in a letter he wrote to Arendt shortly after his topical book on German politics, *Wohin treibt die Bundesrepublik,* was published in 1966: "I'm calling it quits for good with politics. . . . This political scribbling is seductive; it's all so much easier than philosophy. It lowers the level of one's inner being. A politician acting in the world, that is another thing" (Letter 398, *Correspondence,* 642).

46. "Memorial Address," *Correspondence,* 685.

47. Margaret Canovan wisely counsels the reader of these pieces to proceed with due caution in drawing conclusions about Arendt's sense of the degree to which Jaspers's notion of philosophy converges with her notion of political freedom. "Like the 1946 article on 'Existenz Philosophy,' however, these essays need to be read with some caution, remembering the strong personal motives Arendt had for expressing loyalty to her teacher and her close friend, particularly in pieces written for celebratory occasions." Canovan, "Socrates or Heidegger? Hannah Arendt's Reflections on Philosophy and Politics," *Social Research* 57.1 (1990): 148–49.

48. "Memorial Address," *Correspondence,* 685.

49. Arendt, "What Is *Existenz* Philosophy?" *Partisan Review* (winter 1946): 55, 52–53.

50. Ibid., 52–53.

51. Ibid., 55.

52. In his 1827 travel report, Heinrich Heine refers to the East Frisians

as a people possessing a distinctive "Talent der Freiheit" (talent for freedom). Heine, *Sämtliche Werke: Band V* (Munich: Kindler, 1964), 92.

53. Arendt, "Karl Jaspers: A Laudatio," *MDT* 75 (emphases added).

54. Measured by this standard, Jaspers's engagement in public life had actually begun, Arendt notes, before the establishment of Hitler's regime with the publication of *Man in the Modern Age* (1933), which appeared in Germany in 1931 as *Die Geistige Situation der Zeit.*

55. Arendt, "Karl Jaspers: A Laudatio," *MDT* 73–74.

56. "The *humanitas* whose existence he guaranteed grew from the native region of his thought, and this region was never unpopulated" (ibid., 76).

57. Ibid., 79.

58. Ibid., 85.

59. *Correspondence,* 94.

60. "Memorial Address," *Correspondence,* 685.

61. Arendt referred to this story in at least two other recorded instances. In her essay on "The Crisis in Culture," she suggests Cicero as a source: "The reason Cicero ascribed this culture to a training in philosophy was that to him only philosophers . . . approached things as mere 'spectators' without any wish to acquire something for themselves, so that he could liken the philosophers to those who, coming to the great games and festivals, sought neither 'to win glorious distinction of a crown' nor to make 'gain by buying and selling' but were attracted by the 'spectacle and closely watched what was done and how it was done'" (*BPF* 219). In a 1972 York University Conference, she was recorded as saying: "There is an old story that is ascribed to Pythagoras, where the people go to the Olympian games. And Pythagoras says: 'The one goes there for trade, and the best ones sit there in Olympia, on the amphitheater, just for looking'." Arendt cited in Hill, *Recovery of the Public World,* 304.

62. See the map of Olympia in Peter Levi, *Atlas of the Greek World* (New York: Facts on File, Inc., 1989), 80. This is not to say that tragic theater is, in the broadest sense, a purely Attic invention. "The sixth-century experiments [in tragedy] seem to have begun in Corinth and Sicyon in the Peloponnese, but once the Athenians took an interest (according to tradition the credit goes to Thespis in the time of Peisistratus) further progress was entirely in their hands." M. I. Finley, *The Ancient Greeks: An Introduction to Their Life and Thought* (New York: Viking, 1963), 84.

63. Jaeger, *Paideia,* 172.

64. Hermassi, *Polity and Theatre,* 6 (emphasis added).

65. "The lyric poet's individual patron was never wholly lost from sight, especially if he was a tyrant. It was no accident that Simonides and Pindar had such close ties to Sicily, or that Pindar, in particular, was identified with the dying world of the traditional aristocracy and with tyranny,

rather than with the new, triumphant classical polis. It was Athens, the democratic city-state par excellence, which produced and which was in the strict sense the patron of tragedy." Finley, *Ancient Greeks*, 80.

66. *Three Theban Plays*, p. 102, ll. 524–46.

67. Luban, "Explaining Dark Times," and Benhabib, "Hannah Arendt and the Redemptive Power of Narrative."

68. Arendt, "Portrait of a Period (October 1943)," in Feldman, *Jew as Pariah*, 117.

69. Ibid. (emphasis added).

70. The Ingram Bywater translation is cited by Walter Kaufmann in *Tragedy and Philosophy* (Princeton: Princeton University Press, 1992), 59. For the full text, see *Aristotle/Horace/Longinus*, 46.

71. See also Arendt, "Imagination," in Beiner, *Kant's Political Philosophy*, 84.

72. See chapters 11 and 16 of Aristotle, *The Poetics*, in Dorsch, *Aristotle/Horace/Longinus*.

73. Thus, for example, the reference to catharsis as that "cleansing or purging of all emotions that could prevent men from acting" (*BPF* 262) occurs in a passage that gathers philosophy (Hegel), short story (Isak Dinesen), novel, and history under the rubric of reconciliatory forms of poetry.

74. For the first quotation, see James Miller, "The Pathos of Novelty: Hannah Arendt's Image of Freedom in the Modern World," in Hill, *Recovery of the Public World*, 177. For the second quotation—"Hannah Arendt discussed revolutions not in order to outline their histories or distinguish their types but in order to present an ideal for practice"—see Young-Bruehl, *For Love of the World*, 406. For the third quotation—"far from a Fable or a simplistic Critique of Modernity, *On Revolution*, as it was to a whole generation of students in the 1960's, is an indispensable Handbook for Revolutionaries"—see Norman Jacobson, in "Parable and Paradox: In Response to Arendt's *On Revolution*," *Salmagundi* 60 (spring–summer 1983), 139.

75. For a similar characterization of the different perspectives brought by the two legendary figures to thier bargain, see André Gide, *Two Legends: Oedipus and Theseus* (New York: Vintage, 1950), 107–9.

76. *Three Theban Plays*, 102.

77. George Steiner's reading of the conclusion of *Oedipus at Colonus* provides an interesting comparison in that he sees the drama of thinking and acting as enacted diachronically in the personal story of Oedipus instead of synchronically in the bargain of Oedipus and Theseus. A further difference in our interpretations follows from his characterization of the reconciliation of thinking and acting as consisting of a setting apart rather than of a convergence. "It is only in *Oedipus at Colonus* that Oedipus' mastering thought yields to the summons of mystery, of that which, very precisely, lies beyond

the intelligible; and that Oedipus' *virtus,* his [*daimon*] for action, surrenders to passivity, to the trance-like motion which transports him beyond doing. It is only in the sacred wood that understanding and deed are again set apart and given piece." Steiner, *Antigones,* 299.

78. *Three Theban Plays,* p. 128, ll. 1488–91 (emphases added).

79. See ibid., p. 104, ll. 588–94; p. 128, ll. 1469–73.

80. Judith Shklar recognizes this when she hedges her designation of Arendt as "monumental historian" with the proviso that she was "unique among monumental historians [in that] she did not, as they did, merely want to move people to action. She had no intention of abandoning the work of philosophy which does not tell people how to behave but how to think." Shklar, "Rethinking the Past," 80–81.

81. Arendt, "Philosophy and Politics," 98.

82. According to the report of the messenger: "In what manner / Oedipus met his doom no mortal knows / Other than Theseus. In that final moment, / No flash of lightning made an end of him, / Nor sudden tempest springing from the sea. / Either some messenger of the gods arrived, / Or the foundations of the earth split open / To take him without pain, indulgently." *Three Theban Plays,* 130.

83. Karen Hermassi's analysis of the political significance of Greek tragedy draws on a long-established notion that tragic spectatorship constitutes a form of symbolic death: "The new Greek [tragic] theatre, in architecture and in meaning, . . . symbolized the city's graveyard—in the sense that it was a place where the spirit of the past could be recalled, action in the present informed, and the city's identity perpetuated." Hermassi, *Theatre and Polity,* 37. In support of the association of theatrical spectatorship with interment, one could also cite H. G. Wunderlich, who has argued that open rectangular courts built on the grounds of mortuary palaces during Crete's Minoan age functioned as staging areas for "theatrical representations of the . . . life and death of significant men." Wunderlich, *The Secret of Crete* (Athens: Efstathiadis Group, 1987), 338, 336. In this reading, these staging areas were the prototypes for the theaters built on mainland Greece during the classical age.

84. Arendt, "Angelo Giuseppe Roncalli: A Christian on St. Peter's Chair from 1958 to 1963" (*MDT* 69). Deathbed reconciliations are made possible by the dying person's contemplation of his or her approaching death and by the sense of liberation from the press of egostic desires and aversions which results from that contemplation. Such scenes of reconciliation have always been a staple of melodrama. This is partly so, I would argue, because audience members can enjoy this sense of liberation through identification with the dying character.

85. The exemplary significance of this scene is widely recognized for its revealing how identification with the dead can foster a reconciliatory sense

of the fundamental frailty of human life. For a fairly recent iteration, see Euben, *Political Theory*, 223–26.

86. Nietzche, *Birth of Tragedy*, 68.

87. On Cedric Whitman's reading of Theseus's first encounter with Oedipus, just such an identification occurs. Theseus experiences "a fore-knowing acceptance of death," expressed in his utterance, "Being a man, I know that I possess / No greater share of tomorrow than you do." Whitman, "Existentialism," 59.

88. Nietzsche, *Birth of Tragedy*, 125.

89. Arendt, "On Humanity in Dark Times: Thoughts about Lessing," collected in *MDT* (see chapter 2).

90. Arendt, "The Moral of History (January 1946)," in Feldman, *Jew as Pariah*, 109; Arendt, "Preface to the First Edition," *OT* viii. Quotation is from Arendt's reply to Eric Voegelin's review of *OT* in *Review of Politics* (January 1953): 83.

91. See the June 1966 "Preface to Part Three: Totalitarianism" (*OT* xxxiv–xl).

92. For a representative example of the charges leveled at Arendt, see Gershom Scholem's letter to Arendt, reprinted in Feldman, *Jew as Pariah*, 240–45.

93. Hannah Arendt, *Eichmann in Jerusalem: A Report on the Banality of Evil* (New York: Penguin, 1985), 251–52; hereafter cited in the text as *Eichmann*, with page reference.

94. The parallels between a tragic protagonist and a criminal defendant may have been suggested to Arendt by her close friend Harold Rosenberg. His argument appears in "Character Change and the Drama," a chapter in his book *The Tradition of the New* (1959), later reprinted in Lionel Abel, ed. *Moderns on Tragedy* (Greenwich: Fawcett, 1967), 56–70. Arendt praised the book in her essay "The Crisis in Culture" (see *BPF* 197).

95. "By denying in her conception of politics the validity of suffering, Arendt . . . risked distortion of the anguish of justice. In incorporating the pleas of the victims, Israel was right to assert universal claims in defense of a particular people. In advancing the responsibility to judge Eichmann, the Israeli legal system was restraining the passion for revenge for the sake of general principles. For justice, Michael Walzer has argued in another context, 'must be done, for the sake of the victims, on behalf of the victims, though in the name of everybody'" (Whitfield, *Into the Dark*, 207).

96. Schmidt acted without seeking payment, a fact to which Kovner and Arendt accord much importance. Perhaps it indicates to Arendt that Schmidt's initiative-taking reflected a capacity to judge, in the sense of thinking in the place of others and seeing others as deserving of both a place in the world and a share in its governance (*Eichmann*, 230).

97. Arendt notes only one occasion where Eichmann "took an initiative contrary to orders": upon witnessing for the first time the mass executions of Jews, he deliberately routed the first shipment of Jewish and gypsy deportees from Germany not to "Russian territory . . . where they would have been immediately shot by the *Einsatzgruppen* . . . [but] to the ghetto of Lódz where he knew that no preparations for extermination had been made" (*Eichmann*, 94).

98. It is unlikely that this interpretation of Arendt's Eichmann, resting as it does on the apparently shocking idea of Eichmann as a sort of "tragic hero," would provoke a serious reconsideration of views on the part of those who have, from the start, found serious fault with Arendt's book. Even if critics were to grant that Arendt in her concluding verdict does indeed reconstrue Eichmann in this way, they would see, in this fact, evidence further confirming their view of the unfortunate, even perverse, working of Arendt's philhellenism. The same would go for her implicit rejection of the prosecution's attempt to use the trial to tell the "tragedy of Jewry." Can any common ground with critics be established on the basis of Arendt's deployment of a tragic framework in the Eichmann case? If tragedy's promise to promote action and judgment supportive of political freedom depends on finding tragic heroes with whom to identify, the history of Jewish resistance, in Warsaw and other places, offers plentiful material. If Arendt did not avail herself of it, this does not mean that others could not.

99. Nietzsche, *Birth of Tragedy*, 125.

5: MORTAL MESSAGES

1. Jenny Ring, "The Pariah as Hero: Hannah Arendt's Political Actor," *Political Theory* (August 1991): 437, 434, 441.

2. Hanna Pitkin, "Justice: On Relating Private and Public," in Hinchman and Hinchman, *Critical Essays*, 271, 272, 281.

3. Pitkin, *Attack of the Blob*, 164.

4. Wolin, "Democracy and the Political," 6, 4, 10, 18.

5. Kateb, *Politics, Conscience, Evil*, 31.

6. Patricia Springborg, "Arendt, Republicanism, and Patriarchalism," *History of Political Thought* 10.3 (autumn 1989): 520–21.

7. Ibid., 507.

8. In Arendt's "central argument that fascism was the outcome of the extension of household politics and collective housekeeping . . . the obvious connection between fascism and ancient militaristic society—note the philological evidence, usually so heavily weighted by Arendt, in the cognates *fasces, phalanx, phalange,* and so on—is disregarded. It is a sad irony that Germany, which, as Marx observed, kept pace with history in thought, should have re-

produced the excesses of antiquity on a larger than life scale" (ibid., 513–14).

9. Pitkin, *Attack of the Blob,* 63.

10. Hanna Pitkin, *Fortune Is a Woman: Gender and Politics in the Thought of Niccolò Machiavelli* (Berkeley and Los Angeles: University of California Press, 1984), 4, 68, 294.

11. See Morris Dees with James Corcoran, *Gathering Storm: America's Militia Threat* (New York: HarperCollins, 1996).

12. Arendt cited in Young-Bruehl, *For Love of the World,* 171.

13. "Die jüdische Armee—der Beginn einer jüdischen Politik?" *Aufbau,* November 14, 1941, p. 1 (my translation from the German original).

14. To Machiavelli one might add Rousseau, whose admiration for the garrison city of Sparta in *The Social Contract* should be unsettling, for republicans as well as for liberals. See, for some examples, Jean-Jacques Rousseau, *Politics and the Arts: Letter to d'Alembert on the Theatre,* trans. Allan Bloom (Ithaca: Cornell University Press, 1991), 133–35; and "First Discourse," in *The First and Second Discourses* (New York: St. Martin's Press, 1964), 55. Thanks to Geoff Gershenson for these references.

15. For example, Madison in *Federalist 10* argues that the mechanism of representation in an extended republic will serve to blunt the impact of passion in politics, particularly the passion of debtors for legislative relief.

16. Alexis de Tocqueville, *Democracy in America: Volume 1,* trans. Henry Reeve (Cambridge, Mass.: Sever and Francis, 1863), 396.

17. Among contemporary Anglo-American liberal theorists, George Kateb appears most to approach a notion of politics' intrinsic dignity. However, his high praise of representative democracy for diffusing a respect for individual rights throughout society and for fostering the conditions under which individuals may form a poetic attachment to existence rests on a notion of politics as an instrument of individual self-development. See his latest book, *The Inner Ocean: Individualism and Democratic Culture* (Ithaca: Cornell University Press, 1992), chapter 1.

18. Max Weber, *The Protestant Ethic and the Spirit of Capitalism* (New York: Scribner's, 1958), 172.

19. As Michael Walzer's trailblazing study of the struggle between Protestant dissenters and Charles I of England suggests, engagement in politics did come to be seen by some Protestant dissenters as a kind of religious calling. Or perhaps it would be more precise to say it was the activity of warfighting that came to be seen as weighted with existential significance for the dissenters. Michael Walzer, *The Revolution of the Saints: A Study in the Origins of Radical Politics* (Cambridge, Mass.: Harvard University Press, 1965).

20. Shklar, *Ordinary Vices,* 5.

21. "Principal Causes which render Religion powerful in America," in de Tocqueville, *Volume 1,* 396; hereafter cited in the text as "Principal

Causes," with page reference.

22. "Why I Am a Destiny," from Nietzche's *"On the Genealogy of Morals,"* *and "Ecce Homo,"* ed. Walter Kaufmann (New York: Vintage, 1989), 327.

23. See also "How Religion in the United States Avails Itself of Democratic Tendencies," chapter 5 in *Democracy in America: Volume 2,* trans. Henry Reeve (Cambridge, Mass.: Sever and Francis, 1863), 22.

24. Jaspers, *Tragedy Is Not Enough,* 29.

25. See Hermassi, *Theatre and Polity,* 200–201; Euben, *Political Theory,* 55; Strong, *Idea of Political Theory,* 61. See also the beginning of section 21 in Nietzsche, *Birth of Tragedy,* for his classic formulation.

26. A. Andrews, "The Growth of the City-State," in *The Greeks,* ed. H. Lloyd-Jones (London: A. C. Watts, 1962).

27. Central among these changes were the opening of membership in the central decision-making institutions (the citizen assembly, the council, and the law courts) to men of low birth and modest means such as peasants, craftsmen, and shopkeepers; the selection of council members and officeholders (with the exception of military generals) by lot, for annual terms, with service restricted to one or two terms; and the use of city funds to subsidize jury and council service. Scholars continue to debate the extent and significance of Athens's shift to more public, impersonal, and popular decision-making practices. For a nuanced treatment of the gains and the limits of the democratization process in fifth-century Athens, see Finley, *Politics in the Ancient World.*

28. Ken Jowitt, *New World Disorder: The Leninist Extinction* (Berkeley and Los Angeles: University of California Press, 1992), 262, 264.

29. Claus Offe, "Capitalism by Democratic Design? Democratic Theory Facing the Triple Transition in East Central Europe," *Social Research* 58.4 (winter 1991): 869.

30. Thomas Hobbes, *Leviathan* (New York: Penguin, 1982), ch. 13.

31. Timothy Garton Ash, "Letter from Warsaw: Helena's Kitchen," *New Yorker* (February 1999): 33.

32. Arendt, "Organized Guilt and Universal Responsibility (January 1945)," in Feldman, *Jew as Pariah,* 232. For a rare and pithy formulation of the totalitarian dynamic in which superfluousness and narrow self-interest converges: "What we have called the 'bourgeois' is the modern man of the masses, not in his exalted moments of collective excitement, but in the security (today one should say the insecurity) of his own private domain" (234).

33. Jowitt, *New World Disorder,* 265.

34. Offe, "Capitalism by Democratic Design?" 881.

35. All quotes ibid., p. 882, except the last, p. 892.

36. Ibid., 887.

37. Margaret Canovan, "Trust the People! Populism and the Two Faces

of Democracy," *Political Studies* 47 (1999): 11.

38. Robert Putnam, "Bowling Alone: America's Declining Social Capital," *Journal of Democracy* 6.1 (January 1995): 67.

39. Clearly, Arendt did not include in her notion of councils many of the forms of association Putnam has in mind in his consideration of the sources of social capital. This does not, however, rule out the possibility that many of the associations Putnam discusses provide (however incompletely or sporadically) the kind of experiences Arendt associated with council participation.

40. In considering the relevance of Arendt's endorsement of councils in estabished democracies, Jeffrey Isaac chooses an apt metaphor: "Arendt sees her elites [self-chosen participants in council forms of self-government] not as alternatives to the formal institutions of representative government but as complements to them, reproaches to their tendency to treat people as subjects rather than as citizens." Isaac, "Oases in the Desert: Hanna Arendt on Democratic Politics," *American Political Science Review* (March 1994): 160.

Bibliography

SELECTED WORKS BY HANNAH ARENDT

Arendt, Hannah. *Between Past and Future*. New York: Penguin, 1978.

———. *Crises of the Republic*. New York: Harcourt Brace Jovanovich, 1972.

———. *Eichmann in Jerusalem: A Report on the Banality of Evil*. New York: Penguin, 1985.

———. *The Human Condition*. Chicago: University of Chicago Press, 1958.

———. *The Jew as Pariah: Jewish Identity and Politics in the Modern Age*. Edited by Ron Feldman. New York: Grove Press, 1978.

———. "Die jüdische Armee—der Beginn einer jüdischen Politik?" *Aufbau*, November 14, 1941, pp. 1, 2.

———. *Lectures on Kant's Political Philosophy*. Edited by Ronald Beiner. Chicago: University of Chicago Press, 1989.

———. *The Life of the Mind: Thinking*. New York: Harcourt Brace Jovanovich, 1978.

———. *The Life of the Mind: Willing*. New York: Harcourt Brace Jovanovich, 1978.

———. *Men in Dark Times*. New York: Harvest/Harcourt Brace Jovanovich, 1968.

———. *On Revolution*. 1963; New York: Penguin, 1979.

———. *The Origins of Totalitarianism*. 1951; New York: Harvest/Harcourt Brace Jovanovich, 1973.

———. "Personal Responsibility under Dictatorship." *Listener* 6 (August 1964): 185–87, 205.

———. "Philosophy and Politics." Edited by Jerome Kohn. *Social Research* (spring 1990).

———. Sonning Prize Address, April 18, 1975. Library of Congress.

———. "Totalitarian Imperialism." *Journal of Politics* 20 (February 1958): 5–43.

———. "Understanding and Politics." *Partisan Review* 20.4 (July–August 1953): 377–92.

———. *Vita Activa*. Munich: Piper, 1989.

———. *Was ist Politik?: Fragmente aus dem Nachlass*. Edited by Ursula Lutz. Munich: Piper, 1993.

———. "What Is *Existenz* Philosophy?" *Partisan Review* 13.1 (winter 1946): 34–56.

————. "What Was Authority?" In *Authority*. Edited by Carl J. Friedrich. 1958; Westport, Conn.: Greenwood Press, 1981.

CORRESPONDENCE AND INTERVIEWS

Arendt, Hannah, and Karl Jaspers. *Hannah Arendt / Karl Jaspers Correspondence, 1926–1969*. Edited by Lotte Köhler and Hans Saner. Translated by Robert and Rita Kimber. New York: Harcourt Brace Jovanovich, 1992.

Arendt, Hannah, and Mary McCarthy. *Between Friends: The Correspondence of Hannah Arendt and Mary McCarthy, 1949–1975*. Edited by Carol Brightman. New York: Harcourt Brace, 1995.

Gaus, Günter. Interview. *Zur Person: Porträts in Frage und Antwort*. Munich: Deutscher Taschenbuch Verlag, 1965.

Roundtable Discussion. "On Hannah Arendt." In *Hannah Arendt: The Recovery of the Public World*. Edited by Melvyn A. Hill. New York: St. Martin's Press, 1979.

REFERENCES

Abel, Lionel, ed. *Moderns on Tragedy: An Anthology*. Greenwich: Fawcett, 1967.

Alison, R. H. "'This Is the Place': Why Is Oidipus at Kolonus?" *Prudentia* 16 (1984): 67–91.

Andrews, A. "The Growth of the City-State." In *The Greeks*. Edited by Hugh Lloyd-Jones. London: A. C. Watts, 1962.

Aristotle. *The Poetics*. Translated by T. S. Dorsch. In *Aristotle/Horace/Longinus: Classical Literary Criticism*. London: Penguin, 1965.

Baldry, H. C. *The Greek Tragic Theater*. New York: Norton, 1971.

Beiner, Ronald. "Interpretive Essay: Hannah Arendt on Judging." In *Hannah Arendt: Lectures on Kant's Political Philosophy*. Edited by Ronald Beiner. Chicago: Chicago University Press, 1989.

————. "Judging in a World of Appearances: A Commentary on Hannah Arendt's Unwritten Finale." *History of Political Thought* 1.1 (1980): 117–35.

————. *What's the Matter with Liberalism?* Berkeley and Los Angeles: University of California Press, 1995.

Benhabib, Seyla. "Hannah Arendt and the Redemptive Power of Narrative." In *Hannah Arendt: Critical Essays*. Edited by Lewis Hinchman and Sandra Hinchman. Albany: State University of New York Press, 1994.

————. *The Reluctant Modernism of Hannah Arendt*. Newbury Park, Cal.: Sage Pubications, 1996.

Blundell, Mary Whitlock. "The Ideal of Athens in *Oedipus at Colonus*." In *Tragedy, Comedy, and the Polis*. Edited by Alan H. Sommerstein. Bari:

Levante Editori, 1993.

Bradshaw, Leah. *Acting and Thinking: The Political Thought of Hannah Arendt.* Toronto: University of Toronto Press, 1989.

Calder, W. M. "The Political and Literary Sources of Sophocles' *Oedipus Coloneus.*" In *Hypatia: Essays in Classics, Comparative Literature and Philosophy.* Edited by W. M. Calder, V. Goldsmith, and P. Kenevan. Boulder: Colorado Associated University Press, 1985.

Canovan, Margaret. *The Political Thought of Hannah Arendt.* London: Dent and Sons, 1974.

———. "Politics and Culture: Hannah Arendt and the Public Realm." In *Hannah Arendt: Critical Essays.* Edited by Lewis Hinchman and Sandra Hinchman. Albany: State University of New York Press, 1994.

———. "Socrates or Heidegger? Hannah Arendt's Reflections on Philosophy and Politics." *Social Research* 57.1 (1990): 135–65.

———. "Trust the People! Populism and the Two Faces of Democracy." *Political Studies* 47 (1999): 2–16.

Chytry, Josef. *The Aesthetic State: A Quest in Modern German Thought.* Berkeley and Los Angeles: University of California Press, 1989.

Cumming, R. D. *Human Nature and History: A Study of the Development of Liberal Thought.* Vol. 1. Chicago: University of Chicago Press, 1969.

Curtis, Kimberley. "Aesthetic Foundations of Democratic Politics in the Work of Hannah Arendt." In *Hannah Arendt and the Meaning of Politics.* Edited by Craig Calhoun and John McGowan. Minneapolis: University of Minnesota Press, 1997.

Dees, Morris, with James Corcoran. *Gathering Storm: America's Militia Threat.* New York: HarperCollins, 1996.

Denneny, Michael. "The Privilege of Ourselves: Hannah Arendt on Judgment." In *Hannah Arendt: The Recovery of the Public World.* Edited by Melvyn Hill. New York: St. Martin's Press, 1979.

Disch, Lisa. *Hannah Arendt and the Limits of Philosophy.* Ithaca: Cornell University Press, 1994.

Dolan, Frederick. *Allegories of America: Narratives, Metaphysics, Politics.* Ithaca: Cornell University Press, 1994.

Euben, J. Peter. *The Tragedy of Political Theory: The Road Not Taken.* Princeton: Princeton University Press, 1990.

Euripides. *Hippolytus.* Translated by David Grene. In *Complete Greek Tragedies,* Vol. IV. Edited by David Grene and Richmond Lattimore. Chicago: University of Chicago Press, 1967.

Finley, M. I. *The Ancient Greeks: An Introduction to Their Life and Thought.* New York: Viking, 1963.

———. *Politics in the Ancient World.* Cambridge, England: Cambridge University Press, 1983.

Flashar, Hellmut. *Inszenierung der Antike: Das griechische Drama auf der Bühne der Neuzeit*. Munich: C. H. Beck, 1991.

Gide, André. *Two Legends: Oedipus and Theseus*. New York: Vintage, 1950.

Gouldner, Alvin. *Enter Plato: Classical Greece and the Origins of Social Theory*. New York: Basic Books, 1965.

Hammer, Dean, Jessica Bleiman, and Kenneth Park. "Between Positivism and Postmodernism: Hannah Arendt on the Formation of Policy Judgments." *Policy Studies Review* 16.1 (spring 1999): 148–81.

Hansen, Phillip. *Hannah Arendt: Politics, History and Citizenship*. Stanford: Stanford University Press, 1993.

Hauser, Arnold. *The Social History of Art*, Vol. 3. Translated by Stanley Godman in collaboration with the author. New York: Vintage Books, 1951.

Hegel, G. W. F. *Hegel on Tragedy*. Edited by Anne Paolucci and Henry Paolucci. Garden City: Anchor Books, 1962.

Heidegger, Martin. *Introduction to Metaphysics*. Translated by Ralph Mannheim. New Haven: Yale University Press, 1959.

———. "Tragedy, Satyr-Play, and Telling Silence in Nietzsche's Thought of Eternal Recurrence." Translated by David Farrell Krell. In *Why Nietzsche Now?* Edited by Daniel O'Hara. Bloomington: Indiana University Press, 1981.

Heine, Heinrich. *Sämtliche Werke: Band V*. Munich: Kindler, 1964.

Heller, Agnes. "An Imaginary Preface to the 1984 Edition of Hannah Arendt's *The Origins of Totalitarianism*." In *Eastern Left, Western Left: Totalitarianism, Freedom, Democracy*. Edited by Ferenc Féher and Agnes Heller. Cambridge, England: Polity Press, 1987.

Hermassi, Karen. *Theatre and Polity in Historical Perspective*. Berkeley and Los Angeles: University of California Press, 1977.

Hill, Melvyn, ed. *Hannah Arendt: The Recovery of the Public World*. New York: St. Martin's Press, 1979.

Hinchman, Lewis P., and Sandra K. Hinchman. "Existentialism Politicized: Arendt's Debt to Jaspers." In *Hannah Arendt: Critical Essays*. Edited by Lewis Hinchman and Sandra Hinchman. Albany: State University of New York Press, 1994.

Holmes, Stephen Taylor. "Aristippus in and out of Athens." *American Political Science Review* 73 (March 1979): 113–28.

Honig, Bonnie. "Declarations of Independence: Arendt and Derrida on the Problem of Founding a Republic." *American Political Science Review* 85 (March 1991): 97–113.

Horowitz, Irving. Review of *On Revolution*. *American Journal of Sociology* (January 1964): 420–21.

Isaac, Jeffrey. "Oases in the Desert: Hannah Arendt on Democratic Politics." *American Political Science Review* 88 (March 1994): 156–68.

Jacobson, Norman. "Parable and Paradox: In Response to Arendt's *On Revolu-*

tion." *Salmagundi* 60 (spring–summer 1983): 123–39.

Jaeger, Werner. *Paideia: The Ideals of Greek Culture*. Vol. 1. New York: Oxford University Press, 1974.

Jaspers, Karl. *Tragedy Is Not Enough*. Translated by H. Reiche, H. Moore, and K. Deutsch. 1952; Hamden, Conn.: Archon, 1969.

Jocylen, H. D. "The Ruling Class of the Roman Republic and Greek Philosophers." *Bulletin of the John Rylands University Library* 59 (1977).

Jowitt, Ken. *New World Disorder: The Leninist Extinction*. Berkeley and Los Angeles: University of California Press, 1992.

Kateb, George. *Hannah Arendt: Politics, Conscience, Evil*. Totowa, N.J.: Rowman and Allanheld, 1984.

———. *The Inner Ocean: Individualism and Democratic Culture*. Ithaca: Cornell University Press, 1992.

Kaufmann, Walter. *Tragedy and Philosophy*. Princeton: Princeton University Press, 1992.

Kazin, Alfred. "Woman in Dark Times." *New York Review of Books*, June 24, 1982.

Kitto, H. D. F. *Greek Tragedy: A Literary Study*. Garden City, N.Y.: Anchor Books, n.d.

Kerényi, C. *The Heroes of the Greeks*. Translated by H. J. Rose. Southampton, England: Thames and Hudson, 1978.

Lacoue-Labarthe, Philippe. *Heidegger, Art and Politics: The Fiction of the Political*. London: Basil Blackwell, 1990.

Lessing, G. E. *The Hamburg Dramaturgy*. Edited by Victor Lange. New York: Dover, 1962.

Levi, Peter. *Atlas of the Greek World*. New York: Facts on File, Inc., 1989.

Loraux, N. *Tragic Ways of Killing a Woman*. Translated by Anthony Forster. Cambridge, Mass.: Harvard University Press, 1987.

Kaufmann, Walter. *Tragedy and Philosophy*. Princeton: Princeton University Press, 1992.

Luban, David. "Explaining Dark Times: Hannah Arendt's Theory of Theory." In *Hannah Arendt: Critical Essays*. Edited by Lewis Hinchman and Sandra Hinchman. Albany: State University of New York Press, 1994.

McGrath, William. *Dionysian Art and Populist Politics*. Hartford: Yale University Press, 1974.

MacIntyre, Alasdair. *After Virtue*. Notre Dame: University of Notre Dame, 1984.

Miller, James. "The Pathos of Novelty: Hannah Arendt's Image of Freedom in the Modern World." In *Hannah Arendt: The Recovery of the Public World*. Edited by Melvyn Hill. New York: St. Martin's Press, 1979.

Nietzsche, Friedrich. *"The Birth of Tragedy," and "The Case of Wagner"*. Edited and translated by Walter Kaufmann. New York: Vintage, 1967.

——. *"On the Genealogy of Morals," and "Ecce Homo"*. Edited by Walter Kaufmann. 1967; New York: Vintage, 1989.

Nussbaum, Martha C. *The Fragility of Goodness*. Cambridge: Cambridge University Press, 1986.

——. *Poetic Justice: The Literary Imagination and Public Life*. Boston: Beacon Press, 1995.

Offe, Claus. "Capitalism by Democratic Design? Democratic Theory Facing the Triple Transition in East Central Europe." *Social Research* 58.4 (winter 1991): 865–92.

O'Hara, Daniel, ed. *Why Nietzsche Now?* Bloomington: Indiana University Press, 1981.

Pitkin, Hanna. *The Attack of the Blob: Hannah Arendt's Concept of the Social*. Chicago: University of Chicago Press, 1998.

——. *Fortune Is a Woman: Gender and Politics in the Thought of Niccolò Machiavelli*. Berkeley and Los Angeles: University of California Press, 1984.

——. "Justice: On Relating Private and Public." In *Hannah Arendt: Critical Essays*. Edited by Lewis Hinchman and Sandra Hinchman. Albany: State University of New York Press, 1994.

de Polignac, François. *Cults, Territory, and the Origins of the Greek City-State*. Translated by Janet Lloyd. Chicago: University of Chicago Press, 1995.

Putnam, Robert. "Bowling Alone: America's Declining Social Capital." *Journal of Democracy* 6.1 (January 1995): 65–78.

Rich, Adrienne. *On Lies, Secrets and Silence: Selected Prose, 1966–1978*. New York: Norton, 1979.

Ring, Jenny. "The Pariah as Hero: Hannah Arendt's Political Actor." *Political Theory* (August 1991): 433–52.

Rosenberg, Harold. "Character Change and the Drama." In *Moderns on Tragedy*. Edited by Lionel Abel. Greenwich: Fawcett, 1967.

Rousseau, Jean-Jacques. *The First and Second Discourses*. New York: St. Martins Press, 1964.

——. *Politics and the Arts: Letter to d'Alembert on the Theatre*. Translated by Allan Bloom. Ithaca: Cornell University Press, 1991.

——. *The Social Contract*. Translated by Maurice Cranston. New York: Penguin, 1968.

Schiller, Friedrich. *Schillers Werke in Fünf Bänden*. Vol. 1. Berlin and Weimar: Aufbau Verlag, 1981.

Schwarz, Benjamin. "The Religion of Politics: Reflections on the Thought of Hannah Arendt." *Dissent* 17.2 (1970): 144–61.

Segal, Charles. *Tragedy and Civilization: An Interpretation of Sophocles*. Cambridge, Mass.: Harvard University Press, 1981.

Silk, M. S., and J. P. Stern. *Nietzsche on Tragedy*. Cambridge, England: Cambridge University Press, 1987.

Shklar, Judith. "Hannah Arendt's Triumph." *New Republic,* December 27, 1975, pp. 8–10.

———. *Ordinary Vices.* Cambridge, Mass.: The Belknap Press of Harvard University Press, 1984.

———. "Rethinking the Past." *Social Research* 44.1 (1977): 80–90.

Slater, Philip E. *The Glory of Hera: Greek Mythology and the Greek Family.* Boston: Beacon Press, 1968.

Sophocles. *Ödipus auf Kolonus.* Edited by Hellmut Flashar. Frankfurt am Main: Insel, 1996.

———. *Oedipus at Colonus.* In *Sophocles II.* Edited by Hugh Lloyd-Jones. Cambridge, Mass.: Harvard University Press, 1994.

———. *Oedipus at Colonus.* In *Three Theban Plays,* trans. Theodore Howard Banks. Oxford: Oxford University Press, 1956.

Springborg, Patricia. "Arendt, Republicanism, and Patriarchalism." *History of Political Thought* 10.3 (autumn 1989): 499–523.

Steiner, George. *Antigones.* Oxford: Oxford University Press, 1984.

———. "Lafayette, Where Are We?" *Reporter,* May 9, 1963.

Strong, Tracy. *The Idea of Political Theory: Reflections on the Self in Political Time and Space.* Notre Dame: University of Notre Dame Press, 1990.

———. "Nietzsche's Political Aesthetics." In *Nietzsche's New Seas.* Edited by Michael Gillespie and Tracy Strong. Chicago: University of Chicago Press, 1988.

———. "Oedipus as Hero: Family and Family Metaphors in Nietzsche." In *Why Nietzsche Now?* Edited by Daniel O'Hara. Bloomington: Indiana University Press, 1981.

Taylor, Charles. *Hegel.* Cambridge, England: Cambridge University Press, 1993.

Tripp, Edward, ed. *The Meridian Handbook of Classical Mythology.* New York: New American Library, 1974.

Turner, Victor. *From Ritual to Theatre: The Human Seriousness of Play.* New York: Performing Arts Journal Publications, 1982.

Villa, Dana. *Arendt and Heidegger: The Fate of the Political.* Princeton: Princeton University Press, 1996.

Vernant, J.-P. *Mortals and Immortals: Collected Essays.* Princeton: Princeton University Press, 1991.

de Tocqueville, Alexis. *Democracy in America: Volume 1.* Translated by Henry Reeve. Cambridge, Mass.: Sever and Francis, 1863.

———. *Democracy in America: Volume 2.* Translated by Henry Reeve. Cambridge, Mass.: Sever and Francis, 1863.

Walzer, Michael. *The Company of Critics: Social Criticism and Political Commitment in the Twentieth Century.* New York: Basic Books, 1988.

———. *The Revolution of the Saints: A Study in the Origins of Radical Politics.* Cambridge, Mass.: Harvard University Press, 1965.

Weber, Max. *The Protestant Ethic and the Spirit of Capitalism*. Translated by Talcott Parsons. New York: Scribner's, 1958.

White, Hayden. *Metahistory*. Baltimore: Johns Hopkins University Press, 1987.

———. *Tropics of Discourse: Essays in Cultural Criticism*. Baltimore: Johns Hopkins University Press, 1978.

Whitfield, Stephen. *Into the Dark: Hannah Arendt and Totalitarianism*. Philadelphia: Temple University Press, 1980.

Whitman, Cedric. "Existentialism and the Classic Hero." In *The Heroic Paradox*. Edited by C. Segal. Ithaca: Cornell University Press, 1982.

Wolin, Sheldon. "Hannah Arendt: Democracy and the Political." *Salmagundi* 60 (spring–summer 1983): 3–19.

———. "Hannah Arendt and the Ordinance of Time." *Social Research* 44.1 (spring 1977): 91–105.

Wunderlich, H. G. *The Secret of Crete*. Athens: Efstathiadis Group, 1987.

Young-Bruehl, Elizabeth. *Hannah Arendt: For Love of the World*. New Haven: Yale University Press, 1982.

———. "Hannah Arendt's Storytelling." *Social Research* 44.1 (1977): 183–90.

———. "Reflections on Hannah Arendt's *The Life of the Mind*." In *Hannah Arendt: Critical Essays*. Edited by Lewis Hinchman and Sandra Hinchman. Albany: State University of New York Press, 1994.

Index